THE
GREAT
DISAPPEARANCE

THE
GREAT
DISAPPEARANCE

31 WAYS TO
BE RAPTURE READY

DR. DAVID
JEREMIAH

W PUBLISHING GROUP

AN IMPRINT OF THOMAS NELSON

To Donna Jeremiah
*For sixty years you have been my greatest love . . . my closest
friend . . . my fiercest encourager. We have done life together.
We have done books together. This one is dedicated to you!*

CONTENTS

CONTENTS

INTRODUCTION

You and I are privileged to stand on the cresting waves of prophecy—to live in a time closer to the return of Jesus Christ than any other generation in the history of the world. We sense the nearness of His return. We see the signs of the times. We know the world is reaching a climactic point of unparalleled crisis.

Nuclear weapons are now sophisticated enough and small enough to be carried by hand; such weapons even have a nickname: "tactical nukes." The global economy is hanging by a spider's thread. Political fragmentation seems to be occurring simultaneously on every continent. And the -isms—secularism, radical Islamism, communism, totalitarianism, and terrorism—are spreading over the nations like a runaway case of poison ivy.

These realities frighten us and are heartrending, but to me they're also exhilarating, for they portend the return of Christ. I've been exhilarated by the thought of seeing Christ for many years, and, like you, I've been privileged to live at a time when we can trace the prophecies of God's Word being fulfilled before our very eyes.

I also feel honored to have been connected in a small way with two of the most important prophecy books or series of books that have ever been written.

I began my pastoral career in 1969 when my wife, Donna, and I, along with seven families, started Blackhawk Baptist Church in Fort

Wayne, Indiana. In 1970, the second year of my pastoral ministry there, Hal Lindsey published a book entitled *The Late Great Planet Earth*. The book came out a few years after the Six-Day War in the Middle East when people were focused on the remarkable events unfolding in Israel.

This book brought the message of biblical prophecy into everyday conversation, and it became the bestselling nonfiction book of the seventies. It sold more than twenty-eight million copies by 1990 and was eventually translated into more than fifty languages. Some pundits have calculated that, all together, Lindsey's book sold more than thirty-five million copies.[1]

Hal Lindsey graduated from Dallas Theological Seminary, the same seminary from which I graduated in 1967. Both of us were privileged to sit under some of the greatest teachers of Bible prophecy in the modern era—professors including Dwight Pentecost, John Walvoord, and Charles Ryrie. In his book, Lindsey took the theological truths he had learned in seminary regarding the prophetic portions of Scripture, as well as insights from his own subsequent studies, and connected them to events in the present and future.

The coauthor of Lindsey's book was a gifted and godly woman named Carole Carlson. In the early eighties, I met Carole and her husband, Ward, at the Forest Home Bible Conference in California, where I was a speaker. Sometime during that week, Donna and I had coffee with Carole, and she suggested she might be able to assist me in putting some of my prophetic sermons into print.

Two books came out of that conversation. The first one, *The Handwriting on the Wall*, was released in 1992. It captured the message of the Old Testament book of Daniel. *Escape the Coming Night*, a contemporary commentary on the New Testament book of Revelation, was released on the first day of the Gulf War and became my all-time bestselling book.

I recall with fondness the hours Carole and I spent together talking about prophecy and discussing how to make it come alive for our readers. Since then, both Carole and Ward have graduated into the presence of the Lord. Yet they're still alive today, not only in heaven but also in the books they helped two authors create.

In the late seventies and early eighties I developed a relationship with a California pastor by the name of Tim LaHaye. By the providence of God, I was called to be his successor at what was then called Scott Memorial Baptist Church in San Diego, California. Today that church is Shadow Mountain Community Church. After forty-two years, I am still the pastor of that church. It fills me with gratitude to think Tim LaHaye and I have pastored the same church for over sixty years.

In the early 1990s, God placed a burden upon Dr. LaHaye's heart as he was flying home from a speaking engagement. After a vigorous study of the Scriptures, he had firmly come to the conclusion that all believing Christians would be removed from the world prior to the Tribulation by means of an event called the Rapture.

On the airplane that day, he couldn't help noticing one of the pilots flirting with a flight attendant. The pilot was wearing a wedding ring. Dr. LaHaye thought to himself, *What if this were the moment God chose to remove His faithful believers from earth, leaving behind billions of bewildered unbelievers? What if the Rapture occurred while I was riding on an airplane?*

It was then he decided to write a fictional account of what could happen on earth in the moments after the Lord returns in the skies to suddenly take all Christians to heaven.

Dr. LaHaye joined forces with an experienced author named Jerry Jenkins to write the series. The first book, *Left Behind*, was published in 1995. If you've read it, you likely remember the opening scene, which features an airline pilot interrupted by a frantic stewardess telling him that dozens of passengers have disappeared. Only the bodies were missing; everything else—clothes, shoes, and even gold fillings—were left behind.

What an opening scene for a novel—especially one based on biblical truths about unfolding prophecy!

That book and the fifteen that followed sold close to eighty million copies. The last six volumes in the series each debuted as number one on all the major bestseller lists, including those of the *New York Times*, *USA Today*, *Publishers Weekly*, and the *Wall Street Journal*. Two of the books were made into movies, and the entire series inspired a children's collection of Left Behind books.

Even as I'm writing these words today, a new *Left Behind* movie has been released, more than two decades after the first book was published.

I had the honor of walking through some of those exciting days with my friend Tim LaHaye. On a number of occasions he'd invite me to lunch and present me with a signed copy of the latest release in the series.

I owe a lot to Hal Lindsey and Tim LaHaye. They helped me understand how important it was to teach the prophetic Scriptures—which, by the way, comprise 27 percent of the Bible. I believe one of the reasons God blessed these remarkable books by Lindsey and Dr. LaHaye was this: the Rapture is the central event in each series.

The Rapture is also the central event in biblical prophecy.

Mark Hitchcock wrote, "More than any other single thing, studying the end times has helped me to understand the whole Bible. And while there are many truths about the end times that have deeply affected my life, one truth stands out above all the others: the Rapture."[2]

Who among the followers of Jesus wouldn't be thrilled to hear the blast of the trumpet, catch the shout of the angel, and feel the upward pull of the magnetic, rapturous grace of God calling us out of this world and letting us see our Lord Jesus face-to-face? In this book, I'll present my deeply held views about the timing of the Rapture in the overall program of God for the Last Days. But the greatest truth about the Rapture is not its timing but its reality—for blessed are all those who long for His appearing (2 Tim. 4:8).

How we need this anticipation! It's our glorious hope in a world filled with hopelessness. Peter spoke of how wonderful it is to be "looking forward to these things" (2 Pet. 3:14).

Yes, but you have questions, don't you? Questions about the Rapture. Questions about timing and sequence. Questions that begin with "Who?" and "What?" and "When?"

That's why I've poured myself into this book. It's the culmination of decades of studying this subject. In the pages to come, I'll explain the meaning of the word *rapture*, the difference between the Rapture and the Second Coming, and the joy of expecting our Savior to come at any moment—a doctrine we call the imminence of Christ's return.

What about the chaos that will ensue on earth? We'll look at that too.

The truth of the Rapture is taught throughout Scripture, but three passages rise above the rest like peaks in the Pyrenees: John 14, 1 Corinthians 15, and 1 Thessalonians 4. We'll study each one in depth.

You might be surprised to learn that some people have already been raptured! *What?* It's true, and I'll introduce them to you.

We'll also deal with very practical questions, such as these: Will children be raptured? What will happen to our bodies at the moment of resurrection? What will our glorified bodies be like? Will we know each other after the resurrection? And what will happen in the days and years immediately after we're raptured? What will happen to us? Will those left behind still have an opportunity to receive Christ as their Savior?

We'll deal with all that and more.

There is one thing you'll *not* find in this book—the day and hour of Christ's return. None of us knows that, and the Bible warns about trying to predict it. We know it's not yesterday, but we don't know if the Rapture could come ten years from now, tomorrow—or today.

But when it *does* come, everyone will know. It will be the Great Disappearance—the moment when billions of people suddenly vanish from the face of the earth, along with billions of dead bodies returning to life and ascending to meet the Lord in the air. Imagine the thrill for those who go and the terror for those who stay!

In this book, we're dealing with scriptural truth—truth to steady you, encourage you, motivate you, purify you, and give you cheerful hope on dreary days. This is something to think about upon rising in the morning and retiring at night. This isn't just the light at the end of the tunnel; it's the light that heralds eternity, heaven, and the fulfillment of all God has promised His children.

This is the truth spoken by the Savior who said, "I will come again and receive you to Myself" (John 14:3).

It's the truth Paul proclaimed when he said the Rapture would happen "in a moment, in the twinkling of an eye, at the last trumpet" (1 Cor. 15:52).

This is the truth expressed in these infallible, unforgettable words: "For the Lord Himself will descend from heaven with a shout, with the voice of an archangel, and with the trumpet of God. And the dead in Christ will rise first. Then we who are alive and remain shall be caught up together with them in the clouds to meet the Lord in the air. And thus we shall always be with the Lord" (1 Thess. 4:16–17).

My prayer for you as you read this book is that you'll become so thrilled with this topic you'll keep it at the forefront of your mind. We must teach these things to our children and grandchildren, share them with others, proclaim them in our pulpits, and preach them from the housetops.

Join me in the following thirty-one chapters to become rapture ready, eager, excited, and filled with a joy that will make others ask you about it when they see the hope that's within you.

May the Lord bless you as you eagerly await His impending appearance in the skies. And as we wait, may we comfort one another with these words.

CHAPTER 1

CHAOS ON EARTH

Imagine a Moment coming soon to our planet that will change everything and everyone forever. Imagine ambivalent, unaware people conducting their business, scurrying around, trying to make sense of their lives. Depending on where you look on our globe, the scene may be very different, yet in many ways it's the same.

In the United States, in China, in Argentina, in Indonesia, in Kazakhstan.

People loving, laboring, longing.

All over the world that day, billions will be eating and drinking, marrying and giving in marriage, celebrating birthdays, battling sickness, digging graves. People will be getting up or going to bed, working or playing, enjoying their pleasures or indulging their vices.

I try to imagine these things happening all over the world, from the rising of the sun to the place where it sets. What will people think when the Moment comes?

I wonder what the headlines will be on the morning of that day. Wars and rumors of war. Earthquakes. Famines. Loud voices deceiving many. New laws. Old lies. New dilemmas. Nation rising against nation, kingdom against kingdom. Parts of the world may report an earthquake, a famine, or a plague.

Will the news be written by artificial intelligence? Will people be able to tell truth from fiction?

I wonder what the weather will be that day. Sunny in one place, cloudy in another? Something is about to happen in the skies—if only people would look up in expectation! In the unseen realms, the glory of the Lord is gathering, the angels are assembling, and the skies are preparing to part. But most people will be looking down at their phones, addicted to the newest messages or oldest sins.

I wonder what Christians will be doing that day. Will they be as surprised as everyone else when the Rapture occurs? Will they be eager, ready, and waiting?

Can't you see the masses moving about as usual? Millions of people walking around all day on the streets of New York, Tokyo, Mumbai, worried about their money, wondering about their relationships, anxious about their images, following the world stock markets, the latest music, the latest sports scores.

It will be an ordinary day on this globe—until, suddenly, it isn't.

One day soon, the world will face the Great Disappearance!

Billions of people. Gone in a flash more powerful than an atomic burst, yet silent. Invisible! Sudden! Inexplicable!

Try to imagine this extraordinary Moment on planet Earth. Every single follower of Jesus Christ, as well as all those under the age of accountability—all the babies, young children, and mentally disabled—gone in a flash, along with all those who have died in Christ.

Bodies will disappear from their coffins at funeral homes all over the world. Patients will vanish from hospital beds. Babies from their cribs. Children from their classrooms.

Imagine cars flying down the freeway with missing drivers, planes with missing pilots, nuclear submarines with missing commanders, nations with missing leaders, parents with missing children.

In various parts of the world, Christian congregations will be meeting for worship. Suddenly the buildings will be empty—or nearly so—as the churches resume their services in the sky! Soldiers will be missing in action. Emergency responders will find their numbers depleted. Prisons will be partially depopulated, especially those filled with Christians under persecution.

News reports will spread like wildfire, but the Christian press will be strangely silent. There'll be no believers to report the news.

People will frantically search for their loved ones, but phone calls will go to voicemail and texts will be unanswered.

In today's world, just one missing-person case can grip the nation. What about a billion? What will people think? What panic will they feel? What theories will they embrace?

The FBI has been tracking missing-person cases for years. The bureau has a website devoted to it with picture after picture of those whose whereabouts are unknown. These people seemingly just vanished. Many times foul play is involved. In virtually every case families are torn apart with grief, community life is disrupted, and law enforcement is focused on solving the mystery.

The oldest active missing-person case in America involves Marvin Clark, who vanished October 30, 1926, while on his way to visit his daughter in Portland, Oregon. He traveled by bus. He boarded the bus in Tigard, Oregon, but failed to get off at his destination. He simply disappeared. He was in his early seventies at the time, and his case is still open. Authorities are still looking for his remains—if there are any.[1]

One of the strangest missing-person cases in Canada involved thirty-two-year-old Granger Taylor of British Columbia. On November 29, 1980, he left a note to his parents saying: "Dear Mother and Father, I have gone away to walk aboard an alien spaceship, as reoccurring dreams assured a 42 month interstellar voyage to explore the vast universe, then return. I am leaving behind all my possessions to you as I will no longer . . . require the use of any."[2]

No one has seen Granger since.

For the record, I don't believe he was abducted by aliens, but I can see how the world will be gripped by a thousand conspiracy theories in the aftermath of the coming Rapture. Global panic will help prepare the way for a one-world government, the emergence of an ironfisted ruler, and the onset of the Tribulation.

It will be utter chaos on an unimaginable scale for those left behind.

For most of my life I've been thinking about this very day: the predicted Moment when Jesus will reenter earth's atmosphere for His church. The reason I'm asking you to imagine it is because I've been doing the same for decades. It's hard to get your head around the pandemonium that will engulf our planet when Jesus fulfills His promise to come for His people.

I think it helps us to visualize that day as best we can.

After I graduated from seminary, I became the youth director of a large New Jersey church. It takes special skill to work with teenagers, and I don't mind telling you I was nervous about relating to them and them to me.

It didn't help when the senior pastor told me that my first contact with the group would be at a summer conference where I was to teach them a weeklong study on Bible prophecy. I've never had a more challenging assignment!

Thankfully, someone had given me a copy of a fictitious newspaper designed to show the events and headlines on the day of the Rapture. The headlines said:

MILLIONS OF PEOPLE DISAPPEAR! AIRPLANES CRASH!
CHILDREN VANISH! PANIC IN THE STREETS!

On the first night of the conference, I asked a few kids to play the historic role of newsboys and go throughout the group, hollering "Extra! Extra! Read all about it!" Soon, the teenagers were devouring the paper.

The lead article began: "At 12:05 this morning a telephone operator reported three frantic calls regarding missing relatives. Within fifteen minutes all communications were jammed with similar inquiries. A spot check from around the nation found the same situation in every city. Sobbing husbands sought information about the mysterious disappearance of their wives. One husband reported, 'I turned the light on to ask my wife if she remembered to set the clock, but she was gone. Her bedclothes were there. Her watch was on the floor, but she vanished.'"

Another headline read:

THRONGS IN THE NATION DIE OF HEART ATTACKS

I can tell you those teenagers didn't just sit idly through my talks about prophecy. They wanted to know the details!

This wasn't hypothetical, I told them, but prophetic. The same Bible that describes our Lord Jesus ascending into the sky and disappearing into the clouds also tells us of His imminent, impending return for His people. For reasons I'll explain in this book, we call it the Rapture. It's the resurrection of those who are dead in Christ, immediately followed by the "snatching up" of the final generation of Christians on earth.

Dr. Tim LaHaye pondered this approaching day at length. He said that at the Moment of the Rapture "a million conversations will end midsentence. A million phones will suddenly go dead. A woman will reach for her husband's hand in the dark, and no one will be there. A man will turn with a laugh to slap a colleague on the back and his hand will move through empty air. A basketball player will make a length-of-floor pass to a teammate streaking downcourt and find there is no one there to receive it."[3]

This isn't science fiction, conspiracy theory, or mindless speculation. When Christ comes for His people, it will be in the twinkling of an eye. The trumpet will sound, the Lord will shout with the voice of authority, the dead will rise, and we who are alive will be caught up in the air to meet the Lord in the sky.

Between the resurrected and the raptured, billions of people will exit this planet in an instant. But billions more will be left behind. It will be chaos on our globe but incredible, glorious joy in the skies.

This is the Rapture—the Great Disappearance. I've been studying this in Scripture all my adult life, and now I want to write about it as fully as I can. It's vital to know what the Bible says about this coming day, the next event on God's prophetic agenda for the earth.

I think you'll be fascinated, motivated, and highly encouraged as you study the pages to come. Most of all I hope you'll be well prepared for that day.

It's one thing to try to imagine that day and another to see what the Bible truly says about its who, why, when, where, and how. I believe the Scriptures are clear on this subject, and I want to show you the pertinent passages in God's Word that discuss it. That's because we're not just to imagine it but to anticipate it with all our hearts and look forward to it with all our souls.

Don't put this book down yet. Just turn the page, and let's get started. After all, time is short. I can't wait for you to see what's just ahead. The Moment can come at any moment.

Even now!

CHAPTER 2

A GREAT DAY

In all of his mansions, there's not a room big enough for all his awards. Sir Paul McCartney may go down in history as the greatest musician of all time—a founding member of the Beatles and a man who became, as the *Guinness Book of World Records* puts it, the planet's "most successful musician and composer in popular music history."[1]

His fans know it's been a rough ride. Some of McCartney's hardest days were after the Beatles broke up. McCartney tumbled into a dark place. He stayed in his Scottish home smoking pot and getting drunk. He lost hope. After all, how do you follow the Beatles? Is there life after that kind of ride?

McCartney's turnaround started when the chords of a song came to him, one he'd worked on from time to time. The music made him feel optimistic, and he crafted it into a song for his children. He didn't record it until years later, but for him it was a personal song of hope.

He called the song "Great Day". The lyrics talked about a future day that was coming. And it was going to be a "Great Day"! And it wouldn't be long in coming, so it was something to look forward to . . . something to celebrate.

McCartney explained, "I liked the idea of a song saying that help is coming and there's a bright light on the horizon. I've got absolutely no evidence for this, but I like to believe it. It helps to lift my spirits."[2]

Paul McCartney doesn't realize how close he is to the truth. There is a Great Day coming—and it won't be long. There's a bright light on the horizon, and we have plenty of evidence for it. We have biblical evidence, and, boy, does it lift our spirits!

Jesus Christ is coming back for us—and soon!

If only McCartney realized that. If only the whole world—this world filled with hopelessness and despair—realized this truth of Scripture: "The great day of the LORD is near; it is near and hastens quickly" (Zeph. 1:14).

The apostle Paul talked excitedly about the heavenly crown awaiting him, "which the Lord, the righteous Judge, will give me on that great day of his return. And not just to me but to all those whose lives show that they are eagerly looking forward to his coming back again" (2 Tim. 4:8 TLB).

This is a book about a Great Day that's coming—the day of the Rapture. The exact date is already circled on God's calendar. We aren't privy to those records, but the year, month, day, hour, minute, and second are locked into God's program for our planet.

The Rapture is an event in the impending future when all of us, living or deceased, who have put our trust in Jesus Christ for salvation and eternal life will be suddenly caught up from this earth into the heavens. We'll be reunited with loved ones who have preceded us in death. We'll be met by the Lord Himself, who will usher us into heaven to live forever in perfect fellowship with God.

John Walvoord considered the Rapture a central event in biblical prophecy, writing, "The Rapture of the church is one of the most important practical prophecies in Scripture for believers today. It is an essential part of the many other prophecies in Scriptures. Though the Rapture is only a small fraction of the large body of prophetic Scripture, it stands out as one of the most important."[3]

Why is this day so great?

I'll deal with that question throughout this book, but let me give you some previews.

IT'S A GREAT DAY OF HOPE

The Bible uses the word *hope* repeatedly to describe the feelings we should currently have because of this imminent event. Peter called it a "living hope" (1 Pet. 1:3), and he said we could rest fully on that hope as we await the coming of Jesus (v. 13). The writer of the book of Hebrews called it "the hope set before us" (6:18) and "an anchor of the soul" (v. 19). The apostle Paul called it "the blessed hope" (Titus 2:13); he said this hope will never disappoint us (Rom. 5:5).

When the Bible uses the word *hope* in this sense, it doesn't simply mean a desire that may or may not occur. It means the "eager expectation" for something that will certainly happen, that is impending and swiftly coming.

Biblical hope is the excitement we feel today about what Jesus will do tomorrow.

In other words, when we grasp the reality of the approaching Rapture, it brings today's events into a happy perspective. There is an end to evil. There is an expiration date on suffering. There's coming a Great Day when we'll realize the sufferings of this present world aren't worth comparing to the glory that's about to be revealed (Rom. 8:18).

The energy that surges through us as we ponder this reality—well, that's what the Bible calls *hope*.

IT'S A GREAT DAY OF HOMECOMING

The Rapture will also be a day of homecoming when we'll be reunited with the entire family of Jesus Christ and we'll meet those who have gone before. In his primary passage about the Rapture in 1 Thessalonians 4, Paul made a point to emphasize this aspect of the Great Day so that bereaved Christians will not "sorrow as others who have no hope" (v. 13).

Mark Hitchcock wrote, "The truth of the Rapture is a source of supernatural comfort and hope to all of God's people when a believing loved one or friend goes home to be with the Lord. These words [in 1 Thessalonians 4] have certainly been read at thousands of funerals throughout the centuries."[4]

Seeing that statement gave me a jolt! I've often read 1 Thessalonians 4:13–18 at funerals and graveside services, but I'd never thought another pastor was doing the same 100 years ago, and 1,000 years ago, and 1,500 years ago, and 1,900 years ago. All of us standing by open graves, reading the same passage, literally from the days of Paul till now. And undoubtedly on this very day around the world, godly pastors are reading this text at the homegoing of faithful Christians!

Perhaps no words have ever given more hope to more people in more places during moments of raw grief.

IT'S A GREAT DAY OF HEALING

As we'll see, the moment of the Rapture is going to be the greatest healing event in human history. Talk about a healing service! During His ministry on earth, Jesus healed quite a few people; but on this day He is going to heal all His believers instantly and totally and eternally, whether they are still alive or have passed away, of any and all ailments of body, mind, or soul.

Imagine a dreaded case like cancer. (Many of us don't have to imagine; we've experienced it.) We're at the hospital receiving doses of medication that seem, at the moment, to make us ever sicker. Suddenly, in the twinkling of an eye, we're totally healed. Old age will be reversed, and physical deformities will be corrected—all in an instant. The total healing of every follower of Christ, immediately.

The dead will be raised imperishable, and all of us who remain will be caught up to heaven with new, glorified bodies. I can't wait to get to the chapter that deals with that promise in detail.

IT'S A GREAT DAY OF HAPPINESS

The very word *rapture* has become a term describing unbridled happiness. People talk about a rapturous event, and this will be the ultimate one. In fact, thinking about the Rapture brings me happiness right now, which is why I'm writing this book—to share the same wonderful information with you.

But our happiness now can't compare to the rapture of the actual Rapture!

And think of this: it's not just a happiness for you and me. Imagine how elated the resurrected saints will feel, how delighted the angels will be, and think of the joy that will flood over the face of our Lord Jesus as He gathers His children home.

Psychologists often talk about "mental triggers." Sometimes these are negative. A certain sound, smell, or memory can trigger a negative emotion, such as for those suffering post-traumatic issues. But there are positive triggers also. A favorite Scripture framed on the wall. A midmorning pause to breathe deeply. A slogan to get the day started. An uplifting hymn.

During the course of this book, I'm going to quote many, many verses of the Bible. Some will be from three major passages in John 14, 1 Corinthians 15, and 1 Thessalonians 4. But there will be many others—too many for me to count right now. I encourage you to select one or more of those verses. Be looking for them. When we get to a verse that especially speaks to you and brings you a ray of cheer, underline or highlight it. Then pick two or three of your favorite ones, memorize them, turn them into little songs, post them where you can see them daily, share them, and let them serve as positive mental triggers for the rest of your life.

The Rapture brings us happiness as we ponder it now, followed by unspeakable joy when it occurs.

IT'S A GREAT DAY OF HOLINESS

The Great Rapture Day will also be characterized by total and all-encompassing holiness. When we're caught up into the sky, we'll leave behind all our faults and failures, our shame and embarrassment, our weaknesses and woes. We'll be transformed not just physically but spiritually. Made holy in every way!

When we receive Christ as Savior, we're declared holy in God's sight. But our condition doesn't always match our position. Every day we're striving to live up to the supreme example of Christ. But on that future day we'll become holy in every thought, word, deed, and attitude.

The apostle Paul said, "Being confident of this, that he who began a good work in you will carry it on to completion until the day of Christ Jesus" (Phil. 1:6 NIV).

Galatians 5:5 says, "But we who live by the Spirit eagerly wait to receive by faith the righteousness God has promised to us" (NLT). I don't know about you, but I'm ready to get beyond the reach of the devil and his temptations.

So there's a bright light on the horizon, and we have plenty of evidence. It's going to be the greatest of all great days—the best day of your life. A Great Day of hope, homecoming, healing, happiness, and holiness. It's going to be a Great Day with Him who is preparing at this very moment to return in the skies *above* us and *for* us.

For the first time ever, the whole family of Christ will be together. No one will be left behind. If you don't think that's important, ask Van Ho.

One day during the Vietnam War, this little Vietnamese girl woke up as usual when the rooster crowed at five. But something was wrong. Her mother, sisters, and brother were gone. She went around the house, but her family had vanished. During the night, they had escaped from the invading Communists. Van Ho was too young for the rigorous trip, and her grandmother was too old, so they were left behind together to care for each other temporarily. When the rest of the family made it to America, they began desperately trying to find a way for the two who were left behind to join them.

In time, Van Ho was reunited with her family in Canada, and her first day there was unbelievable. For the first time, she saw modern conveniences like a bathroom with running water, a television with moving pictures, and cold milk from the refrigerator.

She later wrote, "I was still scared about leaving everything behind that was familiar. I was not sure about Canadian food or the snow. It bothered me that I couldn't understand everything my family talked about. . . . But I didn't care. For the first time since I was three years old, my whole family was together again. Nobody was left behind."[5]

That's what Jesus and Paul want us to know. For those of us who are followers of Christ, the Lord has gone ahead of us, but we're not forgotten. The whole family of God will be together again on that great and coming day.

None of His children will be left behind.

Certainly not you!

CHAPTER 3

THE RULE OF THREE

On May 13, 1940, Winston Churchill delivered his first speech as prime minister of the United Kingdom. The nation was already in the early stages of World War II, and Churchill's speech—like the man himself—was a powerful combination of the practical and the inspirational.

It was during that speech that Churchill delivered the now-famous promise "to wage war by sea, land and air, with all our might and with all the strength that God can give us; to wage war against a monstrous tyranny, never surpassed in the dark, lamentable catalogue of human crime."[1]

But there's a moment earlier in the same speech that I want to focus on right now. Speaking to both Parliament and the nation about his qualifications for leadership, Churchill said, "I have nothing to offer but blood, toil, tears, and sweat."[2]

Linguists have identified that moment as the likely origin of the phrase "blood, sweat, and tears."

You might be wondering, *Where did the "toil" go? How did "blood, toil, tears, and sweat"* become pared down to just *"blood, sweat, and tears"?*

The most likely answer is what communication experts call "The Rule of Three."

Speaking generally, The Rule of Three states that ideas or concepts are most understandable, relatable, and retainable when expressed in groups of three. For example:

- Life, liberty, and the pursuit of happiness.
- Calm, cool, and collected.
- I came; I saw; I conquered.

Part of the reasoning behind this rule is based on the way human brains are constructed. We have limited short-term memory, which means we often find it difficult to hold or process more than three separate blocks of information. At the same time, ideas presented in groups of one or two can feel boring or unappealing.

Perhaps that's why most plays are written with three acts. Perhaps that's why the best speakers often build their presentations around three points. And perhaps that's why Dale Carnegie famously said, "Tell the audience what you're going to say, say it, then tell them what you've said."[3]

By the way, even Jesus used The Rule of Three in His stories—in the parable of the good Samaritan, for example. First a priest, then a Levite, but it's the Samaritan who stopped and helped the beaten man on the side of the road (Luke 10:25–37). In Jesus' parable of the sower, He described the good soil as that which produces a crop, "some thirtyfold, some sixty, and some a hundred" (Mark 4:8). And probably most famous of all is Luke 15, where Jesus strung together a story about a lost sheep, a story about a lost coin, and a story about a lost son to show God's love for the wayward and the wandering.

Three seems to be the chosen number for effective communication. How interesting, then, that God provided a triad of passages in

Scripture that outline His prophetic plan for the Rapture. Those passages are found in John 14, 1 Corinthians 15, and 1 Thessalonians 4. Jesus provided the executive summary for the Rapture in the first passage, and Paul filled in the details in his two epistles.

There are other verses that mention or reflect the Rapture, of course, but these three chapters contain the core of God's teaching about that event. For that reason, these three chapters will serve as the foundation for this book.

JOHN 14:1–3

We begin in John 14, where Jesus talked with His disciples in the Upper Room just four days before His resurrection. His words were filled with comfort, instruction, and emotion. In the middle of that message, Jesus said:

> Let not your heart be troubled; you believe in God, believe also in Me. In My Father's house are many mansions; if it were not so, I would have told you. I go to prepare a place for you. And if I go and prepare a place for you, I will come again and receive you to Myself; that where I am, there you may be also. (vv. 1–3)

Highlight those words, "I will come again and receive you to Myself." That's Rapture talk. During one of the most comforting messages Jesus ever gave His followers, including us, the Rapture was at the forefront of His mind.

To give some context, our Lord Jesus opened His public ministry with the Sermon on the Mount in Matthew 5–7. Three years later, He closed His earthly work with the Upper Room Discourse, which is recorded in John 13–17. Remember, Jesus knew everything that was about to transpire: His arrest, the false accusations, the trial, His crucifixion, His resurrection, and His ascension soon after. The disciples, on the other hand, knew nothing about the chaos they were about to endure. Therefore, Jesus sought to prepare them and comfort them in advance.

As we read the Upper Room Discourse today, it's apparent that the Rapture was heavily on Jesus' thoughts. In fact, He spoke eagerly and wistfully about His future absence and His eventual return.

He told His followers, "Little children. . . . 'Where I am going, you cannot come'" (John 13:33).

That disturbed the disciples, and Peter asked Him about it: "Lord, where are You going?" (v. 36).

In response, Jesus told them about His Father's house and its many rooms. He told them about preparing a place designed specifically for them, and for us. Then Jesus spoke those wonderful words: "I will come again and receive you to Myself" (John 14:3).

Shortly after, He prayed, "Father, I desire that they also whom You gave Me may be with Me where I am" (John 17:24).

How Jesus loves us! How He loves you! Don't let your thoughts about the Rapture be confined to people vanishing or trumpets sounding. Instead, focus on the truth that Christ came and died to save you, returned to heaven to prepare a place for you, and is shortly coming to receive you to Himself.

Why? Because He wants you to be where He is, to see and to share in His glory!

1 CORINTHIANS 15:51–58

Next we come to Paul's first letter to the Corinthians, where the apostle connected the resurrection of Jesus Christ with the future resurrection of Christians at the time of the Rapture. He wrote:

Behold, I tell you a mystery: We shall not all sleep, but we shall all be changed—in a moment, in the twinkling of an eye, at the last trumpet. For the trumpet will sound, and the dead will be raised incorruptible, and we shall be changed. For this corruptible must put on incorruption, and this mortal must put on immortality. So when this corruptible has put on incorruption, and this mortal has put on immortality, then shall be brought to pass the saying that is written: "Death is swallowed up in victory."

"O Death, where is your sting?

O Hades, where is your victory?"

The sting of death is sin, and the strength of sin is the law. But thanks be to God, who gives us the victory through our Lord Jesus Christ.

Therefore, my beloved brethren, be steadfast, immovable, always abounding in the work of the Lord, knowing that your labor is not in vain in the Lord. (1 Cor. 15:51–58)

This is the second Scripture passage that provides the foundation for our understanding of the Rapture.

More broadly, Paul wrote 1 Corinthians 15 as a response to people connected with the church in Corinth who doubted the reality of a physical, bodily resurrection for believers. Without the completed New Testament, some of the early believers held mistaken views about the future, and they were often vocal about proclaiming those views. (Some things never change!)

Truthfully, the church in Corinth was confused about many theological and doctrinal issues. That church was the "problem child" among Paul's congregations, which I'm sure was frustrating at the time. But as a result of their need for correction, Christians throughout history have access to important teachings we wouldn't have received otherwise.

Many Bible scholars call 1 Corinthians 15 "The Resurrection Chapter of the Bible," for Paul defended the resurrection of Christ, explained the nature of the resurrection body, and ended the chapter at the zenith of prophecy: his description of the Rapture.

1 THESSALONIANS 4:13–18

Finally, we find our most detailed and, I think, most helpful depiction of the Rapture in 1 Thessalonians 4:13–18:

> But I do not want you to be ignorant, brethren, concerning those who have fallen asleep, lest you sorrow as others who have no hope. For if we believe that Jesus died and rose again, even so God will bring with Him those who sleep in Jesus.
>
> For this we say to you by the word of the Lord, that we who are alive and remain until the coming of the Lord will by no means precede those who are asleep. For the Lord Himself will descend from heaven with a shout, with the voice of an archangel, and with the trumpet of God. And the dead in Christ will rise first. Then we who are alive and remain shall be caught up together with them in the clouds to meet the Lord in the air. And thus we shall always be with the Lord. Therefore comfort one another with these words.

Once again, context is helpful for fully engaging these verses. Acts 17 describes the moment Paul planted a church in the great city of Thessalonica, located in the northern region of modern-day Greece. According to Acts 17:2, he was with them for only about three weeks before he was driven away by persecution. Paul didn't have ample time to plant deep spiritual roots or answer all the Thessalonians' theological questions. But he did speak often about the Lord's return as he presented the gospel.

As a result, the Thessalonians were gripped by the reality of Christ's return. To think they would see the Lord face-to-face! He was coming for them! They knew they needed to be ready for Christ to come again at any moment, and they looked for Him every day—as we all should. Yet there was also confusion.

When some of their church members died, the others grieved because those members hadn't lived long enough to see Christ come again. They were afraid their deceased loved ones had missed the Rapture—indeed, that those loved ones had missed heaven itself.

Paul wrote back to reassure them, teach them, and offer the comforting answers they needed. He introduced his message by saying, "For this we say to you by the word of the Lord" (1 Thess. 4:15). That indicates Paul's teaching on the Rapture was a direct communication received from Almighty God.

The apostle told the Thessalonian believers not to grieve like people who haven't discovered the hope Jesus gives us, and then he went on with the wonderful passage I quoted previously, saying that

- God will bring all His children to Himself, even those who "sleep" in death;
- the dead will rise first on the day of the Rapture;
- those still alive on that day will be "caught up together" to be with Christ;
- we shall "always" be with the Lord our God.

I find it helpful to compare the first and last of these three passages—John 14 with 1 Thessalonians 4—because they offer several powerful parallels and comforting collaborations. Here's what I mean:

	John 14:1–3	1 Thessalonians 4:13–17
The Problem	"Let not your heart be troubled" (v. 1)	"lest you sorrow as others who have no hope" (v. 13)
The Point	"believe in God, believe also in Me" (v. 1)	"if we believe that Jesus died and rose again" (v. 14)
The Proclamation	"told you" (v. 2)	"this we say to you" (v. 15)
The Promise	"I will come again" (v. 3)	"the coming of the Lord" (v. 15)
The Purpose	"to Myself" (v. 3)	"to meet the Lord" (v. 17)
The Plan	"receive you" (v. 3)	"caught up" (v. 17)
The Place	"that where I am, there you may be also" (v. 3)	"shall always be with the Lord" (v. 17)

Try to imagine what it would be like to receive these incredible teachings in the ancient world. Put yourself in the Upper Room, hearing Jesus' matchless words about His Father's house. Visualize yourself among the crowd in Corinth hearing Paul's letter for the first time. Think of what it meant to the Thessalonians to realize the Lord Himself would descend from the sky, and that His coming is imminent.

As we'll see in the pages to come, the message of the Rapture is just as urgent for you and me today—in fact, even more so.

I've always enjoyed news stories about overseas military members returning home early or unexpectedly to surprise their loved ones. One Florida elementary school conspired with the military to surprise ten-year-old Evan Ellinor right before Christmas break. During an all-school event in the cafeteria, principal Andrea Hall called Evan to the front and asked him what he wanted for Christmas. Evan said it was to see his brother, Private First Class James Ellinor, whom Evan had missed so badly it had affected the whole family. The little boy said it felt like his brother had been away for three hundred days (although it hadn't actually been that long).

You know what happened next. As the principal chatted with Evan, suddenly the lights flickered and the stage curtain opened—and there was James, dressed in his fatigues and standing with a bright smile in a classic army stance. When Evan saw him, he jumped over a table, clambered onstage, and leaped into his brother's arms, hugging him so tightly he almost had to be pried off. There wasn't a dry eye in the room.[4]

In the early days of reality TV there was a series called *Surprise Homecoming* that spotlighted these tear-jerking clips. The host would profile a wife or children who were wistful and lonely for their loved one, and then he would rip the yellow ribbon from around the tree in front of their house and say, "What these loved ones don't realize is the wait is over!"

In many ways, that is the message of these three key passages from God's Word. Jesus is coming. He will bring us to Himself, and I believe the wait is nearly over. The Lord's reunion *of* His people and *with* His people is close at hand.

CHAPTER 4

THE NOAH FACTOR

They call it "Johan's Ark."

Built by Johan Huibers in 2012, the boat is a reproduction of the vessel God commanded Noah to construct in the book of Genesis. At 390 feet long and 75 feet high, the ship is huge. It boasts numerous animal stalls, larders, and gutters for the disposal of refuse. There's an open amphitheater in the center and a series of labyrinthine stairs leading from deck to deck.

Best of all, it really floats! The boat currently sits in the harbor of Krimpen, a small Dutch town along the Maas River.

Why did Johan Huibers build his ark? "I wanted to spread God's Word in the Netherlands. . . . I wanted children to come here and feel the texture of the wood, see the nails and see that what is written in the book is true."

Specifically, Huibers wants people to recognize the danger of our current age. "I believe we are living in the end of times," he says. "We're not conscious of it. People never are."[1]

In one of his final messages, Dr. Billy Graham was also thinking about the ark—Noah's, not Johan's. Dr. Graham wrote in *Christian*

Post, "The days of Noah are returning to the Earth, and a catastrophe as great and terrible awaits those who refuse to enter into the ark of salvation, which is Jesus Christ."[2]

He was referring to our Lord's message on the Mount of Olives. Jesus said in Matthew 24:36–37: "But of that day and hour no one knows, not even the angels of heaven, but My Father only. But as the days of Noah were, so also will the coming of the Son of Man be."

Jesus did not promise to return when world conditions resembled the days of Abraham, or the days of Daniel, or the days of Paul. He will come suddenly during a period of history resembling the days of Noah.

In his book *As It Was in the Days of Noah*, Jeff Kinley wrote, "Jesus links the historicity of Noah and his Ark to the certainty of coming prophetic events and His physical return to this planet."[3]

But how? In what ways will the times parallel the times of Noah?

Jesus went on to explain in verses 38 and 39: "For as in the days before the flood, they were eating and drinking, marrying and giving in marriage, until the day that Noah entered the ark, and did not know until the flood came and took them all away, so also will the coming of the Son of Man be."

Let's take a deeper look at the comparisons between Noah's day and our own.

A CAVALIER GENERATION

The word that first comes to mind when I read Jesus' words is *cavalier*—a dismissive attitude that disregards all the warnings that should be heeded. Notice Jesus was not talking about people doing bad things, just normal things. They were eating, drinking, having weddings, and taking life as it came. All while Noah was hammering away and preaching about the danger to come. Like our Lord Jesus, Noah was both carpenter and evangelist. But everyone disregarded his message and considered him a fool.

How long did Noah preach to his generation about salvation from the flood? One hundred and twenty years! But rather than turning to God in repentance, those who heard him said, "I don't have time to study prophecy. I have to go to a wedding." "We're having dinner at our house." "I've got a career to pursue."

Jesus said the days before the Rapture will be just like that. People will continue to live as they have always lived despite cataclysmic warnings and predictions. They will focus on the present. They will make plans for the future only to ensure their physical comfort. They will not give one thought to the possibility that the prophets were right.

Jeff Kinley wrote,

> The days of Noah give us a sneak preview of things to come, an advance viewing of humanity in the last days. The generation witnessing the Ark's construction was a God-hating breed, and their kind will return again in the end times. Noah's contemporaries ignored Heaven's message and its messengers. They carried on day after day, year after year, century after century—eating, drinking, and pursuing relationships—without even the slightest acknowledgment of their Creator or a reflection of their responsibility to Him.[4]

Luke added this context in his account of the Lord's message on the Mount of Olives: "Likewise as it was also in the days of Lot: They ate, they drank, they bought, they sold, they planted, they built; but on the day that Lot went out of Sodom it rained fire and brimstone from heaven and destroyed them all. Even so will it be in the day when the Son of Man is revealed" (Luke 17:28–30).

A CARELESS GENERATION

We learn something more about the days of Noah from the book of Hebrews. While listing the heroes of the faith, the author wrote, "By faith Noah, being divinely warned of things not yet seen, moved with godly fear, prepared an ark for the saving of his household, by which he condemned the world and became heir of the righteousness which is according to faith" (11:7).

When God spoke to Noah, the old man believed, being moved with godly fear. He was concerned for his family, and his concern and care for the Lord served to condemn everyone else who was careless with the things of God and heedless to things as yet unseen.

People who have visited most of America's parks often say Glacier National Park is the most beautiful—a showcase of melting glaciers, breathtaking valleys, alpine meadows, and picturesque lakes in northern Montana. But since the park started keeping records in 1913, a total of 264 people have died there, many of them due to sheer carelessness.

John G. Slater was a summer employee of the park in the 1960s. He recalled that all the workers were shown a film entitled *The Mountains Don't Care*, about the dangers they might encounter at Glacier. But the movie didn't make much impact on him because he was young enough to think he "was bulletproof"—that nothing bad could happen to him.[5]

He learned his lesson after a nearly fatal experience on Mount Clements; thankfully, he lived to talk about it. Not everyone is so fortunate.

The book *Death in Glacier National Park* reports, "Supervisors make every effort to impress upon summer employees that Glacier has a wide range of unique hazards [including] snow bridges that conceal crevasses in the ice, ledges that can give way underfoot, and wind-created slabs of snow that can break free and become deadly avalanches. Warnings often go unheeded, however, in the face of peer pressure."[6]

The problem of carelessness can be seen far beyond Glacier National Park. So many people around us ignore the spiritual warning signs in God's Word because they feel bulletproof. It's inconceivable to them that anything cataclysmic could happen. Peer pressure seems stronger than prophetic warnings, and a careless attitude has swept the land.

Just as in the days of Noah.

A CORRUPT GENERATION

Nor can we miss the corruption that fouled the population of Noah's day. The Bible says, "The earth also was corrupt before God, and the earth was filled with violence. So God looked upon the earth, and indeed it was corrupt; for all flesh had corrupted their way on the earth" (Gen. 6:11–12).

Genesis 6:5 adds, "The wickedness of man was great in the earth, and . . . every intent of the thoughts of his heart was only evil continually."

Every intent of his heart! Only evil! Continually!

In Noah's day, people had vile imaginations. That hasn't changed over the course of history, but now we have the technology to put all these images—even worse ones than what you or I can conceive—on screens and instantly transport them to a billion depraved minds with the click of a button. Research shows over a third of all internet downloads are related to pornography, and nearly 10 percent of all viewers are under the age of twelve.[7]

The book of Genesis also described the violence of Noah's day, and I don't need to draw a parallel to our modern times. Paul wrote, "But know this, that in the last days perilous times will come" (2 Tim. 3:1).

Peter, undoubtedly thinking about what he'd heard from Jesus on the Mount of Olives, said, "Scoffers will come in the last days, walking according to their own lusts, and saying, 'Where is the promise of His coming . . . ?' For this they willfully forget: that by the word of God . . . the world that then existed perished, being flooded with water" (2 Pet. 3:3–6).

Noah's generation, like ours, was cavalier, careless, and corrupt. For those reasons and more, they were caught off guard!

A "CAUGHT OFF GUARD" GENERATION

Jesus went on to say in Matthew 24: "As the days of Noah were, so also will be the coming of the Son of Man. . . . Then two men will be in the field: one will be taken and the other left. Two women will be grinding at the mill: one will be taken and the other left" (vv. 37, 40–41).

Can you think of a more vivid way of describing the Rapture? Two people working side by side in a field. One is taken; the other is left. Two women grinding grain. One is taken, the other left.

The word *taken* is the Greek term *paralambano*. Just two days later, Jesus used that exact word in the Upper Room on the night before His crucifixion. He told His disciples, "If I go and prepare a place for you, I will come again and *receive* you to Myself" (John 14:3).

Remember, John 14 is one of our three primary passages on the Rapture.

People are going to be caught off guard! Look at this entire passage and notice the first and last sentences, which I've italicized and which bookend Jesus' teaching:

> *But of that day and hour no one knows, not even the angels of heaven, but My Father only.* But as the days of Noah were, so also will the coming of the Son of Man be. For as in the days before the flood, they were eating and drinking, marrying and giving in marriage, until the day that Noah entered the ark, and did not know until the flood came and took them all away, so also will the coming of the Son of Man be. Then two men will be in the field: one will be taken

and the other left. Two women will be grinding at the mill: one will be taken and the other left. *Watch therefore, for you do not know what hour your Lord is coming.* (Matt. 24:36–42)

As we've already seen in these pages, the seven-year agenda of the Tribulation is plainly laid out in Scripture. Jesus will return just as the armies of the Antichrist are attacking Jerusalem. The Rapture, on the other hand, is unannounced, coming at a time we know not.

Therefore, Jesus said, we must watch and be ready! Right now, the door to salvation is wide-open, just like the door of the ark.

One of the interesting things about the original ark was the fact that it had only one door. Dr. W. A. Criswell explained, "There was not a door above for the birds to come in, nor a little hole in the floor for the humble creatures of the earth to creep in, nor a big door for the elephant to lumber in; but there was one door, and everyone that was saved entered that door. The great eagle swooped out of the blue of the sky and entered in that door; the little wren hopped to safety through that door; the snail crawled slowly through that door. Noah and his wife, Shem, Ham, and Japheth and their wives, all alike, entered that one door."[8]

Perhaps you've heard stories of Muslims around the world having dreams that eventually lead them to Christ. One missions organization told of an Islamic man named Laddi who felt unsatisfied with his life. He prayed, "God, who are You? Tell me the truth!"

One night Laddi had a dream in which he saw a very old door. He opened the door and saw a man standing behind it—Jesus. Shortly afterward he found a local church's Facebook page online, and there was the image of the very door he had seen in his dream! Through that church Laddi learned the gospel, came to salvation through the doorway of Jesus Christ, and found what he most needed in life.[9]

Without Christ, you're living as in the days of Noah: cavalier, careless, corrupt, and about to be caught by surprise. At any moment, the door will swing shut, the Lord will come for His church, and you'll be left behind.

The Carpenter of Nazareth and the Preacher of Galilee said to you with all the amazing grace of His heart: "I am the door" (John 10:9). Come and enter—and you'll find what you most need in life!

CHAPTER 5

THE RETURN

"It's a piece that feels like it was written by God."[1]

That's how composer and jazz trumpeter Terence Blanchard described "Fanfare for the Common Man"—one of the most inspirational and majestic musical compositions ever performed. Even if you don't recognize that title, you've likely heard the song featured at sporting events and concerts and in documentaries, movies, TV shows, and more.

"It starts with percussive drums, gong, and timpani, rumbling like a distant battle," writes one critic. "Then the clear, clarion call of three trumpets, playing in unison, establishes the main theme. French horns join the trumpets, building support and harmony. Finally, the growls of trombones and tuba emerge from below as the fanfare builds to its climax—the brass ensemble establishing a powerful wall of sound."[2]

Aaron Copland composed "Fanfare for the Common Man" in 1942 as part of a broader artistic effort to fan the flames of patriotism once the United States entered World War II. While fanfares are typically reserved for the elite of society, Copland specifically dedicated his masterpiece to regular people.

"It was the common man, after all, who was doing all the dirty work in the war and the army," said Copland. "He deserved a fanfare."[3]

Throughout history, fanfares have been used to announce important events: royal coronations, presidential inaugurations, the beginning of battles, and more. The bright call of trumpets and other brass instruments has a wonderful way of grabbing our attention, spurring deep emotions, and calling us to action.

We're going to explore a specific fanfare in this chapter. One that announces a critical event in God's eschatological calendar: the return of the Lord.

What do I mean by "return"? When Jesus ascended from the Mount of Olives after His resurrection from the grave, He departed from our physical world and reentered the throne room of heaven. He retook His rightful seat at the right hand of the Father, where He remains to this day. Unencumbered by the chains of time, our Lord is enthroned in glory, honor, and praise.

Yet He will not remain there forever. One day soon, He will return to our world. In the words of one scholar, "At some point in the future, Jesus will come out of the Heaven of heavens and descend into the atmospheric heavens."[4]

That moment when Christ once again steps away from His rightful station will be the initiating event of the Rapture. And because the Rapture will be the initiating event of the Tribulation—and because the Tribulation is the initiating event of the Millennium—we can say with some certainty that this return of our Lord Jesus will be the catalyst that commences the End Times.

Now, here's an important distinction that sometimes causes confusion among those who anticipate the End Times. The return of Jesus that initiates the Rapture is not the same thing as the Second Coming of Christ. Those are two different events on the eschatological calendar, although they both involve Jesus physically reaching down to our world to fulfill His promises and complete His mission.

The Second Coming will be the moment Christ returns as the

Righteous King to end the rebellion of the Antichrist, defeat the assembled forces of the nations, and break the power of Satan over our world. We will discuss that glorious and gratifying event in a later chapter because the Second Coming will herald the end of the Tribulation Period and the beginning of the Millennium.

The Rapture, by contrast, will signal the start of the Tribulation. That event will be more of a rescue mission in which Christ the Savior emancipates His people from the chains of death and extricates His living servants from a world on the brink of chaos.

According to Scripture, the return of the Lord at the Rapture will be announced by three distinct, sensational, and spectacular sounds: "For the Lord Himself will descend from heaven with *a shout*, with *the voice of an archangel*, and with *the trumpet of God*. And the dead in Christ will rise first" (1 Thess. 4:16).

More glorious by far than the "Fanfare for the Common Man," this will be the "Fanfare for the Return of Christ." Let's explore each of those sounds in greater detail.

THE SOUND OF THE LORD'S COMMAND

The Greek word used to describe the Lord's shout "is that of a command of a military leader who comes out of his chief commander's tent and issues a command. One day the Chief Commander will come out of His heavenly tent and give a shout, a command for the resurrection and the translation to occur."[5]

Scripture shows us a similar shout in the Gospel of John, when Jesus stood outside the tomb of His friend and shouted: "Lazarus, come forth!" (11:43). It was a resurrection command. I've heard Bible students speculate as to what might have happened had Jesus failed to mention Lazarus's name. Would all the dead within the sound of His voice have emerged from their graves?

At the Rapture, that's exactly what will happen. Jesus' shout of

"Come forth" will not name a single individual but will be heard by every believer in every grave around the world. All those tombs will empty, and the resurrected believers will fly skyward.

THE SOUND OF MICHAEL'S VOICE

Ringing out along with the Lord's command will be the thunderous voice of the archangel. We know from Scripture just who this archangel is. He is Michael, the only archangel named in the Bible and the chief of all the angels (Dan. 12:1; Jude v. 9).

In the entire Bible, only three angels are mentioned by name. The first is Lucifer, who was the greatest of God's heavenly forces yet chose in his pride to rebel against his Creator, becoming Satan. Second is Gabriel, who told Mary she would give birth to Jesus. Gabriel is God's announcing angel. Third, Michael is God's warring angel, a role that makes the sound of his voice at the Rapture significant.

Dr. Arnold G. Fruchtenbaum wrote:

> Angels are often used to put God's plan into motion. Michael the Archangel will be used in the case of the Rapture. The content of what the voice says is not stated. But if known military procedure can be applied to this situation, then, this is simply the repetition by the sub-commander of the order (shout) of the chief commander. Jesus gives the shout or command for the program of the Rapture to begin, and it is Michael's task to set it into motion, so he repeats the command.[6]

Michael's shout at the return of the Lord may be a command to his legions upon legions of angelic warriors, calling them to defend believers from Satan's forces and escort them safely to heaven the moment Christ calls them home.

THE SOUND OF THE TRUMPET

The third sound heard at the Rapture will be "the trumpet of God." In 1 Corinthians 15:52, Paul referred to this as "the last trumpet."

Perhaps you've read about the strange phenomenon occurring around the world as people report hearing eerie sounds of trumpets. This has been going on since 2008, when a video was posted by someone in Belarus.

The website GotQuestions.org reported:

Strange sounds in the sky, which some call "sky trumpets" or "sky quakes," have been reported from around the world in recent years. People in the United States, Canada, Costa Rica, Russia, the Czech Republic, Australia, and other places have been puzzled by what they describe as low frequency hums, trumpets, or horns that seem to emanate from the top of the sky or from under the earth. Most of these sounds have never been heard before now, which makes the phenomenon unnerving.[7]

Residents in Brooklyn heard those sounds on November 11, 2022.[8] On January 17, 2023, residents of Kingston, Ontario, heard trumpet sounds that seemed to emanate from the skies. One resident said, "For the last hour or so, every 10 to 20 minutes the sound appears. It woke me up. . . . [It was] like a trumpet. [It's] coming from the sky."[9]

Well, I have no idea what those strange sounds are, but when the Rapture trumpet blows, the blast will surround the earth like an echo chamber, reverberating into the soul of every ascending Christian. It'll be loud enough to wake the dead—literally!

John Walvoord wrote:

The Rapture trumpet will call all Christians to rise from the earth to meet the Lord in the air and from there they will go to heaven, as Christ promised in John 14:3. The last trumpet for the church may be analogous to the last trumpet used in the Roman army. Soldiers were awakened by a first trumpet blast in the morning which served as their alarm clock. A second trumpet assembled them for instructions for the day. At the third and last trumpet they marched off to their assignments.

Similarly, receiving salvation is like hearing a trumpet call. Then God's call to service is like the second trumpet. At the third or last trumpet, believers go to heaven.[10]

Winston Churchill incorporated this meaning of the trumpet into his own funeral service. He arranged for a trumpeter to sound "the last post" (or taps, as we know it) from the highest reaches of the dome of Saint Paul's Cathedral. The long, slow ballad echoed mournfully throughout the ancient church as diplomats and dignitaries bowed their heads. The dirge was a ruthless reminder that Britain's hero had finally been conquered.

Or had he?

As the last sorrowful note faded, a second trumpeter suddenly sounded the reveille high from another gallery. This, too, was arranged by Churchill. The great statesman wanted the somber call to sleep to be followed by a more triumphant call to rise.[11]

For all who perish before the return of the Lord, our lives will follow a similar pattern. Yes, we will sleep. But at the Rapture, the trumpet blast will be a reveille, calling us to awaken and ascend.

And Jesus will be waiting.

CHAPTER 6

IF WE DIE

The Lord of the Rings movie trilogy is an epic story about the fight between good and evil. Near the conclusion of that story, two characters believe they have come to the end of their personal fight—they are trapped in a doomed city about to be overrun with hordes of evil creatures bent on destruction.

Gandalf is old and wise. His young friend Merry is inexperienced and terrified at the concept of death. As the city gates begin to splinter, Merry turns to Gandalf and says, "I didn't think it would end this way."

"End?" The look on Gandalf's face is one of genuine surprise. Then he smiles. "No, the journey doesn't end here. Death is just another path—one that we all must take."

Merry looks confused, so Gandalf elaborates. "The gray-rain curtain of this world rolls back, and all turns to silver glass. And then you see it."

"What?" asks Merry. "Gandalf, see what?"

"White shores. And beyond, a far green country into a swift sunrise." Gandalf sighs with anticipation just thinking about that heavenly vision. He smiles wide, hopeful even in the face of death.

"Well," answers Merry. "That's not so bad."

"No," says Gandalf, his smile even wider than before. "No it isn't."[1]

One way or another, our journey here on earth will end. Either we will experience death, or we will be part of that fortunate generation who witnesses the Rapture firsthand. That's the unchanging reality of the future. Of *your* future and mine.

For most people, that reality is terrifying. But what if I said we could forever change the way we look at death? What if I promised we could take death out of the fear category entirely? It's true. It's possible. Let's take on this important subject and—with the Bible as our guide—let's pull death out of the darkness once and for all.

THE FACT OF DEATH

Have you noticed the way our culture tries to hide from death? Or, perhaps more accurately, have you noticed the way our culture tries to hide death from us? It's taboo to talk about death. We pretend it doesn't exist.

The Bible isn't afraid to speak of death. It calls it what it is. Words such as *die* or *death* occur nearly nine hundred times throughout God's Word. Oftentimes Scripture uses terms for death that are graceful and poetic: "gathered to my people" (Gen. 49:29); "gather[ed] to your fathers, and you shall be gathered to your grave in peace" (2 Kings 22:20). Who isn't moved by the image of "the valley of the shadow of death" (Ps. 23:4)?

I consider the following to be the most beautiful verse in the Bible concerning the death of God's people: "Precious in the sight of the LORD is the death of His saints" (Ps. 116:15).

Importantly, the Bible does not describe death as the end of something but as a transition into something new. The New Testament is especially filled with passages conveying this positive, transitional perspective on death:

- Jesus referred to death as being "carried by the angels to Abraham's bosom" (Luke 16:22).
- Jesus told the repentant thief who died beside Him, "Today you will be with Me in Paradise" (Luke 23:43).
- Paul described death as being "absent from the body and . . . present with the Lord" (2 Cor. 5:8).
- More than a dozen times death is described as "sleep"—the temporary status of the body from which it will be awakened in resurrection at the end of the age (John 11:11; Acts 7:60; 1 Thess. 4:13).
- Paul said to die is to "gain," meaning being with Christ, and called death "far better" than being on earth (Phil. 1:21, 23).

THE FACES OF DEATH

The word *death* means "separation." What many people find surprising is that the Bible speaks about three kinds of death.

The first is physical death, when our souls and spirits are separated from our bodies. As the apostle James wrote: "The body without the spirit is dead" (James 2:26).

When Rachel, wife of the Old Testament patriarch Jacob, died while giving birth to their son, Scripture describes that moment as the separation of her body and soul: "And so it was, as her soul was departing . . . that she called his name Ben-Oni" (Gen. 35:18).

The second type of death is spiritual death. According to Paul, "The wages of sin is death" (Rom. 6:23).

Spiritual death is the separation of the natural man from God. When sin entered the world through Adam, it spread to everyone so that all unregenerate men and women are dead spiritually—they are separated from God.

Last is what Scripture calls the "second death," which is best described in the book of Revelation: "The sea gave up the dead who were in it, and Death and Hades delivered up the dead who were in them. And they were judged, each one according to his works. Then Death and Hades were cast into the lake of fire. This is the second death. And anyone not found written in the Book of Life was cast into the lake of fire" (20:13–15).

This last form of death, the second death, is the final banishment from God and the final misery of the wicked in hell following the Great White Throne Judgment at the end of the Millennium. From the second death, there is no recovery.

I have tried to bring understanding to this subject by using a little mathematical formula: "If you have been born only once, you will have to die twice. But if you have been born twice, you will have to die only once (and you may even escape that one death if Jesus returns to the earth during your lifetime)."[2]

All of us are born once (our physical birth), but if we are not "born again" through the Spirit and the Word of God (John 3:3–8; 1 Pet. 1:23), we will die twice: once physically when our body expires, and again at God's final judgment. But if we are born the second time through trusting in Jesus Christ as our Savior, we will die physically, but we will never, ever die again. This is what our Lord meant when He said, "I am the resurrection and the life. He who believes in Me, though he may die, he shall live. And whoever lives and believes in Me shall never die" (John 11:25–26).

THE FEAR OF DEATH

There are only two ways to face the future: with fear or with faith. Those who live by faith will find all their fears—especially the fear of death—consumed by the beauty of God's Person and the certainty of His promises.

Let's conclude this chapter with three truths the Bible gives us to defeat the fear of death.

THE PRINCE OF DEATH HAS BEEN DEFEATED

The author of Hebrews wrote, "Inasmuch then as the children have partaken of flesh and blood, He Himself likewise shared in the same, that through death He might destroy him who had the power of death, that is, the devil, and release those who through fear of death were all their lifetime subject to bondage" (2:14–15).

By His death and resurrection, the Son of God played the devil's own trump card. Just as David took the sword of Goliath and cut off his head with it, Jesus took the weapon of Satan and defeated him with it. The cross must have seemed like the ultimate victory for Satan, but it was precisely the opposite. When Jesus stepped from the open tomb on Resurrection Sunday, Satan's defeat was certain. His weapon of death had been destroyed.

Steve and Ann Campbell of Hampton, Tennessee, were sitting in their breakfast room one day, reading and relaxing. Their little dog, Gigi, a Maltipoo (Maltese and poodle mix), was asleep on the bench in the bay window. Suddenly a jolt rocked the room and toppled Gigi from the bench. Nothing was hurt but the little dog's pride.

The couple wondered what caused all the commotion. They could find no clue until they spotted a large hawk outside, lying beneath the bay window. The bird had swooped down, talons out, for Gigi with no regard for the protective pane of glass. A few minutes later the hawk shook off its stupor and vanished into the sky, minus its canine snack.[3]

The devil wants to get his talons into us. The power of the resurrection, however, provides a pane of protection that cannot be broken. Satan may knock himself out trying, but he can't claim us.

Because Christ died, we have lives that are forgiven; because Christ rose, we have lives that are forever.

THE POWER OF DEATH HAS BEEN DESTROYED

In 1 Corinthians 15, Paul said, "'O Death, where is your sting? O Hades, where is your victory?' The sting of death is sin, and the strength of sin is the law. But thanks be to God, who gives us the victory through our Lord Jesus Christ" (vv. 55–57).

There's no way to miss the certainty of Scripture when it comes to this truth: Death has been destroyed. The power of death is no longer powerful.

In the book of Revelation, the apostle John described what life will be like in heaven: "And God will wipe away every tear from their eyes; there shall be no more death" (21:4).

THE PROCESS OF DEATH HAS BEEN DESCRIBED

Perhaps no single verse of Scripture gives us a more comforting picture of death than the widely quoted Psalm 23:4: "Yea, though I walk through the valley of the shadow of death, I will fear no evil; for You are with me; Your rod and Your staff, they comfort me."

The sheer beauty of the passage never fails to move us, and its truth offers a depth of healing even in times of suffering. When you face death—your own or the death of a loved one—this verse should be held close to your heart.

What can it teach us? First, that *death is a journey, not a destination.* Death takes us "through the valley" and then out to someplace new—someplace infinitely better. This is a journey we make with God's hand in ours. My friend Pastor Rob Morgan describes how this journey reveals the transitory nature of death:

Psalm 23:4 does not speak of a cave or a dead-end trail. It's a valley, which means it has an opening on both ends. . . . The emphasis is on *through*, which indicates a temporary state, a transition, a brighter path ahead, a hopeful future. For Christians, problems are always temporary and blessings always eternal (as opposed to non-Christians, whose blessings are temporal and whose problems are eternal). Valleys don't go on forever, and the road ahead is always bright for the child of God, as bright as His promises. There are no cul-de-sacs on His maps, no blind alleys in His will, no dead ends in His guidance.[4]

Paul spoke of being "absent from the body and . . . present with the Lord," indicating that the two conditions are one and the same (2 Cor. 5:8).

As James M. Campbell observed, death is an exit gate, and heaven is an entrance. But the two are arranged so closely that one opens as the other shuts. When one person says that a dying person is "lying at the gate of death," another could say no, he is "lying at the gate of heaven." And both would have it right.[5]

Second, *death is a shadow, not a reality.* David called it "the valley of the shadow."

As Dr. Donald Grey Barnhouse was driving home from the funeral of his first wife, he and his children were overcome with grief. As he sought some word of comfort for his kids, a huge moving van passed them, and its shadow swept over the car. Dr. Barnhouse said, "Children, would you rather be run over by a truck or by its shadow?"

"The shadow, of course," said one of the children. "It's harmless."

"Two thousand years ago," said the father, "the truck ran over the Lord Jesus . . . in order that only its shadow might run over us."[6]

For the Christian, death is but a shadow. No longer is it the true substance of our fear; it's just a momentary obscuring of the light. Look again at Jesus' promise to every believer: "I am the resurrection and the life. He who believes in Me, though he may die, he shall live. And whoever lives and believes in Me shall never die" (John 11:25–26).

Finally, *death is lonely, but we are never alone.* David wrote, "You are with me" (Ps. 23:4).

I've counseled many people as they sat in death's waiting room, and experience has proven to me that God makes His presence known as they walk through that valley. He reaches for their hand.

He whispers words of comfort and promise. And it's not limited just to the dying; it's also for those who grieve for them.

Never must we walk that road alone. The Shepherd appears at our shoulder, and as we reach the gate, angels are there to attend us and usher us into the wonderful surprises that await us.

On December 7, 1941, Peter Marshall, chaplain of the US Senate, was speaking to the cadets at Annapolis. A "day of infamy" was in progress at Pearl Harbor, which now lay in the flames of an enemy attack. The room was filled with young men who would soon give their lives sacrificially. Marshall told them the story of a dying child—a little boy with a disease who asked his mother, "What is it like to die? Does it hurt?"

The mother thought for a minute, then said, "Do you remember when you were smaller, and you played very hard and fell asleep on your mommy's bed? You awoke to find yourself somehow in your own bed?"

The boy nodded.

"Your daddy had come along, with his big, strong arms and lifted you, undressed you, put you into your pajamas as you slept. Honey, that's what death is like. It's waking up in your own room."[7]

So let the future come. Let the next phase of life present itself in God's timing, whether through death or the Rapture. No matter which way we take the next step in our eternal journey, we will do so in our Father's arms.

CHAPTER 7

THE RESURRECTION

Modern science is filled with wonders, but there are many things even the most eminent scientists don't fully understand. Like string theory. And the composition of the universe. And what causes Alzheimer's disease.

And butterflies.

Yes, that's correct. Butterflies.

Those who study bugs for a living have no idea how a caterpillar wraps itself in a chrysalis or a cocoon, rests for a period of days or weeks, and then reemerges as a butterfly. We do know the caterpillar becomes completely dissolved during that process. When scientists cut open those cocoons in the middle of a metamorphosis, all they find is a sticky, slimy goo. Nothing more than a puddle of DNA. Then, somehow, that goo reforms itself into an entirely new creature.

Biologist Bernd Heinrich caused a stir in the entomological community by suggesting caterpillars and butterflies are actually two separate organisms. According to this theory, a caterpillar is born, lives a normal life, and then enters its cocoon as a kind of grave. Its body decomposes. Most of its cells literally die.

Heinrich refers to this stage as a "deathlike intermission."

Then comes a kind of genesis. New cells are created seemingly out of nothing. New organs begin to function as a new organism emerges from the grave. According to Heinrich, "Most of one body dies, and the new life is resurrected in a new body."[1]

We don't know if Dr. Heinrich's hypothesis is correct. But we do know butterflies have been associated with Easter for centuries. They are living, fluttering reflections of resurrection.

We've seen already in these pages that the Rapture will begin with the audible return of Jesus. Accompanied by the voice of the archangel and a divine trumpet call, our Savior will step back into our atmosphere with a shout of command: "Come forth!"

It is Jesus' return that will commence the next phase of the Rapture: the resurrection.

THE SLEEP BEFORE RESURRECTION

When Christ descends from heaven with a shout, He will begin by summoning to Himself "those who are asleep" (1 Thess. 4:15). Paul's terminology is New Testament language for identifying Christians who have died. It's interesting that Bible writers never use the words *sleep* or *asleep* to describe the death of an unbeliever, but they use them often to describe the death of a believer.

Consider these examples:

- "These things He said, and after that He said to them, 'Our friend *Lazarus sleeps,* but I go that I may wake him up'" (John 11:11).
- "Then [Stephen] knelt down and cried out with a loud voice, 'Lord, do not charge them with this sin.' And when he had said this, *he fell asleep*" (Acts 7:60).

- "For David, after he had served his own generation by the will of God, *fell asleep*, was buried with his fathers, and saw corruption" (Acts 13:36).
- "Now Christ is risen from the dead, and has become the first-fruits of those who have *fallen asleep*" (1 Cor. 15:20).

These word choices were not random. Instead, they offer a powerful redefinition of death itself. When viewed through the lens of sleep, the end of a human life is not the end at all. Just another form of "deathlike intermission."

As one commentary noted:

This metaphorical use of the word sleep is appropriate because of the similarity in appearance between a sleeping body and a dead body; restfulness and peace normally characterize both. The object of the metaphor is to suggest that, as the sleeper does not cease to exist while his body sleeps, so the dead person continues to exist despite his absence from the region in which those who remain can communicate with him, and that, as sleep is known to be temporary, so the death of the body will be found to be.[2]

Sleep has its waking, and death will have its resurrection.

Dr. Arnold G. Fruchtenbaum offers a helpful definition for the Bible's redefinition of death:

The Bible views the death of a believer as a temporary suspension of physical activity, until the believer awakens at the Rapture. Just as physical sleep is temporary (a temporary suspension of physical activity until one awakens, yet there is no suspension of mental activity), so death is a temporary suspension of physical activity until one awakens at the resurrection. . . . There is no cessation of spirit-soul activity, only physical activity.[3]

This proper understanding of death is emphasized in the word early Christians adopted for the burying places of their loved ones. It was the Greek word *koimeterion*, which means "a resting house for strangers, a sleeping place." This is the same word from which we get our English term *cemetery*. In Paul's day, this word was used for what we would call a hotel. When we check in at a hotel, we expect to spend a night in sleep before we wake up in the morning, refreshed and raring to go.[4]

Likewise, when Christians die, it is as if they are slumbering peacefully in a place of rest, ready to be awakened at the return of the Lord. Because of Christ's victory on the cross, death is not a tragic finality but only a temporary sleep.

You and I set our alarm clocks every night expecting to awaken in the morning. If we die before Christ's return, we know that one day our bodies will be awakened by the alarm clock of our Lord's coming in the clouds. At that resurrection moment, God will miraculously assemble the necessary molecules and reconstruct our physical bodies.

As Paul wrote, all genetic flaws will be corrected, all illnesses healed, and all damage repaired to perfection: "The body is sown in corruption, it is raised in incorruption. It is sown in dishonor, it is raised in glory. It is sown in weakness, it is raised in power. It is sown a natural body, it is raised a spiritual body. . . . The trumpet will sound, and the dead will be raised incorruptible" (1 Cor. 15:42–44, 52).

THE SEQUENCE OF RESURRECTION

Looking back at 1 Thessalonians 4, we can see a clear chronological sequence connected with this future resurrection. The Bible teaches that those who are asleep in Jesus—Christians who have died—will not be left out of the Rapture. In fact, they will have the prominent place when Jesus comes in the skies: "We who are alive and remain until the coming of the Lord will by no means precede those who are asleep. . . . The dead in Christ will rise *first*" (1 Thess. 4:15–16).

In other words, if I am still alive when Jesus comes back, I will not ascend skyward before my parents. They will be "caught up" first. The Rapture is initially for those who have been saved and whose bodies are resting in the cemeteries. Then, those of us who still have breath in our lungs will also be caught up to join our predecessors in the presence of Christ.

William Barclay wrote the following about the believer's resurrection from the dead:

> The man who has lived and died in Christ is still in Christ even in death and will rise in him. Between Christ and the man who loves him there is a relationship which nothing can break, a relationship which overpasses death. Because Christ died and rose again, so the man who is one with Christ will rise again.[5]

Nineteenth-century Bible teacher A. T. Pierson made an interesting observation about these things:

> It is a remarkable fact that in the New Testament . . . it is never once said, after Christ's resurrection, that a disciple died—that is, without some qualification. . . . Peter says, "Knowing that I must shortly *put off this my tabernacle* as the Lord showed me." Paul says, *"The time of my departure is at hand."* . . . The only time where the word "dead" is used, it is with qualification: "the *dead in Christ,*" "the *dead which die in the Lord.*"[6]

The point here is that Scripture regularly and consistently teaches the reality of the resurrection. Why? Because God created us with eternity in our hearts. Each of us is made for something more than planet Earth; we're meant to matter longer than a shadow or a vapor. We're made for heaven, and we aren't going to exist there in a disembodied form.

THE SECURITY OF RESURRECTION

Dallas Willard once told the story of a woman who refused to talk about life beyond death. She was afraid to discuss the afterlife because she didn't want her children to be disappointed if it turned out there was no afterlife. Willard pointed out the futility of that line of thinking. If there is no afterlife, no one will have any consciousness with which to feel disappointment!

On the other hand, he said, "If there is an afterlife, whoever enters that next life unprepared may experience far more than mere disappointment."[7]

Of course, the Bible teaches the reality of the afterlife from cover to cover, and its teachings change the way we think about death. Or at least, those teachings *should* change the way we think about death.

In my experience, most people today are terrified of dying. Even Christians. They do everything possible not only to avoid the physical moment of death but also to avoid thinking about the reality of death. How often in our culture do we pretend death doesn't exist?

Paul addressed the foolishness of such avoidance when he wrote these words to the Corinthian believers: "Foolish one, what you sow is not made alive unless it dies" (1 Cor. 15:36).

I think Paul was chiding the Corinthians a bit. He was saying to them, "Why are you so worried about death? Don't be silly; you can't have a resurrection if you don't die."

Later in that same chapter, Paul asked, "O Death, where is your sting?" (v. 55).

This is the Bible's way of scolding us, too, for being too worried about the sting of death. If we don't die, we'll have to live in our old, failing, fallible, sickly, weary bodies throughout eternity, just getting weaker and weaker. Anyone who wants to do this is thinking like a foolish person. How much better to let our bodies sleep awhile, then awaken in resurrection glory for eternal life!

The well-known Bible teacher Joni Eareckson Tada tells about the time her mother-in-law bought a grave plot at Forest Lawn Cemetery for her family but wouldn't sign the papers until Joni and her husband, Ken, inspected the lot and gave their approval.

One Sunday afternoon, Ken and Joni drove out there and found the location of their gravesites in a section called Murmuring Pines. They listened to the sales representative as she spoke about what a good view it was, where her feet would be and where her head would be, and so forth. Joni was a little disinterested in the presentation.

A few minutes later, while the family conferred over the paperwork, Joni said, "I powered my wheelchair onto the top of my grave site and turned to gaze at the range of mountains. A gust of wind rippled the grass, and the pines above me did, indeed, murmur. A breeze tossed my hair. A profound peace settled over the scene. Suddenly, it struck me that I was sitting on the exact spot where my actual body will rise, should I die before Christ comes."

Joni thought about the wonder of that moment when her spirit will reinhabit her body and she will suddenly be raised in perfection and glory. For her, it was a moment of profound worship. That hill became holy ground, for she knew she was sitting on the exact spot not simply of her burial but of her resurrection.[8]

CHAPTER 8

THE MYSTERIES

Can you name the bestselling novelist of all time? I'll give you a few clues to solve the mystery. Well, there you already have one—the person is a mystery writer. Second, the writer is a woman. Here's a third clue—she died in 1976 at age eighty-five.

Solve the case? It's Agatha Christie, of course, the author of sixty-six detective novels featuring two primary heroes: Hercule Poirot and Miss Marple. She wrote books such as *Murder on the Orient Express*, *Death on the Nile*, and *The Murder of Roger Ackroyd*. Christie was also a playwright, and *The Mousetrap* remains the world's longest-running play to this day.

She also wrote an autobiography in which she shared the story of her own life and what led to her fascination with the concept of mystery. She wrote, "To be part of something one doesn't in the least understand is, I think, one of the most intriguing things about life."[1]

You might be surprised to learn that the Bible, and particularly the New Testament, is filled with mysteries—though not the type we find in novels.

Here's an example from the book of 1 Corinthians: "Behold, I tell you a mystery: We shall not all sleep, but we shall all be changed—in a moment, in the twinkling of an eye, at the last trumpet. For the trumpet will sound, and the dead will be raised incorruptible, and we shall be changed" (15:51–52).

In this case, Paul was not shedding light on a problem to solve or a crime to investigate. Instead, he was referring to a truth that had never before been revealed: the reality of the Rapture.

When you find the word *mystery* in the Bible, it always describes something God has waited until the right time to tell us. These truths or realities have always existed—they have always been part of God's plan—yet were only disclosed at a specific point in history.

Biblical mysteries are an important part of the New Testament. The word *mystery* occurs twenty-six times from Matthew to Revelation (it's found nowhere in the Old Testament). These mysteries are theological truths connected to salvation, the church, God's kingdom, and other important topics.

According to Fruchtenbaum: "For something to qualify as a New Testament mystery, it must be something totally unrevealed anywhere in the Old Testament. If it is knowable from the Old Testament, it is not a mystery."[2]

As I mentioned, there are many mysteries revealed in the writings of the New Testament. But for the purposes of this chapter, we will focus on five specific mysteries connected with the church—including the critical mystery of the Rapture.

THE MYSTERY OF THE STARS AND LAMPSTANDS

We'll begin our mysterious exploration with the first chapter of Revelation: "The mystery of the seven stars which you saw in My right hand, and the seven golden lampstands: The seven stars are the angels of the seven churches, and the seven lampstands which you saw are the seven churches" (v. 20).

The revealer of this mystery is none other than Christ as He reintroduced Himself to the apostle John on the island of Patmos. John saw the Lord standing "in the midst of . . . seven lampstands" and "had in His right hand seven stars" (1:13, 16). Christ's appearance was overwhelming in every way, causing John to fall "at His feet as dead" (v. 17).

Christ touched John's shoulder and began speaking. After comforting John, and before dictating His letters to the seven churches in Asia, Jesus revealed the mystery of the stars and lampstands.

The stars represent angels that watch over the seven churches, which are represented by the seven golden lampstands. The mystery is this: Each of the seven churches to which Christ addressed a message was watched over by a heavenly messenger (angel) to carry out blessings, provide discipline, or deliver information directed to the church. Nowhere was this truth prophetically revealed in the Old Testament.

THE MYSTERY OF THE BODY OF CHRIST

Next is a subject that feels commonplace for Christians today but was revolutionary for the early church: "[God] made known to me the mystery . . . that the Gentiles should be fellow heirs, of the same body, and partakers of His promise in Christ through the gospel" (Eph. 3:3, 6).

Ephesians 3:1–12 is a detailed description of God's revelation of the existence of His church. Paul used the word *mystery* six times throughout Ephesians and three times in Ephesians 3:3–9. This mystery was never revealed nor even hinted at in the Old Testament: that God would "create in Himself one new man from the [Jew and the Gentile], thus making peace, and that He might reconcile them both to God in one body through the cross" (Eph. 2:15–16).

In other words, God always planned for the church to be multi-national—to include both Jews and Gentiles—but He kept the plan secret until after the resurrection of Christ.

It's clear in the Old Testament that the Jews are God's chosen people. It's also clear they were called to be a "light to the Gentiles" (Isa. 42:6; 49:6; Acts 13:47). God desired to display His glory to the Gentile world through Israel and attract the world to Himself through His chosen people.

But nowhere in the Old Testament was it revealed that the Messiah would create "one new [spiritual] man," the church. It is now possible for Gentiles to share in the promises of Abraham by being grafted into the olive tree that is Israel (Rom. 11:11–24).

THE MYSTERY OF THE INDWELLING MESSIAH

Our personal connection with the Creator of the universe is another biblical mystery worth exploring: "To [the church] God willed to make known what are the riches of the glory of this mystery among the Gentiles: which is Christ in you, the hope of glory" (Col. 1:27).

In verse 26, Paul offered a clear definition for a New Testament mystery: "The mystery which has been hidden from ages and from generations, but now has been revealed to His saints." That mystery is this: "Christ in you, the hope of glory."

While the Old Testament is filled with references to the coming Messiah, the fact that the Messiah would indwell every one of His subjects and followers—that God would actually become part of us by means of the Holy Spirit—was never mentioned or considered. It was a brand-new truth.

Jesus hinted at this mystery in His Upper Room conversation with His disciples. He told them that soon—after the resurrection—they would realize "I am in My Father, and you [are] in Me, and I [am] in you." He promised that whoever loved Him, "My Father will love him, and We will come to him and make Our home with him" (John 14:20, 23).

The full meaning of that, however, only came with the Day of Pentecost and the teaching of Paul and the apostles. The church would come to realize that "it is no longer I who live, but Christ lives in me" (Gal. 2:20).

THE MYSTERY OF THE CHURCH AS THE BRIDE OF CHRIST

Not only are we connected with Christ as individuals, but also as a community, which is described as the Bride of Christ. Paul said this "is a great mystery" (Eph. 5:32).

This is the only time Paul described what he was revealing as a "great mystery." That mystery has to do with the relationship between Christ and His body, the church. Several times in the Old Testament God is implied to be the husband of Israel—an expression of His sacrificial love for His chosen people (Isa. 54:5; Jer. 31:32). But nowhere does the Old Testament reveal that the Messiah will take a bride for Himself, and that the bride will be His church, for which He will lay down His life sacrificially. This is, indeed, a "great mystery."

Throughout Ephesians 5, Paul used human marriage as a way of illustrating this truth (vv. 22–33). The husband is expected to love his wife sacrificially, and the wife is expected to submit to her husband. It's the husband's great love for his wife that motivates her honor and respect. The husband is called to love and nurture his wife and to promote her holiness. Such a mutual relationship also exists between Christ and His church. His sacrificial love for His bride becomes the impetus for the church's willing reverence for Him as Lord.

Paul deepened the significance of this mystery by quoting from Genesis 2:24 in verse 31: a man will leave his parents and become one flesh with his wife. So the church is one with Christ: we died with Him, were buried with Him, and were raised to new life with Him (Rom. 6:1–10; Eph. 2:5). No wonder Paul called this a "great mystery"!

THE MYSTERY OF THE RAPTURE

Now let's look at 1 Corinthians 15 once more, because it's time to explore the mystery most connected with the theme of this book: "Behold, I tell you a mystery: We shall not all sleep, but we shall all be changed—in a moment, in the twinkling of an eye, at the last trumpet. For the trumpet will sound, and the dead will be raised incorruptible, and we shall be changed" (1 Cor. 15:51–52).

The Old Testament was clear about the coming of the Messiah to establish His kingdom on earth at the end of the age. Less clear, but still expressed, was the understanding that a resurrection would take place (Job 19:25–27; Ps. 16:9–11; Dan. 12:2). What was not revealed at all was any understanding about the return of the Messiah coupled with the resurrection of the righteous. That is, the Old Testament didn't reveal there would be a generation of saints alive at the hour of the Messiah's return who would pass into eternity without first going into the grave.

This is the mystery of the Rapture—the translation of living saints from mortality to immortality, from perishable to imperishable, in the "twinkling of an eye."

In 1 Corinthians 15:50–58, Paul explained the instant "translation" from the mortal state to the immortal state. In 1 Thessalonians 4:16–17, he explained the bigger picture: at the sound of the trumpet the dead in Christ will rise first, followed by the translation of those living at the moment. Thus, all who belong to Christ—those who died in Christ and those living in Christ—will be instantly caught up to meet the Lord in the air.

This was the mystery Paul revealed in 1 Corinthians 15, where we learn of God's unfolding plan for our future.

I recently read about a visit made by Queen Elizabeth II to Sydney, Australia, in 1986. What caught my attention wasn't the visit itself but a letter the queen wrote to the citizens of that city. What does the letter say? We don't know! And that's the point.

Near the end of her stay Down Under, the queen presented the letter to Sydney's mayor with the following instructions: "On a suitable day to be selected by you in the year 2085 AD, would you please open this envelope and convey to the citizens of Sydney my message to them."[3]

To this day, the letter has not been opened. It rests somewhere in a glass case within a restricted room at the top of Sydney's Queen Victoria Building. Decades from now, that letter will be opened, and the good people of Sydney will finally hear what the queen wanted to tell them—in her timing.

That's akin to the idea of mystery in the Bible. A biblical mystery is not a problem to be solved but a truth to be revealed. Yes, there will be murder and mayhem during the Tribulation. But the best mysteries are those given to us by God to inform, encourage, and prepare us.

From the beginning of history, God planned to call His people to Himself through the vehicle of the Rapture. But that plan wasn't revealed until God wanted us to know. He delivered those plans through the Gospels and the epistles of the New Testament. He waited until the timing was right to give us the information we need.

So it's the Bible after all—not Agatha Christie's novels—that represent the bestselling mysteries of all time.

CHAPTER 9

THE EXTREME MAKEOVER

He was known as the man with the perfect body.

Born in Prussia (modern-day Germany) in 1867, Eugen Sandow spent much of his early life traveling around Europe as a wrestler or a circus performer. During his travels, he often studied the marbled perfection of sculptures from ancient Greece and Rome, searching for secrets to the perfect physique. Sandow even developed his own system of weight training and exercises based on dumbbells.

Then came his big break. When the United Kingdom created an elaborate competition to discover "the world's strongest man," Sandow entered. Immediately, he was a smash hit with the Victorian public. He signed a contract with a wealthy promoter and went on a kind of bodybuilding tour around the world, including the United States. He even created a special wooden box that shined light on specific, individual muscles.

Though he's largely forgotten today, many credit Eugen Sandow with establishing the modern ideal for male fitness—broad shoulders and chest, narrow waist, muscular legs, and chiseled abs. According to one biographer, "He created a craze for physical culture."[1]

Wouldn't we all like to have "the perfect body"? I'm not interested in looking amazing, but wouldn't it be wonderful to have a body that never broke down? One that wasn't plagued by the imperfections of age and ailments, sickness and senility?

Here's some wonderful news: if you are a follower of Jesus, you will receive such a body! At some point in the future, you will upgrade your current model to one that is top-of-the-line in every respect.

Paul described this upgrade in his first epistle to the church at Corinth: "So also is the resurrection of the dead. The body is sown in corruption, it is raised in incorruption. It is sown in dishonor, it is raised in glory. It is sown in weakness, it is raised in power. It is sown a natural body, it is raised a spiritual body" (1 Cor. 15:42–44).

As we've seen, the Rapture will spark a resurrection renaissance across the globe. Christians who died will live again—not only in a spiritual sense but physically as well. The bodies of believers buried in the ground will come out of the ground. They will be raised up.

Those bodies will be the same ones that went into the grave, though they will be transformed in profound ways. Assuming you and I die before the Rapture, our resurrected bodies on that day will be the same in essence—we will still be humans, and you will still be you. But the resurrection body that emerges will be superior to the old body you are inhabiting now.

These words apply not only to those who will be resurrected at the Rapture but also to those who are alive when Jesus returns. Everything that happens to a resurrected body will also happen to a body "caught up" to heaven in the Rapture.

Specifically, here are six things the Bible tells us will be true of our new bodies in that day.

OUR NEW BODIES WILL BE INCAPABLE OF SICKNESS OR DEATH

Throughout the history of time as we know it, there has been only one body not subject to corruption: the body of the Lord Jesus. Psalm 16:10 says prophetically of Him, "For You will not leave my soul in Sheol, nor will You allow Your Holy One to see corruption." Jesus was buried, but on the third day He came out of the grave. His body incurred no corruption.

Unlike Jesus, when our earthly bodies die and are buried, they see corruption. But Paul told us that when we are raised up on the day of resurrection, we will be raised in incorruption. Our present bodies wear out and grow old, but our resurrection bodies will have no capacity for deterioration or decay. Your new body will be designed for eternity. It will not be subject to accident, disease, aging, or death. It will be pain-free and disease-free. It will never die; it will outlive the stars!

The exclamation point to this truth is found in Romans 6:8–9 where the resurrection body of Jesus is described like this: "Now if we died with Christ, we believe that we will also live with him. For we know that since Christ was raised from the dead, he cannot die again; death no longer has mastery over him" (NIV).

Notice those words about Jesus: *He cannot die again.*

From the moment He arose from the tomb of Joseph of Arimathea on Easter Sunday, there is one thing Jesus Christ cannot do. He did it once, but He can never repeat the action. It is impossible for Him to die again. His glorified body is imperishable and indestructible.

"It is appointed for men to die *once*" (Heb. 9:27). Our bodies are sown in corruption; they will be raised in incorruption.

OUR NEW BODIES WILL BE IDENTICAL TO THE BODY OF THE RESURRECTED JESUS

As several Scriptures tell us, the Lord Jesus Christ in His own resurrection provides the pattern for our resurrection. The Bible says:

- "For our citizenship is in heaven, from which we also eagerly wait for the Savior, the Lord Jesus Christ, who will transform our lowly body that it may be conformed to His glorious body, according to the working by which He is able even to subdue all things to Himself" (Phil. 3:20–21).
- "Beloved, now we are children of God; and it has not yet been revealed what we shall be, but we know that when He is revealed, we shall be like Him, for we shall see Him as He is" (1 John 3:2).
- "And as we have borne the image of the man of dust, we shall also bear the image of the heavenly Man" (1 Cor. 15:49).

The heavenly Man is Jesus. Just as we now bear the image of old Adam in our current bodies, we will bear the image of the Man of heaven, Jesus, in our resurrection bodies.

The Bible gives us a few glimpses of our Lord's resurrection body by telling us some of the things that happened during the forty days between His resurrection and ascension. From what we know in the New Testament, Jesus appeared perhaps ten or twelve times during this period. And when we look at those passages, we see our Lord in His glorified body.

The most important thing about Jesus' body—and He emphasized this repeatedly—is that it was real, literal, physical, and tangible. It was the very body that had been crucified. On one occasion when Jesus appeared to His disciples, He told them, "Behold My hands and My feet, that it is I Myself. Handle Me and see, for a spirit does not have flesh and bones as you see I have" (Luke 24:39).

This tells us we aren't going to be some kind of ghostlike phantoms that float around forever. We're going to have our same literal, physical bodies, but they will be risen, resurrected, and glorified—equipped for eternity.

During two of His post-resurrection appearances, Jesus ate with His disciples, which shows us our glorified bodies will be capable of eating. I have been asked if we will need to eat in heaven. I don't know if we will need to eat, but we certainly will enjoy eating and drinking since Jesus did. In Luke 24, Jesus clearly ate with His disciples, and in John 21, He prepared breakfast for everyone.

The body of Christ was also touchable. It could be held. In John 20:27, Jesus told Thomas, who had a hard time believing that Jesus had really risen from the dead, "Reach your finger here, and look at My hands; and reach your hand here, and put it into My side. Do not be unbelieving, but believing."

In John 20:17, Jesus had to tell Mary to quit clinging to Him. "Do not cling to Me, for I have not yet ascended to My Father."

OUR NEW BODIES WILL BE IDENTIFIABLE BY ALL WHO KNEW US ON EARTH

Over the years, I have been asked these questions: "In my new resurrection body, will people know me? Will they recognize me? And will I know others?"

The Bible is very clear in its answer.

After the resurrection, Jesus knew His disciples, and they knew Him. They recognized the glorified Jesus as the very same One they had known before His death. They were so convinced of the identity of the risen Christ that they all went to their deaths proclaiming the reality of the message of everlasting life.

When you get to heaven, you're going to know all of the people you met down here—and they will know you. It is unthinkable to me that in heaven we will know less than we do here; we will know much more! The Bible says, "For now we see in a mirror, dimly, but then face to face. Now I know in part, but then I shall know just as I also am known" (1 Cor. 13:12).

We will have a greater sense of recognition in heaven than we've ever had here on this earth. When Moses and Elijah appeared out of heaven to stand with Christ on the Mount of Transfiguration, the disciples instinctively recognized Moses and Elijah as real people. They knew them. When Jesus described heaven in Matthew 8:11, He said, "And I say to you that many will come from east and west, and sit down with Abraham, Isaac, and Jacob in the kingdom of heaven."

OUR NEW BODIES WILL BE ILLUMINED IN BRILLIANCE

Paul wrote, "It is sown in dishonor, it is raised in glory" (1 Cor. 15:43). We could accurately translate the word *glory* as "brilliance." Our new bodies may actually have a luminescent quality to them.

In Exodus 34:29, something unusual happened when Moses spent time with the Lord. His face became radiant and began to shine. The same thing happened to Jesus on the Mount of Transfiguration (Luke 9:28–30). In Revelation 21, we're told the entire city of New Jerusalem will be luminescent, brightly illumined by the light that radiates from the resurrected Christ. Daniel 12:3 says the resurrected saints "shall shine like the brightness of the firmament." Matthew 13:43 says, "Then the righteous will shine forth as the sun in the kingdom of their Father."

The glory the Lord Jesus had in His glorious body is a pattern for the glory we will have in our own bodies when we're resurrected.

OUR NEW BODIES WILL BE INFINITE IN PHYSICAL POWER

Paul wrote this about our new body: "It is sown in weakness, it is raised in power" (1 Cor. 15:43).

We will be buried in weakness. A dead body has no strength or power. It cannot lift a finger. But when we come out of the grave, we'll have so much energy we'll think a lightning bolt has supercharged us with electricity.

Our resurrection bodies will be incredible, full of enthusiastic power, and capable of extraordinary functions. When you read about the Lord Jesus after His resurrection, He could enter sealed rooms without going through the door: "Then, the same day at evening, being the first day of the week, when the doors were shut where the disciples were assembled, for fear of the Jews, Jesus came and stood in the midst, and said to them, 'Peace be with you'" (John 20:19).

If the glorified body of Christ could pass through walls and travel by impulses of thought, perhaps the same will be true for us. Without being dogmatic on the specifics, I'm convinced our glorified bodies will not have the same limitations we are forced to endure today.

OUR NEW BODIES WILL BE INCREDIBLY SUITED FOR HEAVEN AND ETERNITY

Paul said our body is "sown a natural body, it is raised a spiritual body. There is a natural body, and there is a spiritual body. As so it is written, 'The first man Adam became a living being.' The last Adam became a life-giving spirit" (1 Cor. 15:44–45).

What did Paul mean by a "spiritual" body? We've already indicated that our heavenly bodies will be literal, physical, touchable, identifiable, and powerful. Therefore, the word *spiritual* in verse 44 does not imply that our bodies will be incorporeal or mere apparitions.

Jesus had a material body, and we're going to have bodies just as He does. But our new bodies will exist on a higher plane. Instead of being governed by our appetites, they will be governed by the Holy Spirit. That's what a spiritual body is.

The basic difference between a natural body and a spiritual body is that the former is suited for life on earth, while our spiritual bodies will be suited for life in heaven for eternity with God. In our current bodies, we couldn't function in the realm of heaven. But God is going to give us new bodies like the ones we have now, only completely made over and transformed—no longer governed by the appetites of the flesh but governed now by the appetites of the Spirit.

Life on earth is fragile and uncertain, but we have a Savior who died for our sins and was buried and raised on the third day according to the Scriptures. And by the grace of God we await that wonderful day when we'll be raised incorruptible and given our new supernatural bodies, made by Christ. This will not be a hard thing for God to do. The Bible says, "Why should any of you consider it incredible that God raises the dead?" (Acts 26:8 NIV). As commentator Matthew Henry wrote:

> Why should it not be as much in the power of God to raise incorruptible, glorious, lively, spiritual bodies out of the ruins of those vile, corruptible . . . ones, as first to make matter out of nothing . . . ? To God all things are possible.[2]

Like the rest of the world, I was struck by the magnitude of the moment when Queen Elizabeth II passed away on September 8, 2022. She was ninety-six on the day of her passing, which means she reigned over the Commonwealth for seventy years and 214 days—the longest verified rule of any female monarch in history.

The United Kingdom observed a ten-day mourning period after her death, during which part of the time the queen lay in state at Westminster Abbey. If you watched the funeral service, you saw that ancient cathedral filled with leaders, dignitaries, and well-wishers from all over the globe.

The queen had ordered several Scripture passages to be read throughout the service, beginning with this crucial verse recited in the old King James as the procession guided her coffin toward the altar: "I am the resurrection, and the life: he that believeth in me, though he were dead, yet shall he live: and whosoever liveth and believeth in me shall never die" (John 11:25–26 KJV).[3]

That is the hope we cling to as followers of Jesus. The Rapture assures us that death is not the end of life—it is simply the beginning of a new existence in our new, perfect, glorious bodies.

CHAPTER 10

THE RAPTURE

Captain William Schaffner vanished without a trace. He was a pilot in the United States Air Force, engaged in an official exchange with the Royal Air Force. On September 8, 1970, he was flying a BAC Lightning over the North Sea. His call sign was Foxtrot 94.

Suddenly an unidentified object was caught on radar, and Schaffner pursued it. He reported it as "glowing in a golden light." The object was later said to be another aircraft, but it eluded Schaffner, who flew at a high speed toward the object.

And then he—well, he simply vanished. Not just from radar. The man simply disappeared.

About a month later his plane was found intact on the bottom of the sea, but the cockpit was closed with the canopy and ejector seat still in place. There was no sign of Captain Schaffner or his remains.

For decades, people have tried to solve the mystery of the vanished airman, and Foxtrot 94 has spawned countless theories. Recently another investigation suggested Schaffner had manually opened the canopy and jumped out in midair; and when his plane hit the water, the pressure closed the canopy.[1]

Maybe. But the case of the vanished air force pilot has puzzled military and civilian investigators for decades. Imagine, then, how officials will try to explain the spontaneous disappearance of millions or even billions of people? How will the governments explain it? What conspiracy theories will grip the popular imagination? What panic will haunt the hearts of those left on earth?

That's the Rapture!

THE PORTRAITS OF THE RAPTURE

Some people question using that word because the term *rapture* is not in the Bible. Yes, but 1 Thessalonians 4:17 says we will be "caught up"! The Greek word Paul used was *harpazo*. When the New Testament was rendered into Latin, the translators used the word *raptura*, which means "to catch up or snatch up." From this, we get our word *rapture*.

You probably seldom think about Greek terms, but this is one you should understand. *Harpazo* is found thirteen times in the New Testament, and it has multiple shades of meaning. Each helps us understand the nature of the Rapture event.

In some instances, the word means "to carry off by force." At the Rapture, the devil and his cohorts may do all in their power to keep Christians here on earth. But the Lord Jesus will overpower them, delivering us by the omnipotent power at His command as if carrying us off by supreme might.

The word can also mean "to claim for oneself eagerly." At the end of this present age of grace, our blessed Savior will come to claim us as His very own.

A third meaning of the word is "to snatch out or away speedily." This emphasizes the sudden nature of the Rapture. In a split second, the Lord will call all believers to Himself to share in His glory. Not one will remain behind.

The fourth meaning of the word is the most definitive. It means "to rescue from the danger of destruction." In his letter to the Corinthians, Paul described the sudden nature of the Rapture as "in a moment, in the twinkling of an eye" (1 Cor. 15:52).

Mark Hitchcock explained it like this:

> The events of the Rapture will happen "in a moment, in the twinkling of an eye" (NASB). The Greek word for *moment* is *atomos* from which we get our English word *atom*. *Atomos* refers to something that is indivisible, that cannot be divided. When Paul wrote these words, no one could imagine splitting the *atomos*. Today, we would translate this "in an instant," "in a split second," or "in a flash."
>
> The second phrase that describes the duration of the Rapture is "in the twinkling of an eye." The Greek word for *twinkling* is *rhipe*. This might refer to the time it takes for light to reflect in the human eye. Others believe that it refers to the time it takes to blink your eye—"in the blink of an eye." Blinking is the quickest movement in the human body. People everywhere understand what "in the blink of an eye" means.

Hitchcock summarized by saying, "The Rapture will occur in a split second. Suddenly corpses all over the world will be raised and reunited with perfected spirits, and living believers everywhere will be caught up to heaven and transformed body, soul, and spirit. The Rapture will shock the world. It will change everything."[2]

In a nanosecond, the Lord will call all believers to Himself to share in His glory. We will simply vanish from the earth. No one who has confessed Christ as Lord will remain behind.

THE PICTURE OF THE RAPTURE

It is hard to imagine just what that will look like, but I read a paragraph recently that created this vivid picture:

Millions of people from all parts of the earth feel a tingling sensation pulsating throughout their bodies. They are all suddenly energized. Those with physical deformities are healed. The blind suddenly see. Wrinkles disappear on the elderly as their youth is restored. As these people marvel at their physical transformation, they are lifted skyward. Those in buildings pass right through the ceiling and roof without pain or damage. Their flesh and bones seem to dematerialize, defying all known laws of physics and biology. As they travel heavenward, some of them see and greet those who have risen from their graves. After a brief mystical union . . . they all vanish from sight.

The world will somehow have to come to grips with *millions* of missing Christians. The ensuing outcry of sorrow, loss, and confusion will make the Rapture a well-publicized event, dominating the media for weeks and weeks.[3]

I recall a depiction of the Rapture in Hal Lindsey's book *The Late Great Planet Earth*:

There I was, driving down the freeway and all of a sudden the place went crazy . . . cars going in all directions . . . and not one of them had a driver. I mean it was wild! I think we've got an invasion from outer space!

It was the last quarter of the championship game and the other side was ahead. Our boys had the ball. We made a touchdown and tied it up. The crowd went crazy. Only one minute to go and they fumbled—our quarterback recovered—he was about a yard from goal when—zap—no more quarterback, completely gone, just like that!

It was puzzling, very puzzling. I was teaching my course in the Philosophy of Religion when all of a sudden three of my students vanished. They were quite argumentative—always trying to prove their point from the Bible. No great loss to the class. However, I do find this disappearance very difficult to explain.[4]

These images help us visualize what the Rapture may be like, though our imaginations aren't big enough to truly envision what the world will experience. Our hearts *are* big enough, however, to realize our Lord wants us to be with Him, and every day we're more eager for His return.

THE PURPOSE OF THE RAPTURE

But why will He come in this way and at this unspecified time? Let me suggest two reasons.

First, the Rapture will end the church age and trigger the stunning sequence of the events of the End Times.

According to Guinness World Records, the largest chain of dominoes so far constructed was at a Michigan school. It consisted of one hundred thousand dominoes, which took a week to assemble into elaborate patterns across the gym floor. One privileged student toppled the first piece, and the chain reaction was unstoppable.[5]

Similarly, the sudden appearance of Jesus Christ in the sky for His children and their sudden disappearance from earth will trigger a nonstop chain of events, lasting seven years, and culminating in His Second Coming.

Every year, more than a billion people tune in across multiple TV networks to watch the ball drop in New York City's Times Square. Tens of thousands flood the streets of the Big Apple to watch the event live. What's interesting is that the ball itself is a symbol of transition. From the moment the ball begins to descend the pole atop One Times Square, viewers know they're witnessing the end of the current year. They are still experiencing that year, but they know something new is coming. When the ball finally finishes its descent, the new year begins. The old is gone and the new has come.

In like manner, the Rapture will be the catalyst, the divine spark, that will signal the end of our current age and begin the prophetic countdown to the end of history as we know it.

The other purpose of the Rapture will be for God to deliver His children from earth before this seven-year Tribulation begins. What will happen during these seven years will eclipse every natural disaster in history. Jesus warned, "There will be great tribulation, such as has not been since the beginning of the world until this time, no, nor ever shall be" (Matt. 24:21). This period is described in vivid detail in Revelation 6–18.

During this period, the world will experience pain and devastation like never before. But according to the Scriptures, Jesus will first "catch away" all those who have put their trust in Him. He will do this before the Tribulation begins.

In Revelation 3:10, Jesus told the church in the ancient town of Philadelphia: "Because you have kept My command to persevere, I also will keep you from the hour of trial which shall come upon the whole world."

Here, then, is a summary of what happens: The Lord Jesus Christ will return from heaven, bringing the souls of those who have already died with Him. The bodies of those dead saints will be resurrected and changed, and then the bodies of those Christians who are alive and remain at His coming will also be changed.

When this happens, God is going to hover over this universe, and all who have accepted Jesus Christ as Savior, those who have been resurrected and those who have never died, are going to be snatched up—pulled right out of the population, suctioned off the planet. It's going to happen instantly. No time to get ready. No prelude. No preliminaries.

In his book *The King Is Coming*, Harold Wilmington provided an illustration I find especially helpful on this topic:

> A man is cleaning out his garage and discovers a small box filled with a mixture of tiny iron nails, wooden splinters, sawdust, and pieces of paper. Suppose he desires to save the nails. How could he quickly separate them from the wooden splinters? If a magnet was

available, the task would be quite simple. He would simply position the magnet over the box. Immediately all those objects possessing the same physical nature would be caught up to meet the magnet in the air.

When Christ appears, he will not come especially for black or white people, for Catholics or Protestants, for Jews or Gentiles, but for those individuals who possess the same nature as Himself.[6]

Those who know Christ share His nature, and we'll be drawn to Him, caught up by His magnetic, rapturous power—and then we will ever magnify our Savior!

The Rapture Sequence
1. The Return "The Lord Himself will descend from heaven with a shout, with the voice of an archangel, and with the trumpet of God" (1 Thess. 4:16).
2. The Resurrection "And the dead in Christ will rise first" (1 Thess. 4:16).
3. The Rapture "Then we who are alive and remain shall be caught up together with them in the clouds to meet the Lord in the air" (1 Thess. 4:17).
4. The Redemption "We shall not all sleep, but we shall all be changed" (1 Cor. 15:51).
5. The Reunion "Then we who are alive and remain shall be caught up together with them in the clouds to meet the Lord in the air. And thus we shall always be with the Lord" (1 Thess. 4:17).

CHAPTER 11

FIVE OTHER RAPTURES

Whether young or old, we never tire of rereading C. S. Lewis's delightful set of books known as The Chronicles of Narnia. In terms of the chronology of the tale, it all starts with *The Magician's Nephew*.

In the story, set in the late 1800s, two neighborhood children, Digory and Polly, became friends and began playing in an old attic room in the row of buildings where they lived. One day they discovered the strange library of Digory's uncle, who had a set of beautiful rings. When Polly touched a yellow ring, she suddenly vanished. The ring had given her the power to travel between worlds. Digory, in great alarm, touched another yellow ring, determined to go after her. He took with him two green rings, which would allow him and Polly to return.

Thus begins the amazing stories that unfold over seven volumes in the world of Narnia.

It's interesting that C. S. Lewis visualized the possibility of someone disappearing on earth and suddenly being in another world. The

Lord had the same thought, and it actually happens in Scripture—not once or twice but six times!

One day soon it's going to happen to the followers of Christ in the twinkling of an eye. They'll vanish from this world and appear with the Lord in glory.

The Bible calls this the Rapture.

While most Christians are familiar with the Rapture of the church—the future moment when Christ will gather His church from the earth to meet Him in the clouds—many are unaware there are other raptures mentioned in Scripture.

As I said, five other "disappearances" are recorded: those of Enoch, Elijah, Jesus Christ, Paul, and two individuals who will appear during the Tribulation.

Let's take a biblical tour of these vanished victors.

THE RAPTURE OF ENOCH

We'll begin with one of the Bible's most mysterious figures: Enoch, who is mentioned five times in the Bible, beginning in Genesis.

In the early days of the human race, people lived much longer than they do now. Consider these life spans listed in Genesis 5: 930, 912, 905, 910, 895, 962, 365, 969, 777.

Does one of those figures seem out of place? One person "only" lived for 365 years, when others lived nearly three times that long. What happened to him? Did he die prematurely due to an accident or illness? Was it a genetic mutation that shortened his life? Was he murdered? Not at all. This man was Enoch. Because of his godliness we would have expected him to live longer than anyone. But it was actually his godliness that cut short his life on earth.

Genesis 5:22–24 says, "Enoch walked with God three hundred years. . . . So all the days of Enoch were three hundred and sixty-five years. And Enoch walked with God; and he was not, for God took him."

I like the way verse 24 is rendered in *The Message*: "Enoch walked steadily with God. And then one day he was simply gone: God took him."

To use Paul's words, Enoch disappeared in the twinkling of an eye. He instantaneously vanished from earth and appeared in heaven.

Enoch was one of only two people in the Bible who are said to have "walked with God." The other was Noah (Gen. 6:9).[1]

This phrase—*walking with God*—has an Edenic ring to it. It was something Adam and Eve did before the fall. It suggests a closeness, an intimacy, that was unique in human history. According to Jude, Enoch was a preacher of righteousness who predicted the Lord's return (v. 14).

Why did God cut short Enoch's earthly life and take him to heaven? We don't know. Perhaps it was a reward for Enoch's remarkable life. J. B. Phillips put it this way in his translation of Hebrews 11:5: "It was because of his faith that Enoch was promoted to the eternal world without experiencing death. He disappeared from this world because God promoted him."

THE RAPTURE OF ELIJAH

Enoch isn't the only person who had this experience. In dramatic fashion, so did the prophet Elijah.

Swashbuckling characters began appearing in some of the earliest movies from the 1920s, people whom today we call heroes. Zorro and Robin Hood were early examples, then came Superman, Batman, and other superheroes. Today we have myriad military and secret agent types, both male and female, who are paid to spike our adrenaline as we follow them from one amped-up adventure to the next.

If I had to pick a biblical character to star as an ancient action hero, I'd pick Elijah. Vocationally, he was a prophet of God who became a thorn in the side of the wicked king Ahab and his wife Jezebel (1 Kings

17–2 Kings 2). God used Elijah to bring about miracles and to defend the true religion of Israel. Besides his miracles, Elijah is best known for his powerful encounter with 850 false prophets atop Mount Carmel. Elijah, whose name means "the Lord is my God," challenged the false prophets to see if their "god" would defend his own name in a contest with Yahweh, Elijah's God—a challenge Elijah won (1 Kings 18).

Like most charismatic figures, Elijah lived a peaks-and-valleys life. After his victory on Mount Carmel, he fled for his life from Ahab's wife Jezebel and hid in a cave in the desert where God restored him physically and spiritually. Refreshed, he confronted kings again while training his protégé, Elisha. When Elijah's ministry came to its end, "a chariot of fire appeared with horses of fire, and separated [Elijah and Elisha]; and Elijah went up by a whirlwind into heaven. . . . So [Elisha] saw him no more" (2 Kings 2:11–12).

Why did God "rapture" this action-oriented prophet to heaven before he died on earth? Only heaven knows. It seems Elijah had completed God's earthly purpose for him, so God called him home in dramatic fashion.

THE RAPTURE OF JESUS CHRIST

God "took" Enoch, and Elijah "went up." When we come to the disappearance of Jesus Christ from earth at His ascension, we find another element to consider: "Now when [Jesus] had spoken these things, while they watched, He was taken up, and a cloud received Him out of their sight" (Acts 1:9).

There is a grammatical point to be made in that passage: "was taken" is a passive verb. That means Jesus didn't ascend to heaven by His own power. Rather, He was drawn up as if by a magnet by the Father. That adds an important dimension to the six raptures detailed in Scripture: they are all acts of God whereby He removes people from earth to join Him in heaven.

Each of these first three examples is different in the details. Enoch apparently vanished in a moment; Elijah rode to heaven in a fiery chariot; and Jesus ascended to heaven gradually as the disciples watched, then disappeared into the clouds of glory. He was drawn up from above.

Yes, Jesus was and is God. But the Bible is clear in stating that when Jesus was sent by the Father to earth (John 20:21), He gave up His divine prerogatives and status (though not His divinity) to become fully human—the last Adam (1 Cor. 15:45; Phil. 2:6–8). The Father sent the Son to earth to accomplish "the work" (John 17:4) of redemption. And when that work was completed, three decades after His arrival, it was time for Him to return to His union and fellowship with the Father and the Spirit until He returns again (Acts 1:11).

In the case of Enoch and Elijah, we don't fully know why they were called from earth to heaven. But in Jesus' case, we do know—and that gives us insight into each of the raptures in Scripture. They all have to do with God's plans and purposes and timing. While we may not know His purposes in every case, we know this: if God chooses to call someone from earth to heaven, there is a divine reason.

THE RAPTURE OF PAUL

Let's look at another case study. In 2 Corinthians 12:2, the apostle Paul said he was "caught up" from earth to the "third heaven." In a moment of time, Paul found himself in the presence of God, not knowing if he was there physically or not (vv. 2–3). He used the Greek word *harpazo*—a sudden catching up—to describe his experience. This is the same term he later used to describe the Rapture of the saints in 1 Thessalonians 4.

Paul used this verb twice: "[I] was caught up to the third heaven . . . [I] was caught up to paradise and heard inexpressible things" (2 Cor. 12:2–4 NIV).

While Paul was in paradise, God told him inexpressible words about the mysteries of heaven, which informed the apostle and strengthened him for all the incredible suffering he endured during his ministry. I believe this is why Paul was so eager, from that point on, to get back to heaven. He told the Philippians, "I am torn between [living or dying]: I desire to depart and be with Christ, which is better by far" (Phil. 1:23 NIV).

This is also why he could tell us, "I consider that our present sufferings are not worth comparing with the glory that will be revealed. . . . For our light and momentary troubles are achieving for us an eternal glory that far outweighs them all" (Rom. 8:18; 2 Cor. 4:17 NIV).

The rapture event was early in Paul's apostolic career, equipping him to later write the theological letters that would shape his world and ours and to have the stamina to withstand the rigors of his ministry.

Paul's rapture was unique in that he went to heaven and returned to earth to continue serving God until his martyrdom. But it was also similar to all the others in that it reflected God's timing and God's purpose—a sudden and sovereign act.

THE RAPTURE OF THE TWO WITNESSES

I mentioned earlier that Elijah might be compared to modern action heroes. A peer in that regard would easily be Moses. He was bold and courageous, a man of military prowess and miracle power. This dynamic duo—Elijah and Moses—will appear on the world stage during the second half of the seven-year Tribulation. Unnamed in the book of Revelation, they are called God's "two witnesses" (11:3).

When they appear, the world will be under the heel of the Antichrist and his False Prophet. The two witnesses will stand for God and testify to His presence and power by working miracles. They will call down fire, cause a drought, turn waters to blood, and strike the earth with plagues (vv. 5–6).

In retaliation, the Antichrist will kill them and display their bodies in the streets of Jerusalem for three and a half days as the godless world erupts in celebration. But after those three and a half days, God will raise His witnesses from the dead, bringing great fear upon all who observe this miracle.

Yet that won't be the end of the story. After this incredible resurrection, "they heard a loud voice from heaven saying to [the two witnesses], 'Come up here.' And they ascended to heaven in a cloud" in the sight of all the people (v. 12).

When this rapturous miracle occurs, the people who praised the witnesses' death will instead praise the God who raptures them to heaven.

The rapture of God's two witnesses is yet to come; it will take place a few years after the forthcoming Rapture of the church. And given present and future video and communication technology, it will be seen worldwide by billions of people as it happens. As the last of the six biblical raptures, it will represent one of the last opportunities for those who have "eyes to see" to recognize the power and presence of God—before it's too late.

All these people, including all of us who will be raptured at the Great Disappearance, will be vanished but not vanquished. We will be victorious!

Since I opened this chapter with C. S. Lewis, let me close by quoting him: "We do not and cannot know when the world drama will end," Lewis wrote in his essay "The World's Last Night." "The curtain may be rung down at any moment: say, before you have finished reading this paragraph. . . . Precisely because we cannot predict the moment, we must be ready at all moments."[2]

Few people understand that sentiment better than the crew of the famed Imperial Trans-Antarctic Expedition from the early 1900s. Sailing from England aboard the schooner *Endurance* and led by national hero Sir Ernest Shackleton, the sailors sought to make history by traversing the Antarctic continent.

Tragically, the *Endurance* was caught within a rapidly freezing ice pack in January 1915. The ship was crushed and ultimately sank, leaving the men to set up camp on the ice itself. When that ice floe began to break apart, the men were forced to cross hundreds of nautical miles in small lifeboats before landing on Elephant Island—an isolated spot of frozen rock in the middle of a frozen wasteland.

Knowing rescue was unlikely in such a desolate place, Shackleton and five others left in a twenty-two-foot lifeboat to seek help. They had to cross almost a thousand miles of open sea in order to reach regular shipping lanes, yet there was no other hope.

Frank Wild was Shackleton's second-in-command, and it was up to him to keep the rest of the crew safe and engaged within the camp. Each day, Wild sought to maintain morale by assigning duties, serving meals, leading sing-alongs, planning athletic competitions, and more. Because the camp was constantly in danger of being buried in snow, Wild and his men fought fiercely against the drifts using only a few shovels.

Throughout the ordeal, Wild never lost faith that Shackleton—whom the men called "the Boss"—would return. He confidently retained a last tin of kerosene and maintained a small supply of dry combustibles ready to ignite at any moment should the rescue party appear.

Every morning, Wild rolled up his sleeping bag and roused the men by saying, "Get your things ready, boys, the Boss may come today!"[3]

Sure enough, 105 days after they set sail in their lifeboat, Shackleton and his volunteers returned on a Chilean fishing vessel to rescue the rest of the crew. Because of Wild's preparation and infectious enthusiasm, he and his men were ready at that moment of salvation. The torches were lit, and the sailors saved.[4]

Unlike that stranded crew, we have a certain promise that the Lord will return. Ours is not a mere longing or a desperate hope, as theirs was, for our Lord is the Creator and Master of all, and His promise is as sure as His very existence.

Therefore, we can rise each day with that same joyous anticipation in our hearts, saying, "Get your things ready. The Boss may come today!"

CHAPTER 12

WHO GETS RAPTURED?

It was supposed to be one of the more memorable games of Jalen Duren's young career, but it turned into a moment of frustration—even embarrassment. Standing at six feet, eleven inches and packed with talent, Jalen had all the makings of an NBA superstar. Yet as the youngest player in the league, he still had a few things to learn.

Duren and his Detroit Pistons were scheduled for a January 2023 series against their rival Chicago Bulls. But more important than the opponent was the destination: Paris. This was a rare sequence of games played outside the United States, and Jalen was meant to be featured on that international tour.

On the day of the trip, Duren made sure his bags were packed. His adrenaline was pumping. Having just returned from a short injury, he was ready to get back on the court.

Yet when the Pistons boarded the airplane bound for Paris, Duren wasn't there. When the team took a photo together at the Eiffel Tower,

Duren was missing. He wasn't even in the same country! He missed the team flight.

Before the game, reporters peppered Pistons head coach Dwane Casey with questions about his young star: "Where's Jalen?"

The coach's answer was both diplomatic and direct: "It is a learning experience," he said, "understanding how important passports are."[1]

Jalen Duren had every intention to be on that plane from Detroit to Paris. He was qualified physically, having healed from his recent injury and received approval from team doctors. He was qualified professionally as an NBA player and a member of the Pistons team. He was even qualified personally, given his desire to represent his league and his team in a different nation.

Yet all of those factors carried no weight when confronted by the qualification that mattered most: his passport. Because Duren did not have the legal right to visit the destination of his choice, he was left behind.

The same will happen at the Rapture for any and all who are missing their spiritual passport to eternal life in heaven. That passport is Jesus Christ. His sacrifice opened the door for redemption and the forgiveness of our sin. Yet we must receive His righteousness in order to enjoy eternity with Him.

We've explored the "what" and "why" of the Rapture in many ways and from many angles throughout these pages. Yet it would be a mistake for us to ignore the "who." Meaning, who will take part in the Rapture? Who will be "caught up" with Christ during that future event?

The answer: not everyone. The Rapture will be restricted only to those—living or dead—who carry the passport called Christ.

I know such a claim clashes with the values and norms of our culture. It's becoming more and more dangerous to even hint that only certain people will experience eternal life. But that's exactly why it's important for us to have a solid understanding of this issue. You could say this chapter explores the apologetics of the Rapture—we'll examine both the reality of and the reasons for the restrictions connected to the Rapture.

THE REALITY OF THE RESTRICTIONS

Each of the three major passages connected with the Rapture makes it clear that only those who are believers in Jesus Christ will be included. Here's how this unfolds in John 14, 1 Corinthians 15, and 1 Thessalonians 4.

In John 14:1–3, Jesus addressed His disciples as those who believe in God and in Him. He spoke to them about "My Father's house." Only family members will be taken to the Father's house. Only those who have put their faith in Jesus Christ as their Savior will be caught up in the Rapture. Jesus added in verse 6 that He alone is the way, the truth, and the life—that no one can have a relationship with God except through Him.

In 1 Corinthians 15, Paul described the participants in the Rapture as "those who are Christ's at His coming" (v. 23). Paul addressed his readers in the first verse as "brethren," a term used in the New Testament almost exclusively to describe Christ-followers. As if to intentionally remove all possibility of misunderstanding, Paul ended this passage on the Rapture with these words: "Therefore, my beloved brethren be steadfast" (v. 58).

In the 1 Thessalonians 4 passage, Paul again referred to his readers as "brethren" (v. 13). He portrayed them in verse 14 as those who "believe that Jesus died and rose again." In verse 16, he defined the deceased family members in the Thessalonian church as being "dead in Christ."

The Bible doesn't use words lightly. These qualifying phrases restrict the Rapture exclusively to followers of Christ. Only the redeemed of the Lord Jesus Christ will be taken in the Rapture.

This theme dominates many other passages in the Bible as well. The apostle Peter told the Jewish leaders in Jerusalem, "Salvation is found in no one else, for there is no other name under heaven given to mankind by which we must be saved" (Acts 4:12 NIV).

Peter may have been thinking back to our Lord's message about His return on the Mount of Olives, which is recorded in Matthew 24 and 25. Jesus used stark language to warn us that not everyone would be raptured, resurrected, glorified, and caught up to be with Him.

The very last sentence of Jesus' Olivet sermon says: "And these will go away into everlasting punishment, but the righteous into eternal life" (Matt. 25:46). That's the way He ended His sermon on the signs of the times and His glorious return!

In Luke 13, Jesus was making His way from Galilee to Jerusalem when someone asked Him, "Lord, are only a few people going to be saved?"

He said to them, "Make every effort to enter through the narrow door, because many, I tell you, will try to enter and will not be able to. Once the owner of the house gets up and closes the door, you will stand outside knocking and pleading, 'Sir, open the door for us.' But he will answer, 'I don't know you or where you come from'" (Luke 13:23–25 NIV).

That reminds me again of the days of Noah. When the door of the ark was closed, it was too late for those left behind.

When Jesus comes in the clouds and calls His children to Himself, many will beg to join them, but that opportunity will be gone. Yes, people will be saved during the Tribulation—the Rapture is not the final deadline in God's prophetic plan—but they will have lost the chance to join our Lord Jesus in the sky. And any who enter the Tribulation Period risk the strong possibility of death without Christ.

At the final judgment, Christ will say to those who refuse to receive Him, "Depart from Me, you cursed, into the everlasting fire prepared for the devil and his angels" (Matt. 25:41).

THE REASONS FOR THE RESTRICTIONS

It's a reality that there will be restrictions attached to the Rapture. It's vitally important to grasp this truth because it stands opposed to the tenor of the times. Most people reject the exclusive claims of Christ as being the one and only pathway to God.

One man asks, "Why is Jesus the only way to a relationship with God? What about Buddha? Mohammed? Can't an individual simply live a good life? If God is such a loving God, then wouldn't He accept all people just the way they are?"

Another person says, "I believe there are many roads to God, just as there may be many roads to the top of a mountain. Some take one road, and some another. Only an ignorant or an arrogant person would claim that their road was the only one."

A student says, "If God grades on the curve, I'll make it." And most people today assume that God does grade on the curve. But He doesn't. He provides salvation through Christ alone.

Here are four compelling reasons why we need to recognize the restrictions God has placed around salvation generally and the Rapture specifically.

IT'S FACTUAL

An honest reading of the Bible tells us the restrictive nature of the gospel is factual. When people accuse Christians of teaching that there's only one way to be saved, they are correct. That is what we teach, that is what the Bible says, and that's how the gospel has been proclaimed since the days of the apostles.

When Billy Graham was eighty-four years old, he was preaching in Louisville, Kentucky, and he said these words, referencing a conviction that showed up repeatedly in his sermons from the days he was a novice evangelist: "Is there another way to heaven, except through Christ? The Bible teaches there's only one way. Other people will come along and try to tell you there are other ways, but the Bible says there's only one way, and that way is by the cross."[2]

IT'S LOGICAL

The exclusivity of Christianity is not only factual but also logical. Spiritual laws are not different from the laws of physics, mathematics, or any of the other disciplines. If everything is true, nothing is true. If we can't depend on the consistency of scientific laws, everything in the cosmos is absurd. If two plus two equaled four on the earth but five on the moon, we'd be living in an Alice-in-Wonderland universe.

The whole message of the gospel is that we have sinned against God. Since God is a pure, perfect, and utterly holy being, we cannot exist in His presence for a moment if we are stained by sin—no more than a snowflake could exist on the sun. Yet He loved us so much He came to earth as a human, took our sins upon Himself, died for us, rose again, and returned to heaven to prepare a place for us.

The apostle Paul said, "For there is one God and one Mediator between God and men, the Man Christ Jesus, who gave Himself a ransom for all" (1 Tim. 2:5–6).

How many mediators are there? How many who can forgive our sin and reconcile us to God?

There is one: Christ Jesus.

Had there been another way of redeeming the human race, do you think Christ would have gone to the cross? He Himself prayed, "Father, if it is possible, let this cup pass from Me" (Matt. 26:39).

But it wasn't possible, for in the spiritual laws that govern the seen and unseen realms—laws that flow from the infallible righteousness of God—there was no other way.

IT'S CRITICAL

We live in a tolerant and accommodating age. Even we Christians get caught up in those pressures, often feeling we have to apologize for the restrictiveness of the gospel.

But Jesus never apologized. He understood the critical nature of the gospel—the urgency.

Our Savior said, "Enter through the narrow gate. For wide is the gate and broad is the road that leads to destruction, and many enter through it. But small is the gate and narrow the road that leads to life, and only a few find it" (Matt. 7:13–14 NIV).

When people questioned Him, He reminded them about the urgency of the gospel and the price at stake: "I told you that you would die in your sins; if you do not believe that I am he, you will indeed die in your sins" (John 8:24 NIV).

We must also remember the urgency of salvation. Being accepted as "nice" or "tolerant" doesn't amount to anything in comparison with eternity. As Hebrews 2:3 says, "How shall we escape if we ignore so great a salvation?" (NIV).

I remember a few years back when a ride malfunctioned at Knott's Berry Farm, which is an amusement park outside Los Angeles. The ride was called the Sky Cabin. As the name suggests, it was a cabin-like room that lifted people high into the sky and offered amazing views of the city. Think of it as a Ferris wheel without the wheel.

The Sky Cabin experienced some kind of glitch while at the top of its extension. Twenty-one people became stuck 148 feet in the air. At that height, there was no hope for those people to rescue themselves. They couldn't climb down. They certainly couldn't jump or slide. They needed to be saved.

Several attempts were made to facilitate that salvation. Rescuers first tried to use ladders to reach the stranded passengers, but the ladders were all too short. They also tried to unlock the mechanisms of the ride and allow gravity to slowly bring the cabin back to earth, but that failed.

In the end, the fire department was forced to create a rope-and-harness system that could slowly lower each passenger from the cabin to the ground.[3]

The Bible is clear that every human being is born under the penalty of sin. We are trapped in our sinfulness with no hope of escape. There is no way for us to save ourselves. We need rescue.

Our culture offers many options to facilitate that rescue—ladders constructed of false religions and false ideas about morality. But the reality is those options fail. They do not provide salvation.

Only Christ can bring us safely out of our sinfulness. He is the strong rope that offers salvation. Our only hope is to cling to Him for all eternity.

I don't want to frighten or alarm you by talking about the restrictions that govern salvation, but I wouldn't be true to my Lord if I didn't include this chapter in this book. The Rapture is an event restricted to those who trust Jesus Christ for the forgiveness of sin and everlasting life. The same is true for salvation in general.

Whether through death or the End Times, our ride will soon come to an end. Whatever else you hear from me in these pages, please hear this: Step forward and take hold of Jesus for salvation. He is the only One who can bring you safely home!

CHAPTER 13

THE REUNION

A few years ago, American author and journalist A. J. Jacobs received an email from a complete stranger in Israel. It read, "You don't know me, but I'm your eighth cousin. And we have over 80,000 relatives of yours in our database."

That email set Jacobs, an obsessive researcher, on a path of discovery. Who else was he related to? He had to know! So he made a deep dive into genealogical and DNA websites, came away with some astounding discoveries, and produced a TED Talk (and wrote a book) on what he found. For example, Jacobs was delighted to learn he is related to Albert Einstein, along with many other prominent celebrities and political leaders—not to mention some infamous characters.

Still reeling from the magnitude of his unearthed family tree, Jacobs attempted to gather as many of those relatives as he could in an effort to produce the world's largest family reunion. He called it the Global Family Reunion, and it took place in June 2015. More than thirty-eight hundred people gathered in a large field outside New York City. More than forty similar reunions took place in other regions around the world.

All told, close to ten thousand people from the same extended family gathered on that same day to celebrate. According to Jacobs, the entire phenomenon was "horrible. And great. It was the best worst day of my life."[1]

The idea of family reunions is not new, of course. Currently, according to Guinness World Records, the largest family reunion was held by the Porteau-Boileve family in France on August 19, 2012, attended by 4,514 relatives. Prior to that reunion, the largest was the 2009 reunion of the Lilly clan in Flat Top, West Virginia, a reunion held annually since its inception in 1929.

Of course, none of this human relatedness should come as a surprise to Bible students. We are all descendants of Adam and Eve and, therefore, all related. The human race as a whole is truly a worldwide family—a "Global Family" in the words of A. J. Jacobs.

But there is a difference between the world family and the family of God—those who are related to God by faith in Jesus Christ. Romans 8 tells us that God is our Father and we have been adopted into His family to share eternally in the inheritance He has prepared for His children. Eternity represents the grandest family reunion one could ever imagine—billions of souls from all nations and all times will meet one another and share in the faith that brought them together.

Before that ultimate regathering takes place, another amazing reunion—actually three reunions in one—is on God's prophetic calendar. And that threefold reunion will take place at the Rapture.

Let's take another look at 1 Thessalonians 4:16–18 to remind ourselves of the order of events on the day of the Rapture. As you do, note the three reunions described in these verses: "For the Lord Himself will descend from heaven with a shout, with the voice of an archangel, and with the trumpet of God. And the *dead in Christ will rise first*. Then we who are alive and remain shall be caught up *together with them* in the clouds to meet the Lord in the air. And thus *we shall always be with the Lord*. Therefore, comfort one another with these words."

THE REUNION OF BODIES AND SOULS

Death is our most universal and dreaded experience, and even Christians can be apprehensive about it. But as we saw in chapter 6, the Bible doesn't define death as the cessation of life, but as separation. Physical death is the separation of the soul from the body.

James wrote, "The body without the spirit is dead" (James 2:26). Paul told the Corinthians, "To be absent from the body [is] to be present with the Lord" (2 Cor. 5:8). And Solomon described the separation this way: "And the spirit will return to God who gave it" (Eccl. 12:7).

The message of Scripture is clear: for God's children, the separation of soul from body that occurs during death is only temporary. On the day of the Rapture when "the dead in Christ will rise first," our bodies will be reconnected with our souls, which have been residing with the Lord in heaven. In a manner of speaking, the shout and the trumpet will "wake up" those who are asleep—that is, those who died as believers and have been buried in their graves.

Just as the battered, bruised, bloodied, and broken body of Jesus Christ came out of the grave in a glorified state (except for the wounds in His hands and side), so the bodies of believers—regardless of their condition—will be raised in an immortal state and be reunited with their souls.

This is the first reunion that will happen on the day of the Rapture of the church: the dead in Christ will be raised and reanimated with new life by being reunited with their souls, which have been present with the Lord in heaven.

THE REUNION OF DECEASED
BELIEVERS WITH LIVING BELIEVERS

Paul said in 1 Thessalonians 4:16–17: "And the dead in Christ will rise first. Then we who are alive and remain shall be caught up together with them [those who died in Christ] in the clouds to meet the Lord in the air." Those who died and were buried in faith will rise first, followed immediately by those who are alive in faith at the time of the Rapture of the church.

Think about what this means from the perspective of we who are alive today and may be alive on the day of the Rapture. First, we all have ancestors we know from family records and stories who were believers in Jesus Christ, but whom we never had the chance to see or meet personally. They lived generations before us and were faithful Christians. Well, we who are alive at the Rapture will be united with them "in the clouds" where we will "meet the Lord in the air."

Talk about a global family reunion!

Second, no family has been spared the loss of someone in this present generation—a parent or grandparent, a spouse, a child, a dear friend. Not a day goes by that we don't mourn the loss of those we loved and were close to. We know they went to be with the Lord when they died, yet still we dearly miss their presence. Even so, we can take comfort in the truth that a day is coming when we will meet them again in their resurrected bodies.

In fact, think of this: On the day of the Rapture, all over the world there will be funerals taking place of Christians who have died. Then, later that same day or night, those who attended a funeral will hear the shout and the trumpet of heaven. And those buried earlier that day will rise from the dead and be reunited with family and loved ones in the clouds.

That's the second reunion on the day of the Rapture: the reunion of deceased believers with living believers. No wonder Paul wrote, "Therefore comfort one another with these words" (1 Thess. 4:18).

THE REUNION OF BELIEVERS
WITH THEIR LORD

Those of us who love and follow Jesus Christ sometimes wonder, *What would it have been like to see Jesus in person? I wish I could have been around Him for just one day!* Time travel not being possible, we try to satisfy our desires to see and know Jesus physically by creating dramatic portrayals of His life.

Every Christian who has ever wished to see Jesus in person will have that desire fulfilled at the Rapture—at the third reunion that takes place on that day. This is the reunion of believers with their Lord. John the apostle told us in beautiful words what that day will be like: "Beloved, now we are children of God; and it has not yet been revealed what we shall be, but we know that when He is revealed, we shall be like Him, for we shall see Him as He is" (1 John 3:2).

Three truths to note. First, we don't know exactly "what we shall be" in the future. As lovely as life can be today, "eye has not seen, nor ear heard, nor have entered into the heart of man the things which God has prepared for those who love Him" (1 Cor. 2:9). What we shall be has not yet been revealed, but it *will be* revealed.

And it *will be* wonderful!

Second, the revelation of what we shall be for eternity will happen "when He is revealed." The result? "We shall be like Him." This is the ultimate goal of our salvation in Christ: "For whom He foreknew, He also predestined to be conformed to the image of His Son, that He might be the firstborn among many brethren" (Rom. 8:29). Believers past and present will have a reunion with Christ, the firstborn in the family of God. We, His brothers and sisters, will become like Him when we are united with Him at the Rapture.

Third, the reunion of believers with their Lord will manifest the final answer to Jesus' prayer to the Father on the night before He was crucified: "Father, I desire that they also whom You gave Me may be with Me where I am, that they may behold My glory which You have given Me" (John 17:24). When we are united with Christ at the Rapture, "we will see Him as He is!"

I wonder: Could any human being see Jesus Christ in all His resurrected, ascended, exalted glory and not be instantly transformed? Is that why "we shall be like Him, for we shall see Him as He is"?

The process of that transformation into the image and likeness of Christ remains to be experienced. But I, for one—and I hope you as well—am anticipating the result of being united with our Lord Jesus Christ and seeing Him as He is.

I mentioned previously the Lilly family's annual reunion in Flat Rock, West Virginia. In the late 1700s, Robert Lilly migrated from Virginia and established the village of Lilly, West Virginia. That town existed until 1946 when it was razed in anticipation of a new dam flooding the site. Since then, the annual Lilly family reunion has attracted thousands of "Lillys" from all over the world. Each year is a family-focused festival where mountain gospel music and fellowship dominate the three-day event.[2]

As remarkable as that family reunion has been, there are some differences between it and the great reunion I've written about in this chapter. For one thing, only living Lillys attend the annual family reunion in West Virginia; at the reunion of the church with her Founder, all who have named His Name will attend—the living and the dead.

Second, the Lilly family reunion only lasts three days. The reunion of the church with her Lord will last forever. Our joy will never cease!

And one final difference: In a spirit of generosity, the Lilly family reunion welcomes all, even those not named Lilly or having a direct connection with the family. But that won't be true at the Rapture family reunion. Only those who have taken the Name of Christ—only those who are Christians, or "Christ-ones"—will be invited to attend the reunion of Christ's family at the Rapture.

Make sure you have taken His Name as your own.

CHAPTER 14

THE RAPTURE EFFECT

Robert Murray M'Cheyne was a brilliant, highly influential pastor and poet in nineteenth-century Scotland. He died of typhus shortly before his thirtieth birthday, causing some to think his enormous potential was wasted. Yet in those brief thirty years, God used M'Cheyne to accomplish more than most of us would ever dream of in a lifetime. He wrote several books, conducted highly successful evangelistic campaigns, and set up a missionary program to reach Jews in Israel.

I'm told M'Cheyne wore a special wristwatch on which he had engraved "The Night Cometh." Every time he checked his watch, he was reminded that a time was coming when he would no longer be able to spread the news of God's love. This reminder motivated him to be fervent.

After completing his description of the Rapture to the Thessalonian believers, Paul concluded his message with a motivational challenge. In this chapter I would like to grab hold of Paul's encouraging words and add a few of my own.

The Rapture must never become just an academic journey. The revelation in the New Testament of this future event is meant to encourage, challenge, and motivate us. If we really, truly comprehend the reality of the Rapture, it will change the way we go about life in the here and now.

Let's look at four words that describe the Rapture effect—four words that will help you determine if you are rapture ready. Not just ready for the Rapture if it should happen today, but ready even if it does not happen in your lifetime.

CONSOLATION

Paul explicitly communicated the truth of the Rapture to the Thessalonians so they would not "sorrow as others who have no hope" (1 Thess. 4:13).

The message for these grieving Thessalonians, and for us, is that death is not final. All who die in Christ will be restored to bodily life and taken up to be with Him when He returns. This certainty offers great comfort to those whose loved ones have died. No matter what happens here on earth, we have the assurance of ultimate resurrection and reunion. The promise of the Rapture removes the poison fang from the jaw of death.

Jesus emphasized that promise on the night before His own death. He told His disciples not to be troubled by His impending absence because He would return and take them to live with Him forever (John 14:1–3). The Rapture signals the fulfillment of that promise, which encourages us to endure as we wait and gives us strength to face whatever trials may assail us in the interim.

In 1 Thessalonians 4:18, Paul urged us to use our knowledge of the Rapture to "comfort one another." He added this sentence to the end of his explanation of the Rapture. Notice he began with the word *therefore*, which introduces an independent-result clause. In other words, "In light of what I have just told you, here is what you should do: comfort one another."

The Greek word for "comfort" is *parakaleo*, which is written in a form that indicates continuous action. As followers of Jesus, we are instructed to comfort one another continually with the message of the Rapture and the resurrection. We are to make this a habitual practice until the Lord returns.

EXPECTATION

Charles Haddon Spurgeon, the great English pastor of the Metropolitan Tabernacle in London, believed the Lord could return at any time. He repeatedly urged his people to cultivate an attitude of continual expectancy.

Listen to this man preach:

> Oh, beloved, let us try, every morning, to get up as if that were the morning in which Christ would come. And when we go up to bed at night, may we lie down with this thought, "Perhaps I shall be awakened by the ringing out of the silver trumpets heralding His coming. Before the sun arises, I may be startled from my dreams by the greatest of all cries, 'The Lord is come! The Lord is come!'" What a check, what an incentive, what a bridle, what a spur such thoughts as these would be to us! Take this for the guide of your whole life—act as if Jesus would come in the act in which you are engaged—and if you would not wish to be caught in that act by the coming of the Lord, let it not be your act.[1]

Wayne Grudem suggested that the degree to which we are longing for Christ's return is a measure of our spiritual condition. As he explained:

> The more Christians are caught up in enjoying the good things of this life, and the more they neglect Christian fellowship, and their

personal relationship with Christ, the less they will long for his return. On the other hand, many Christians who are experiencing suffering or persecution, or who are elderly and infirm, as well as those whose daily walk with Christ is vital and deep, will have a more intense longing for his return.[2]

As Dr. Grudem noted, the idea is not merely to watch for Jesus' coming as we might watch for a storm in a black cloud, but rather to anticipate it as something we look forward to and long to see.

CONSECRATION

Many New Testament passages use the impending return of the Lord to motivate us toward greater consecration and service to Him. The apostle John wrote: "Beloved, now we are children of God; and it has not yet been revealed what we shall be, but we know that when He is revealed, we shall be like Him, for we shall see Him as He is. And everyone who has this hope in Him purifies himself, just as He is pure" (1 John 3:2–3).

As followers of Jesus, we live our lives as a continual journey of sanctification—of being daily transformed into the image of Christ. When the Rapture comes, we will finally reach the end of that journey. "We shall be like Him" (1 John 3:2). In the meantime, our task is not to focus solely on ourselves but to accomplish the work of Christ by loving our neighbors and investing our resources in the proliferation of the gospel.

John Walvoord wrote:

The rapture not only confronts people with the challenge to receive Christ before it is too late; it also challenges Christians to live with eternal values in view. Since the rapture can occur at any moment, and believers lives on earth will thus be cut short, we need to maximize our commitment to Christ, doing all we can for the Lord in upright living and service to Him and to others.[3]

The late Dr. Renald Showers concluded his book on the Rapture with these words:

The fact that the glorified, holy Son of God could step through the door of heaven at any moment is intended by God to be the most pressing, incessant motivation for holy living and aggressive ministry (including missions, evangelism, and Bible teaching) and the greatest cure for lethargy and apathy. It should make a difference in every Christian's values, actions, priorities, and goals.[4]

Our objective as Christians is not merely to be included in the Rapture but to take as many people with us as we can.

EXAMINATION

Suppose the Lord Jesus chose this very moment to return. Would you be ready? Jesus warned us that He is coming quickly (Rev. 22:12). When that moment strikes, there will be no time for you to get ready for heaven. So the question you must ask is this: "Have I committed myself to Jesus Christ and submitted to Him as my Lord and Savior?"

Everything you need to know in order to make that decision lies before you in the Bible.

After Jesus promised His disciples that He would leave to prepare a place for them and return to take them there, He added, "And where I go you know, and the way you know" (John 14:4).

Immediately, His analytical "show me" disciple, Thomas, said, "Lord, we do not know where You are going, and how can we know the way?" (v. 5).

Jesus answered with one of the most important statements in the

Bible. It is heaven's answer to anyone seeking salvation from eternal death. He said, "I am the way, the truth, and the life. No one comes to the Father except through Me" (v. 6).

You may be reading this book as an unbeliever, perhaps out of simple curiosity. You have never recognized Christ as your Lord or submitted your life to Him. You may or may not have grasped everything you've read here, but I hope you can at least see that God will bring an end to the chaos of this sin-damaged world and restore His perfect rule over it. He wants you to be a part of that new beginning. He has delayed His return for centuries to give you, and others like you, the opportunity to come to Him before the door closes—which will inevitably happen either at His return or at your own death.

There is a book in heaven, a registry, called the Lamb's Book of Life, in which the names of all who will be in heaven are recorded. Jesus said to His disciples on one occasion after they had reported great success in their ministries, "Nevertheless do not rejoice in this, that the spirits are subject to you, but rather rejoice because your names are written in heaven" (Luke 10:20).

Is your name written in heaven? Do you have a reservation there? One day you'll stand before God and He will say to you, "Why should I let you into My heaven?"

You must be able to say, "My name is in the Lamb's Book of Life. I have a reservation. I have put my trust in Jesus Christ as my Savior and therefore I qualify to come into Your heaven."

Ruthanna Metzgar was once asked to sing at a wedding in Seattle, where she lives. It was an upscale wedding. One of the wealthiest families in the city had a daughter getting married, and Ruthanna considered it a great honor to be chosen as the soloist. She was particularly excited because the wedding reception was to be held on the top two floors of the Columbia Center, the tallest building in the Northwest.

The whole event was exclusive, and Ruthanna couldn't help thinking about how fun it would be to go there with her husband, Roy.

After the wedding, Ruthanna and Roy drove to the beautiful

facility and approached the reception desk. They watched as the maître d', who was decked out in a splendid tuxedo, admitted and introduced the guests and ushered them toward luscious hors d'oeuvres and exotic beverages.

Soon after, the bride and groom approached a beautiful glass and brass staircase leading to the top floor, and someone ceremoniously cut a satin ribbon draped across the bottom of the stairs and announced that the wedding feast was about to begin.

As Roy and Ruthanna approached the top of the stairs, the maître d' asked them, "May I have your name, please?" Before him was a bound book.

"I am Ruthanna Metzgar and this is my husband, Roy."

The maître d' searched through the listings in the book, then he looked again. He asked Ruthanna to spell her name, and he searched again. Finally he looked up and said, "I'm sorry, but your name is not here."

"Oh, there must be some mistake," Ruthanna said. "I am the singer. I sang for this wedding!"

"It doesn't matter who you are or what you did," said the man. "Without your name in the book you cannot attend this banquet." He motioned to a waiter and said, "Show these people to the service elevator please."

The Metzgars were unceremoniously ushered past beautifully decorated tables laden with shrimp, whole smoked salmon, and magnificent carved-ice sculptures. They passed the orchestra, preparing to perform. All the musicians were resplendent in white tuxedos. The Metzgars were led past the guests enjoying the food, the fellowship, the views, and the opulence of the moment.

The waiter took Ruthanna and Roy to the service elevator, ushered them in, and pushed G for the parking garage. The Metzgars were stunned to find themselves out on the street, driving home in silence. Somewhere along the way, Roy looked over and asked, "Sweetheart, what happened?"

She said, "When the invitation arrived for the reception, I was very busy and I never bothered to return the RSVP. Besides, I was the singer, surely I could go to the reception without returning the RSVP!"

Then, as Ruthanna later recalled, she started to cry—not only because she had "missed the most lavish banquet" she'd ever been invited to but also because she'd suddenly had a small taste of what it will be like someday for people as they stand before Christ and find their names missing from the Lamb's Book of Life.[5]

CHAPTER 15

WILL CHILDREN BE RAPTURED?

Ashley Irwin was slightly amused and slightly alarmed when her young son, Wyatt, asked her to pull down his Marvel-themed duffel bag. "I've got a big trip tomorrow," he said.

At first, Ashley thought her son was talking about church, since this all took place on a Saturday night. But Wyatt had a bigger goal in mind—a higher destination.

"I'm going to heaven," he told his mom.

In that moment, Ashley understood. Her husband, Tyler, had passed away almost two years before. Wyatt was planning a trip to visit his dad. Asking no more questions, Ashley handed the duffel to her son and allowed him to pack in private.

Later, when the boy was asleep, she looked through the bag and found a wonderful assortment of supplies. First were superhero masks and capes. Then a whistle. Then two baseball gloves and a ball. A collection of foam darts. And two wallets—one belonging to Wyatt and the other to his dad. And Wyatt's wallet was stuffed with family photos.

Last of all, Ashley found a bottle of her husband's cologne tucked deep inside Wyatt's shoe.[1]

I don't know if I've heard anything more touching than a boy packing his bag—with two gloves, not one—to meet his father on a trip to heaven. No matter how long I live, I'm confident I will never plumb the depth of a child's imagination, nor of a child's faith.

But Wyatt's desire to see his father in heaven raises an interesting and important connection with the subject of this book. Namely, what will happen to young children on the day of the Rapture? What will happen to those little ones who are too young to make a decision about eternity when eternity crashes into our world? Does the Bible offer any clarity for parents and grandparents—any hope?

Yes. What happens to children when they die is the key to understanding what will happen to them should they be living on earth when the Rapture takes place.

Thankfully, Scripture gives us four solid reasons for believing that children who die—and children who are living when the Rapture occurs—will go straight to heaven.

THE CHARACTER OF GOD

The Bible is full of information about the nature of God—His character, personality, and attributes. Scripture calls Him our *Father*, and that ought to tell us something. He isn't simply a distant force in the universe. He is, as Jesus put it, "our Father in heaven" (Matt. 6:9).

There's a tender passage describing God's fathering love in Deuteronomy 1:29–31: "Do not be terrified, or afraid of them. The LORD your God, who goes before you, He will fight for you, according to all He did for you in Egypt before your eyes, and in the wilderness where you saw how the LORD your God carried you, as a man carries his son, in all the way that you went until you came to this place."

God is full of compassion, tenderness, and mercy. He carries us through tough patches like a father carrying his son. Psalm 145:9 says, "The LORD is good to all, and His tender mercies are over all His works."

If God is good to all, that would surely include infants; and if His tender mercies are over all His works, that would certainly include children. He knows, as we do, that babies cannot understand the witness of God, either in creation or in Scripture. He knows that little children cannot comprehend the truth of the gospel. Yet God loves them deeply. He loves the children, and He delights in the babies He has created. He loves the preborn and the newborn. He loves the infant and the toddler.

The word *children* appears more than fifty times in the Gospels alone. The Bible teaches that God knows and loves children with special tender care. Furthermore, according to Scripture, life begins from the moment of conception. Accordingly, God knows and loves the unborn baby, even in the womb.

The psalmist wrote,

> For you formed my inward parts; You covered me in my mother's womb. I will praise You, for I am fearfully and wonderfully made. . . . Your eyes saw my substance, being yet unformed. And in Your book they all were written, the days fashioned for me, when as yet there were none of them. How precious also are Your thoughts to me, O God! How great is the sum of them! (Ps. 139:13–17)

On a number of occasions God refers to these little ones as "innocents" (Jer. 2:34; 19:4). That does not mean children are "sinless." Instead, they are not yet responsible for their sins in the same way as those whose sins are willful and premeditated. And God understands the difference.

The character of God lays the foundation for the realization that children who cannot understand the gospel are enveloped within the grace and mercy of our Lord. On them, God has a tender heart. On them, His compassion reigns.

THE CONDITION FOR SALVATION

There's another reason why children go straight to heaven when they die—and why they will be raptured into Jesus' arms if they are living when He comes back. This second reason has to do with the condition for salvation.

Let's ask this question: "What must a person do to be lost?" Answer: They must refuse the free offer of God's saving grace.

Children too young to know and understand the gospel cannot willfully reject it. As John MacArthur wrote: "Little children have no record of unbelief or evil works, and therefore, there is no basis for their deserving an eternity apart from God. . . . They are graciously and sovereignly saved by God as part of the atoning work of Christ Jesus."[2]

Infants are shielded by the blood of Him who loves all the little children of the world and who is not willing for even one of them to perish.

THE COMPASSION OF THE SAVIOR

When we read the stories of Jesus in the Gospels, we discover that our Lord had an incredible love for children, and He demonstrated that love on many occasions. One example is so important that it is recorded by Matthew, Mark, and Luke. Here is Matthew's account: "Then little children were brought to Him that He might put His hands on them and pray, but the disciples rebuked them. But Jesus said, 'Let the little children come to Me, and do not forbid them; for of such is the kingdom of heaven'" (Matt. 19:13–14; see also Mark 10:13–14 and Luke 18:15–16).

Additionally, we have a wonderful passage in Matthew's gospel that is as definitive as any verse in the Bible on the eternal love that Jesus has for children: "Even so it is not the will of your Father who is in heaven that one of these little ones should perish" (18:14).

This is a good place for me to deal with the subject of children who perish before they are even born. What about babies that are never born because of miscarriages or abortions? Will they be present with God in heaven?

Yes. Our conviction about this is based on the biblical belief that a child is a person from the moment of conception. Since that is true, all preborn babies who perish—whether through miscarriage, abortion, or tragic accidents—go straight to heaven.

J. Vernon McGee wrote, "I believe with all my heart that God will raise the little ones such that the mother's arms who have ached for them will have the opportunity of holding them. The father's hand which never held the little hand will be given the privilege. I believe that little ones will grow up in heaven in the care of their earthly parents if they are saved."[3]

If you have had an abortion, I want to tell you that God knows how to pour His forgiveness and healing into your life through the merits of Christ. Abortion is not the unpardonable sin. God not only forgives you; He goes far beyond that. Because of His mercy, that little one now lost will be waiting for you in heaven, and you will enjoy an eternity of loving fellowship with that precious child.

Jesus loves you, and He loves every child from conception. In fact, He loves us from before time began.

THE CHILD OF DAVID

The pages of the Old Testament tell the sordid story of King David's adultery with Bathsheba and his conspiracy to have her husband killed. For a year after those foul deeds, David had this sin in his heart, but finally the Lord sent the prophet Nathan to confront him. Nathan predicted that the child conceived by David and Bathsheba would be taken away in death. When the child got sick, David pleaded with God for the child's life. He fasted and lay all night on the ground. The child was sick for seven days before he finally died.

When David found out that the child had died, he did something that seemed very strange at the time. "So David arose from the ground, washed and anointed himself, and changed his clothes; and he went into the house of the LORD and worshiped" (2 Sam. 12:20).

If you are confused by David's actions, you're not alone.

"Then his servants said to him, 'What is this that you have done? You fasted and wept for the child while he was alive, but when the child died, you arose and ate food'" (v. 21).

David's answer to his questioning servants has brought peace to many grieving parents. Here is what he said: "While the child was alive, I fasted and wept; for I said, 'Who can tell whether the LORD will be gracious to me, that the child may live?' But now he is dead; why should I fast? Can I bring him back again? I shall go to him, but he shall not return to me" (vv. 22–23).

The last sentence in that passage—2 Samuel 12:23—is arguably the greatest sentence in the Bible on the subject of what happens to children when they die. David's hope at that moment resided with eternity in heaven. He knew he would see his child again. He said in essence, "I cannot bring the child back, but one day I will go where my child is, and we will be reunited."

David wasn't talking about being united with his child in death, because the attitude behind his words was one of hope and cheer. It was the thought of an eternal reunion that buoyed him. Where did he think the reunion would be? Not in the grave. Not in hell. David was anticipating heaven! He expressed the belief that his baby had gone before him to that blessed place, and the idea of meeting his child in heaven so encouraged David that he quit weeping and fasting, dressed himself, and went out to meet with people.

David knew this truth: when little ones die or the Rapture happens before they understand the gospel, they go straight to heaven.

There was a family whose baby boy had died. Their little girl came to the mother and asked her where her baby brother had gone. "To be with Jesus," answered the mother.

A few days later the mother was visiting a friend. "I am so grieved to have lost my baby," she told her. The little girl, overhearing the remark, came to her mother and said, "Mama, is something lost when you know where it is?"

"No, of course not," replied the mother.

"Well, how can a baby be lost when he has gone to be with Jesus?"

Isn't that a wonderful truth to remember? If we know where they are, they're not lost. We're just waiting for the time when we will be reunited in the future.

CHAPTER 16

LIVE LIKE YOU WERE DYING

"Live Like You Were Dying." That was the title of a Tim McGraw hit song from years ago. The lyrics spoke of loving deeper, speaking sweeter, and giving forgiveness once denied. The final thought in the song went like this: "Someday I hope you get the chance to live like you were dying."[1]

About the same time as that song was released, Carnegie Mellon University professor Randy Pausch was invited to be a speaker in an ongoing series asking thoughtful lecturers to assume they were giving their last presentation—to lecture as if they were dying. It turned out, this was really the case with Pausch, who became a victim of pancreatic cancer at forty-seven. He delivered an unforgettable talk that became a book with more than ten million copies sold. The book was called *The Last Lecture*.[2]

The country singer and the university professor hit a common chord: the importance of living on purpose—of moving through life with a sense of urgency based on something higher than the pursuit of pleasure.

We've spent several chapters exploring the "what" of the Rapture. What it is. What will happen in that moment. What will change when Christ returns for His church. Now it's time to examine the "why" of the Rapture. Specifically, why it matters for you and me today.

Perhaps you've been wondering about the relevance of the Rapture. If the Rapture is coming in the future, why does it matter now? And if the Rapture is the moment when all Christians—living and dead—are reunited with our Lord in heaven, why should that event affect my life on earth?

The answer is connected to the themes highlighted by Tim McGraw and Randy Pausch. In the same way death can help all people recognize the value of life, the reality of the Rapture must motivate followers of Jesus to make proper use of our time in the here and now. History will not endure forever. There is an end coming—and perhaps coming soon. Therefore, we are responsible to love God and love others to our fullest capacity while we still have the opportunity to impact eternity.

If ever there was a time for the church of God and the people of Christ to catch this sense of urgency, that time is now.

That's the essence of Paul's challenge to us in Romans 13:11–14:

> And do this, knowing the time, that now it is high time to awake out of sleep; for now our salvation is nearer than when we first believed. The night is far spent, the day is at hand. Therefore let us cast off the works of darkness, and let us put on the armor of light. Let us walk properly, as in the day, not in revelry and drunkenness, not in lewdness and lust, not in strife and envy. But put on the Lord Jesus Christ, and make no provision for the flesh, to fulfill its lusts.

Using terse, blunt words, Paul offered four keys to resisting the seductiveness of our generation and remaining alert to the coming of Christ. I like to think of those keys as Rapture Priorities for the people of God.

WATCH VIGILANTLY

It has always been important to understand the times. In the Old Testament, a group was appointed for the specific purpose of discerning the times on behalf of the nation of Israel. The people who were assigned this task were "the sons of Issachar who had understanding of the times, to know what Israel ought to do" (1 Chron. 12:32).

When you get to the New Testament, you hear the Lord Jesus scolding His critics: "You know how to discern the face of the sky, but you cannot discern the signs of the times" (Matt. 16:3).

In other words, the spiritual leaders of Jesus' day watched for the rain or for the setting of the sun, but all the while they were remarkably blind to the workings of the Holy Spirit in their lives.

Evangelist Vance Havner once put it this way: "The devil has chloroformed the atmosphere of this age. Therefore in view of the sure promises of Christ's return, as believers, we are to do more than merely be ready; we are to be expectant. In our day of anarchy, apostasy, and apathy, we need to take down our 'Do Not Disturb' signs . . . snap out of our stupor, come out of our coma and awake from our apathy."[3]

Ready or not, the Lord is coming. His return is certain and, according to Paul, it is also imminent: "For now our salvation is nearer than when we first believed" (Rom. 13:11).

When I use the word *imminent*, I'm not using a calendar word. I am not setting a date for the Lord's return. *Imminence* does not mean *immediate*. It simply means that something could happen at any moment—that nothing has to occur before that something happens. (We'll explore this idea further in chapter 21.)

Paul expressed the truth about our Lord's return in this passage in a unique way, writing, "For now our salvation is nearer than when we first believed."

If you want a good answer for those who ask when the Lord is coming back, here it is: Just tell them that His coming is nearer now than it was when you first believed. You will always be accurate when you answer that way!

But what did Paul mean when he said our salvation is nearer than when we first believed? I mean, after all, isn't our salvation in the past?

When Paul used the word *salvation* here, he was seeing that concept in its completeness—in its fullness. The moment we say yes to Christ, we are sealed by the Holy Spirit and our sins are washed away. Next comes the ongoing growth process in which we are conformed, spiritual molecule by spiritual molecule, to the image of Christ through the redeeming work of the Holy Spirit. Last will be the future moment Paul was talking about in Romans 13. There will be a day when we are finally freed from the very presence of sin.

Here's a good way to remember this threefold salvation:

- Past: I have been saved from the penalty of sin.
- Present: I am being saved from the power of sin.
- Future: I will be saved from the presence of sin.

My salvation will be complete when Jesus takes me unto Himself in the future—when sin is forever destroyed, and life with Christ is perfected. And that day, said Paul, "is nearer than when we first believed." Therefore, you and I must watch vigilantly in the present as we allow Christ's victory in the past to lead us into our glorious future.

Charles Spurgeon preached to Victorian England about the problem of apathy in his day. He made a point I will not soon forget. He said: "You can sleep, but you cannot induce the devil to close his eyes. . . . The prince of the power of the air keeps his servants well up to their work. . . . If we could, with a glance, see the activities of the servants of Satan, we would be astonished at our own sluggishness."[4]

WAR VALIANTLY

I know "watching" can feel like a relatively passive activity. Like watching paint dry. But Paul had other plans—and other priorities—in mind for followers of Jesus: "The night is far spent, the day is at hand. Therefore let us cast off the works of darkness, and let us put on the armor of light" (Rom. 13:12).

There are two critical commands in that verse, and the first is to "cast off the works of darkness." What does that mean?

Darkness is a term used often in Scripture to describe the life we lived before we trusted Christ as Savior. For example: "For you were once darkness, but now you are light in the Lord. Walk as children of light" (Eph. 5:8).

Many followers of Christ are surprised to discover that when they become Christians, their old nature is still present with them. We still struggle with sin. More specifically, we still carry the desire to sin—which is why it is necessary for us to fight against those old impulses. We wage war against our old nature.

As the old saying goes:

> Two natures beat within my breast.
> The one is foul, the one is blessed.
> The one I love, the one I hate.
> The one I feed will dominate!

Paul's second command is more positive: "And let us put on the armor of light" (Rom. 13:12).

Here, Paul was using imagery connected with the New Testament picture for walking in fellowship with God.

John said, "But if we walk in the light as He is in the light, we have fellowship with one another, and the blood of Jesus Christ His Son cleanses us from all sin" (1 John 1:7).

I have been told that, scientifically, there is no such thing as darkness. Darkness is simply the term we use to describe the absence of light. Which means whenever light shows up, darkness cannot exist. It vanishes.

In the same way, when we walk in the light of Christ, any spiritual darkness will have to flee.

WALK VIRTUOUSLY

What does it mean to "walk in the light"? How do we live out true virtue as followers of Christ? Once again, the first step is to reject the parts of us we know to be sinful.

Let's continue exploring Paul's urgent words to the Christians in Rome, and to us: "Let us walk properly, as in the day, not in revelry and drunkenness, not in lewdness and lust, not in strife and envy" (Rom. 13:13).

Paul focused specifically on six actions that prevent us from walking "properly": revelry, drunkenness, lewdness, lust, strife, and envy. At first glance, that may seem like a random selection of vices. But these six sins are unusually dangerous because they can hide in the night of the human heart before they are manifest in the light of day.

If no one else knows about my little struggles, we think, *they aren't really that harmful. I'll get it figured out later.* We deceive ourselves.

Again, that's the power of the Rapture. It reminds us that "later" isn't good enough. Christ is coming! There is a cosmic plan of which each of us is a tiny part, yes—but still a part. God has work for us to accomplish before the day of His return. Therefore, we can choose to walk virtuously.

WAIT VICTORIOUSLY

Watch vigilantly, war valiantly, walk virtuously, and finally—wait victoriously. In light of the reality of the Rapture, we anticipate God's future victory over evil even as we enjoy Christ's current victory over our sin.

"But put on the Lord Jesus Christ, and make no provision for the flesh, to fulfill its lusts" (Rom. 13:14).

What does it mean to "put on the Lord Jesus Christ"? Ray Stedman suggested this approach:

> When I get up in the morning, I put on my clothes, intending them to be part of me all day, to go where I go and do what I do. They cover me and make me presentable to others. That is the purpose of clothes. In the same way, the apostle is saying to us, "Put on Jesus Christ when you get up in the morning. Make Him part of your life that day. Intend that he go with you everywhere you go, and that He act through you in everything you do. Call upon His resources. Live your life IN CHRIST!"[5]

When we live in this way, we "make no provision for the flesh." We don't allow ourselves any possibility to gratify our evil desires.

"Do not plan for sin; give it no welcome; offer it no opportunity. Kick the sin off your doorstep and you won't have it in the house."[6]

There's an old saying that goes like this: "Call upon God, but row away from the rocks." The idea is to put yourself in the best situation to succeed and move as far away as possible from the place of failure.

When we become Christians, Christ comes to live His life in us, and we learn to be uncomfortable with everything that grieves Him. Just knowing, really knowing, that Christ lives in you is the greatest motivation toward godliness that you will ever experience. In so many ways, that knowing is the key to victory in our spiritual lives.

The epic war movie *Saving Private Ryan* tells the story of a rescue mission centering on young private James Ryan during World War II. When a senior official in Washington, DC, learns that three of James's brothers were killed in action within days of each other, he orders a special mission to bring the young man home to his mother. The last of her sons.

Unfortunately, James's unit is missing in action somewhere in France. So, Captain John Miller is tasked with assembling a squad and finding Private Ryan—a mission he accomplishes. But when young Private Ryan refuses to abandon his fellow soldiers, Captain Miller and his squad are forced to defend him in the middle of a terrible battle against enemy forces. James Ryan survives that battle, but Captain Miller and most of his squad are killed.

At the end of the film, a mortally wounded Captain Miller pulls the stunned private forward and says, with his final breath, "James, earn this—earn it!"

The scene flashes forward to the present, where James Francis Ryan, now in his eighties, pays homage at Captain Miller's grave at Omaha Beach in Normandy. Overcome with emotion and perhaps some guilt, James speaks to the grave marker as if addressing Miller and the rest: "I hope . . . I've earned what all of you have done for me."[7]

Of course no one could ever merit such a great sacrifice. Nobody could "earn it." Thankfully, no gift is ever earned, especially the gift of life.

That is the truth about salvation as well: we can never earn it. But we can, in the words of Paul, "live a life worthy of the calling you have received" (Eph. 4:1 NIV).

That's the message I want to communicate in this chapter. Because of what Jesus has done for us and due to the reality of the Rapture, let us avoid anything that will sully the splendor of His sacrifice. As followers of Christ, let us be alert, watchful, and vigilant—with one eye on the headlines and the other on the eastern skies. Let us learn to live like we were dying!

CHAPTER 17

WHAT'S UP WITH HEAVEN?

As far as my staff and I can determine, there is no city, community, or township in America called "Heaven."

But there used to be.

According to the Texas State Historical Association, the little settlement of Heaven, Texas, was organized in 1924. It was located near Farm Road 769 in Cochrane County. Other than the name, Heaven's main attraction seems to have been its proximity to the Atchison, Topeka, and Santa Fe Railroad.

Sadly, things didn't pan out for the residents of Heaven. The town was caught up in a bitter struggle with its neighbor—Morton, Texas—in 1925. Both towns wanted to be recognized as the Cochrane County seat. There was an election that year, which was won by rival Morton.

Unsatisfied, Heaven contested the results, even insinuating the election had been rigged. Eventually, higher powers officially awarded the county seat to Morton.

Soon after, the township of Heaven was abandoned.[1]

It's somewhat humorous to imagine a group of people trying to set up their version of heaven on earth. But it does raise the question, "What will the real heaven be like?"

We've spent many pages exploring and seeking to understand the Rapture of the church, during which Jesus will escort believers to heaven to live with Him forever. We know amazing new experiences are in store for believers in heaven, and we will learn about some of them in this chapter.

But what, specifically, can we expect to encounter there? What will we find?

In a word, everything! Everything that is most precious and dear to you and me, everything that is important to Christ-followers, is currently in heaven. Everything we need or desire will be found in heaven once we pass through its magnificent gates, either by death or by being caught up with Christ at the Rapture.

Here are seven examples to show you what I mean.

OUR REAL ESTATE IS IN HEAVEN

Let's begin with a foundational truth about heaven: it's a place. Unlike Heaven, Texas, it currently exists and will always exist.

The word *heaven* is mentioned almost seven hundred times in the Bible. Thirty-three of the thirty-nine Old Testament books talk about heaven along with twenty-one of the twenty-seven books in the New Testament. The word *heaven* refers to something that is raised up or lofty. So the language of the Bible speaks of heaven as a place that is high, lofty, and lifted up.

In John 14:1–3, Jesus said, "Let not your heart be troubled; you believe in God, believe also in me. In my Father's house are many mansions; if it were not so, I would have told you. I go to prepare a *place* for you. And if I go and prepare a *place* for you, I will come again and receive you to Myself; that where I am, there you may be also."

The Bible refers to heaven as a "place"—a word that implies a specific, literal location. The Greek word used for "place" is *topas*, which strictly refers to a geographic area that can be located. A real place.

Jesus spoke these words in the Upper Room on the night before His death. He had just told His disciples that He would die for them on the cross. He explained that He would be buried and resurrected and that He would return to heaven. They were confused by this and filled with sorrow. But Jesus told them they should not be troubled. He said, "I go to prepare a *place* for you."

The apostle Paul spoke of Christ as ascending to heaven to sit at God's right hand "in the heavenly *places*" (Eph. 1:20).

Jesus does not intend for us to live in a vapory nether land, in a disembodied haze, or in a blissful but intangible state of mind. No, the Bible refers to heaven as a specific place.

Sometimes the Bible refers to heaven as a country, which implies vastness of territory. Sometimes it's referred to as the celestial city, which brings to mind buildings, streets, residents, and activity. Sometimes heaven is referred to as a kingdom, which speaks of organization and government. In the passage I quoted from John 14:1–3, Jesus referred to heaven as "My Father's house."

For me, there's something intimate, sweet, and personal about heaven when we talk about it as "My Father's house." It's no longer an empty space. In my mind's eye, I see a home. Jesus promised that if we put our trust in Him, He would prepare a place for us in our Father's house that will serve as our heavenly home. There is nothing imaginary, hypothetical, or intangible about that.

OUR REDEEMER IS IN HEAVEN

Next, our Redeemer is in heaven. Hebrews 9:24 says, "Christ has not entered the holy places made with hands, which are copies of the true, but into heaven itself, now to appear in the presence of God for us."

Just imagine the moment we get to heaven—and we see Jesus! Right now we don't see Him in a visual way. But the Bible says that when Jesus returns for us, "we shall be like Him, for we shall see Him as He is" (1 John 3:2).

The book of Revelation describes what it will be like in heaven throughout eternity: "The throne of God and of the Lamb shall be in it, and His servants shall serve Him. They shall see His face" (22:3–4).

Think of the joy that will be ours when we get to heaven and see the One who gave His life for us so that we could spend forever with Him in paradise!

OUR RELATIONSHIPS ARE IN HEAVEN

I remember a conversation I had with my father toward the end of his life. He was a great man who had developed many relationships, which meant he both attended and presided over more than his fair share of funerals.

"You know, David," he told me, "one of the things about getting old is this: one day you begin to realize you have more friends in heaven than you have here on the earth."

He was right about that! It happens gradually, but it happens inevitably as we age. The longer we live, the more our loved ones precede us into eternity.

Thankfully, we have confidence that our loved ones who died in Christ are all in heaven.

We will join them soon.

OUR RESOURCES ARE IN HEAVEN

Fourth, our resources are in heaven. The Bible says, "Blessed be the God and Father of our Lord Jesus Christ, who according to His abundant mercy has begotten us again to a living hope through the resurrection of Jesus Christ from the dead, to an inheritance incorruptible and undefiled and that does not fade away, reserved in heaven for you" (1 Pet. 1:3–4).

When you become a Christian, God becomes your Father and makes you an heir. That means you have an inheritance in Christ that will never be touched by inflation. It won't be lost in an economic crash. Its value will never decline or decrease, and it is both reserved and preserved for you. Your name is on it.

Those eternal resources include the rewards we will receive from Christ. Jesus told His followers during a time of persecution, "Rejoice and be exceedingly glad, for great is your reward in heaven, for so they persecuted the prophets who were before you" (Matt. 5:12).

OUR RESIDENCE IS IN HEAVEN

Heaven is also precious to us because our residence is there. I'm not just talking about where we will live; I'm talking about our citizenship. When we become Christians, we become residents of heaven: "Our citizenship is in heaven, from which we also eagerly wait for the Savior, the Lord Jesus Christ" (Phil. 3:20).

When you apply for a passport, you have to state where you were born, where you currently live, your birthdate, and so forth. If approved, the government issues you a passport to let other governments know you are a citizen of the United States, Germany, Mexico, or wherever. I was born in Toledo, Ohio, and I live in San Diego, California. I have a United States passport. But my real residence is in heaven. I am a citizen of that land, and I'm currently on earth as an ambassador.

As believers in Jesus, we are not citizens of earth who are going to heaven. We are citizens of heaven who are traveling through earth. Let that reality change the way you live each day!

OUR RICHES ARE IN HEAVEN

Heaven is also precious to us because it's where our riches are stored: "Do not lay up for yourselves treasures on earth, where moth and rust destroy and where thieves break in and steal; but lay up for yourselves treasures in heaven, where neither moth nor rust destroys and where thieves do not break in and steal. For where your treasure is, there your heart will be also" (Matt. 6:19–21).

What a statement! How can we lay up for ourselves riches in heaven? The only way we can get our treasures from here to there is by investing in God's work. We can't take our money with us to heaven, nor our homes, cars, boats, or articles of clothing. But we can take other people with us by investing our lives and resources in the spreading of God's kingdom.

The only things going from earth to heaven are human souls and the Word of God. So, if you're trying to build equity in heaven, invest your time, talents, and treasure in the Word of God and the souls of men and women who need the message of Jesus Christ.

OUR RESERVATION IS IN HEAVEN

Finally, heaven is precious because our reservation is there. In chapter 14 I described the registry in heaven called the Lamb's Book of Life, in which the names of all who belong to Christ are recorded. Is your name written in heaven? Do you have a reservation there?

Recently a collection of nearly four hundred hotels, regional tourism boards, tour operators, and others in the hospitality industry sent a letter to Chuck Sams, the director of the National Parks Service, and Deb Haaland, who is the US Department of the Interior secretary. The reason for that letter? Frustration with the national parks' reservation website Recreation.gov.

For many years, tourists from all across America have seethed when trying to reserve camping sites or hotel accommodations at Yellowstone, Yosemite, Great Smoky Mountains National Park, and more than 4,200 other federally managed properties. The main issue seems to be the reservation system, which allows would-be visitors to book only between thirty and sixty days prior to a visit—a window that manages to thwart people who plan ahead and those who live spontaneously.

Aline Prado is one of those would-be visitors. She spent months logging on to Recreation.gov in an effort to secure lodging for her family's summer vacation at Glacier National Park. "There were never any reservations available, and I was always told to check back again. But when? How is everything booked already?"[2]

It's strange to think that gaining access to a national park is more difficult than gaining access to heaven, but that is the case! Faith in Jesus is all that's required to secure your reservation for eternal salvation.

If you are reading these words and aren't sure your reservation is secure, I urge you to pray right now. Confess your sins. Acknowledge Jesus Christ as your Lord and Savior. Do it now. Turn your life over to His control and accept His free offer of the gift of eternal life.

CHAPTER 18

MINDFUL OF HEAVEN

Are you addicted to looking down? It's a global epidemic. In America, the average person spends more than five hours a day scrolling on their smartphone—sometimes while walking, jogging, or even riding a bicycle or scooter.[1]

That's causing problems!

In Hong Kong, officials are installing a new kind of streetlight that casts a red glow on the sidewalk, warning pedestrians who are looking down at their cell phones of upcoming intersections.[2] In Spain, new laws target "distracted walkers" who are looking down at their phones instead of paying attention to their surroundings.[3]

On one April Fools' Day in Philadelphia, city officials used tape to create an "e-lane" on city sidewalks outside downtown office buildings. What's an e-lane? A fake path for distracted pedestrians to use while walking with their heads down and staring at their electronic devices. The whole thing was supposed to be a funny way to remind citizens of keeping their heads up while navigating city streets.

Most people didn't get the joke, thinking the e-lane was real. In fact, when the tape on the sidewalk was removed, city hall received complaints from citizens who thought the smartphone lane was a great idea!

As a result, Philadelphia officials began drafting a safety campaign aimed "at pedestrians who are looking at their devices instead of where they're going." Rina Cutler, deputy mayor for transportation and public utilities, explained, "One of the messages will certainly be 'pick your head up'—I want to say 'nitwit,' but I probably shouldn't call them names."[4]

"Pick your head up" is good advice for a lot of situations. It's practical, but it's also spiritual—as in "Keep your eyes focused upward on heaven." In discussing the signs of the times, the Lord Jesus said exactly that: "When these things begin to happen, look up and lift up your heads, because your redemption draws near" (Luke 21:28). The Bible tells us to set our minds "on things above, not on things on the earth" (Col. 3:2).

Now that we know a little more about what heaven is and what we will experience there, let's learn how the reality of heaven impacts our lives here on earth. The New Testament constantly affirms that what we believe about heaven affects how we live now. How we view the future has a tremendous influence on how we conduct ourselves in the present.

The apostle Peter devoted a powerful chapter to prophecies about the end of the world when he wrote his second letter, and his takeaway is timeless: "Therefore, since all these things will be dissolved, what manner of persons ought you to be?" (2 Pet. 3:11).

What manner, indeed!

In light of 2 Peter 3, let's discuss the difference it makes when we know God's future plans for us. How should we live today in light of what we've learned about heaven, the Rapture, and eternal life?

Peter answered that question in straightforward language, and I think it's helpful to see the practicality of his insights. He offered five characteristics true of rapture ready people.

PEOPLE OF PURITY

Look again at 2 Peter 3:11: "Therefore, since all these things will be dissolved, what manner of persons ought you to be in holy conduct and godliness?"

In this verse, Peter described the lifestyle of a Christian who understands the future plan of God. He said we ought to be people of holy conduct. He also added the word *godliness*, which means to have a Godward attitude and to do the things that are pleasing to Him.

The apostle John agreed: "All who have this hope in him purify themselves, just as he is pure" (1 John 3:3 NIV).

In his first letter to Timothy, Paul exhorted us to make godliness the object of determined effort and pursuit. He said, "Exercise yourself toward godliness" and "pursue . . . godliness" (1 Tim. 4:7; 6:11). This affects the words we speak, the things we watch, the thoughts we indulge, and the habits that shape our lives.

Let me ask you plainly: In light of the imminent Rapture, is there any change you need to make in your daily life, entertainment, spending, attitudes, and use of time?

In his book *Heaven*, Randy Alcorn helps us understand how God's revealed future should motivate us to live holy lives:

> If my wedding date is on the calendar, and I'm thinking of the person I'm going to marry, I shouldn't be an easy target for seduction. Likewise, when I've meditated on Heaven, sin is terribly unappealing. It's when my mind drifts from Heaven that sin seems attractive. Thinking of Heaven leads inevitably to pursuing holiness. Our high tolerance for sin testifies of our failure to prepare for Heaven.[5]

PEOPLE OF PROMISE

In addition to lifting up godliness and holy conduct, Peter encouraged Christ-followers to be "looking for and hastening the coming of the day of God" (2 Pet. 3:12).

In other words, Peter instructed us to be mindful of God's promises for the future, specifically the Rapture and the Second Coming. C. S. Lewis showed us what this looks like on a practical level when he wrote: "I must keep alive in myself the desire for my true country, which I shall not find till after death; I must never let it get snowed under or turned aside; I must make it the main object of life to press on to that other country and to help others do the same."[6]

According to Peter, it is easy to become indifferent to the coming of the Lord and His future plans for us. He encouraged us to live as those "looking for and hastening the coming of the day of God." The words translated as "looking for" mean "to expect or wait for."

When Peter wrote in verse 12 that we are "hastening" the coming of the day of God, he was reminding us we are to earnestly desire the coming of the Lord. Paul put it this way toward the end of his life: "Finally, there is laid up for me the crown of righteousness, which the Lord, the righteous Judge, will give to me on that Day, and not to me only but also to all who have loved His appearing" (2 Tim. 4:8).

I love the word *anticipation*. We have an inborn psychological need to look forward to coming events, to enjoy thinking about them, to plan for them, to relish the thought of our upcoming vacation or visit with a grandchild or holiday meal. How much more should we anticipate the sure promise of Christ's return for us!

PEOPLE OF PURPOSE

Next, because the Rapture and heaven are a future reality, Peter urged believers in Jesus to remain mindful about their purpose. He wrote,

"Therefore, beloved, looking forward to these things, be diligent to be found by Him in peace, without spot and blameless" (2 Pet. 3:14).

The instruction to "be diligent" means to "do your best, make haste, take care, hurry on." This is the third time Peter used the word *diligent* in his second epistle. Here are the first two:

- "But also for this very reason, giving all diligence, add to your faith virtue, to virtue knowledge, to knowledge self-control, to self-control perseverance, to perseverance godliness, to godliness brotherly kindness, and to brotherly kindness love" (1:5–7).
- "Therefore, brethren, be even more diligent to make your call and election sure, for if you do these things you will never stumble" (1:10).

In Peter's day, there were some who thought that since the Lord was coming back soon, they should just take it easy and coast into heaven. The very opposite is true. Because Christ is coming back, we're to be filled with urgency. We are to be diligent, consistently mindful of our purpose.

Jesus affirmed this instruction when He told us to "do business till I come" (Luke 19:13). We are to use the gifts and callings He has placed upon us and take advantage of every opportunity that He puts in front of us.

Oh, what urgency these truths ought to put into our daily routine! Our Lord has assigned work for each of us to do, and this work is daily. We have a task to finish, a race to run, and a job to do. How we serve the Lord this week is determined by our zeal for His swift return.

PEOPLE OF PERSISTANCE

Peter also wrote this sentence of warning: "You therefore, beloved, since you know this beforehand, beware lest you also fall from your own steadfastness, being led away with the error of the wicked" (2 Pet. 3:17).

The word *beware* is the translation of a Greek military term that means "to guard or to be on guard." Peter told us that because we know Jesus is returning soon, we are to constantly guard against being deceived by the error of unbelievers, and, as a result of that deception, lose our own steadfastness.

The word *steadfast* means to be firmly fixed in our faith or duty, constant, unchanging, steady. That term is associated throughout the New Testament with the coming of the Lord and His plan for the future. Why? Because this is no time for weakness or cowardice.

Elsewhere the Bible says:

- "But hold fast what you have till I come" (Rev. 2:25).
- "Behold, I am coming quickly! Hold fast what you have, that no one may take your crown" (Rev. 3:11).

Because we know the truth about the future, we patiently walk and work alongside the Lord, unfazed by the errors of wicked people. They may ridicule us, mock us, oppose us, and try to intimidate us. But our heads are high and our eyes are on heaven's future. We are steadfast people!

PEOPLE OF PROGRESS

Finally, we are called to be people of progress. Peter ended his chapter saying, "But grow in the grace and knowledge of our Lord and Savior Jesus Christ. To Him be the glory both now and forever. Amen" (2 Pet. 3:18).

These are actually the last recorded words of the apostle Peter. What he offered here is a challenge that will occupy our attention until we enter heaven. We're to grow in grace and in the knowledge of our Lord and Savior Jesus Christ.

How do we do that? The Bible offers four ways, which I'd like to explore as we wrap up this chapter.

First, growth comes through *the will of God*. It's His desire for us to grow in all areas of life, and He has the ability to accomplish what He desires. Paul wrote, "Being confident of this very thing, that He who has begun a good work in you will complete it until the day of Jesus Christ" (Phil. 1:6).

Second, growth comes through *the watchfulness of prayer*. Peter wrote this in his first epistle: "But the end of all things is at hand; therefore be serious and watchful in your prayers" (1 Pet. 4:7). All Christians understand prayer to be a necessary part of loving God and living as a member of His kingdom. The question is this: Do we pray? Are we people of prayer? If not, we won't be people of progress.

Third, growth comes through *the Word of God*. Jesus told us, "Behold, I am coming quickly! Blessed is he who keeps the words of the prophecy of this book" (Rev. 22:7). It was A. W. Tozer who said, "Nothing less than a whole Bible can make a whole Christian."

And finally, growth comes through *the work of the church*. Believers were never meant to seek progress on our own. We're part of a community. A kingdom. A church. The author of Hebrews wrote, "Let us consider one another in order to stir up love and good works, not forsaking the assembling of ourselves together, as is the manner of some, but exhorting one another, and so much the more as you see the Day approaching" (Heb. 10:24–25).

So you see, the coming of Christ and the doctrine of eternity provide the strongest motivations for living the Christian life *today*. The Rapture makes us mindful of heaven even in the here and now, moving us onward toward purity, promise, patience, purpose, and progress.

I've mentioned C. S. Lewis a few times in these pages, including earlier in this chapter. I want to quote him again, because perhaps no one has written more helpfully about heaven than he has. He offers a perspective on this topic that is both simple and profound.

In *Mere Christianity*, Lewis wrote, "If you read history, you will find that the Christians who did most for the present world were just those who thought most of the next. . . . It is since Christians have largely ceased to think of the other world that they have become so ineffective in this. Aim at Heaven and you will get earth 'thrown in': aim at earth and you will get neither."[7]

CHAPTER 19

THE TRIBULATION

For more than a month in 2022, Nadezhda Sukhorukova endured the fury of the Russian army. So did three hundred thousand other residents of Mariupol in the southeast region of Ukraine. That fury included rockets. Tanks. Drones. Artillery fire. Infantry with guns and grenades. The entire city was trapped in a literal war zone with no access to water, electricity, or communication with the outside world.

When Nadezhda finally managed to escape, she began posting on Facebook to inform the rest of the world about the horrors she'd seen, heard, felt, and lived. "The dead lie in the entrances, on the balconies, in the yards," she wrote. "The biggest fear is night shelling. Do you know what night shelling looks like? Like death."[1]

In another post she tried to describe the experience of waiting out missile attacks in the early hours of the morning: "A huge hammer is pounding on the iron roof and then a terrible rattle, as if the ground was cut with a huge knife, or a huge iron giant walks in forged boots on your land and steps on houses, trees, people."[2]

"My city is dying a painful death."[3]

Reading those words as a human being causes me to experience a whole range of emotions. Sorrow and grief because so many lives were devastated. Anger because of the injustice involved. Helplessness at my inability to provide assistance in a tangible way.

Reading those words as a student of biblical prophecy causes me to think about what our entire world will experience in the future. Reading about the trials and tribulations of people throughout Ukraine reminds me that *the* Tribulation is coming—and perhaps coming soon.

Remember, the Rapture will not occur in a vacuum. The moment Jesus steps through the gates of heaven and returns to rescue His people from this world, the countdown to Tribulation will begin. Therefore, it's important for us to learn more about that seven-year period looming on the horizon of human history.

THE PICTURE OF THE TRIBULATION

According to God's Word, the Tribulation will be a period filled with unprecedented horrors, upheavals, persecutions, natural disasters, massive slaughter, and political turmoil in the years immediately prior to Christ's Second Coming. All who accept the authority of the Bible believe the Tribulation will occur. And the spiraling chaos of today's world leads many to fear it may be upon us.

The word *tribulation* is rarely used in ordinary conversation today. Translated from the Greek *thlipsis*, the term calls to mind the giant weights used throughout the ancient world to crush grain into flour.[4]

So the idea behind *tribulation* is utterly crushing, pulverizing, or grinding a substance into powder. What a powerful picture!

That is the image we should focus on whenever we think about the Tribulation—the seven-year period that will be one of the prominent features of the prophetic End Times. Let's explore what the Bible tells us about this terrible time.

SEVEN YEARS OF SURPRISE

Once again, the Rapture will signal the beginning of the Tribulation. That is the moment when Christ appears, raises the dead who believed in Him, and draws living Christians from the earth to be with Him.

The next natural question for Paul's readers would have been "When will this happen?" Paul anticipated the question and began 1 Thessalonians 5 with these words: "But concerning the times and the seasons, brethren, you have no need that I should write to you. For you yourselves know perfectly that the day of the Lord so comes as a thief in the night" (vv. 1–2).

That phrase "the day of the Lord" is a synonym for what we call the End Times. It includes everything that will happen beginning with the Rapture and extending all the way through the Tribulation and the Millennium.

Paul was saying that you cannot know when the Rapture will occur any more than you can know when a thief is planning to ransack your house. No thief sends a letter announcing he will arrive tomorrow at 2:00 a.m. Likewise, we are not given the ETA of the Rapture. It will come upon us unexpectedly, and the Tribulation will follow in its wake.

SEVEN YEARS OF SEVERITY

Nowhere in Scripture will you find one word or description that says anything good about the Tribulation Period (unless it is the promise that it will end after seven years). Moses called it "the day of their calamity" (Deut. 32:35). Zephaniah said it was "the day of the LORD's anger" (Zeph. 2:2). Paul referred to it as "the wrath to come" (1 Thess. 1:10). John called it "the hour of trial" (Rev. 3:10) and "the hour of His judgment" (14:7). Daniel described it as "a time of trouble, such as never was since there was a nation" (Dan. 12:1).

According to the prophet Zephaniah, "That day is a day of wrath, a day of trouble and distress, a day of devastation and desolation, a day of darkness and gloominess, a day of clouds and thick darkness, a day of trumpet and alarm against the fortified cities and against the high towers" (Zeph. 1:15–16).

Jesus told us that the Tribulation will be a time of terror and horror without precedent: "For then there will be great tribulation, such as has not been since the beginning of the world until this time, no, nor ever shall be. And unless those days were shortened, no flesh would be saved; but for the elect's sake those days will be shortened" (Matt. 24:21–22).

The central chapters of Revelation give us a vivid description of the horrors of the Tribulation Period. Great wars will ravage the world as nations rise up, lusting for conquest. All peace will end, and rampant slaughter will bloody the earth. Hail and fire will burn up the planet's grass and destroy a third of all trees. Intense famine will dry up food supplies. Rivers and seas will become too polluted to sustain life. Many rivers will dry up entirely. The sun will scorch the earth and its inhabitants like fire. A quarter of the world's population will die from war, starvation, and beastly predators. Giant earthquakes, accompanied by thunder and lightning, will destroy cities. Mountains will crash into the seas, killing a third of the fish. Tidal waves from the cataclysm will sink a third of all the world's ships. A massive meteor shower will strike the earth. Ashes and smoke rising from its devastation will hide the sun and moon. Swarms of demonic insects will darken the sun and inflict painful stings. Rampant, epidemic plagues will kill one-third of all mankind. Everyone, from national leaders to servants and slaves, will flee the cities to hide in caves and under rocks (Rev. 6:2–17; 8:8–13; 9:1–20; 16:1–21).

To make matters even worse, a maniacal despot known as the Antichrist will rise to power. He will be multiple times more demonic than Antiochus IV, Nero, Stalin, and Hitler combined. He will demand total allegiance to his satanically inspired program, and those who resist will be barred from buying or selling food or any other product.

His lust for power will not cease until the entire civilized world chokes in his tyrannical grasp (13:1–18).

It is not an overstatement to say that the Tribulation will be hell on earth, from which Dr. J. Dwight Pentecost tells us there will be no escape and no relief: "No passage can be found to alleviate to any degree whatsoever the severity of this time that shall come upon the earth."[5]

THE PURPOSE OF THE TRIBULATION

Of course, God will not be absent during those seven years of terror. As always, He will remain actively involved in all aspects of life.

Yes, the Tribulation will be brought on the earth by humanity's increasing rebellion and rampant sin. But God's hand will be heavily involved, just as it was when He brought the plagues on the defiant nation of Egypt. The Tribulation is a planned program designed to accomplish three important goals.

TO PURIFY ISRAEL

The Jewish nation exists as a result of God's promise to Abraham that his seed would be as numerous as the stars in heaven and would endure throughout all eternity (Gen. 12:1–3; 15:5). The Jewish nation has tested God's patience throughout the many centuries of its existence, turning away from Him time and time again. But despite Israel's persistent rebellion, God will keep His promise, not only because He is God and does not break His promises, but also because of His deep love for Israel.

One of the last phases of His promise to Israel was fulfilled in 1948, when the nation was reestablished on its originally promised land. Yet after all God's care to preserve the scattered Jews through the centuries, enabling them to remain intact so they could inherit their land, they remain disobedient even today.

The first purpose of the Tribulation is to purge out the Jewish rebels and bring about the final conversion of the nation. The Tribulation will be the fire that purifies Israel by burning out all the dross and impurities. As the prophet Ezekiel recorded: "I will make you pass under the rod . . . I will purge the rebels from among you, and those who transgress against Me" (Ezek. 20:37–38; see also Deut. 4:30–31).

The apostle Paul left no ambiguity as to whether this purging prophesied by Ezekiel would be effective: "And so all Israel will be saved, as it is written: 'The Deliverer will come out of Zion, and He will turn away ungodliness from Jacob; for this is My covenant with them, when I take away their sins'" (Rom. 11:26–27).

TO PUNISH SINNERS

The overall purpose of the Tribulation will be to execute God's wrath upon those who oppose Him—first upon the Jews, and then upon the Gentiles. As Paul wrote, "For the wrath of God is revealed from heaven against all ungodliness and unrighteousness of men, who suppress the truth in unrighteousness" (Rom. 1:18).

We like to think and speak about the love of God, but not so much about His wrath. But wrath goes hand in hand with judgment, and it is as much an expression of His goodness as His love. In fact, love and wrath are two sides of the same coin. One who is infinitely good, as God is, rightly abhors evil because evil is the enemy of goodness. Evil is, in fact, like a parasite, a blight, or a cancer on goodness. It feeds on and destroys what is good. Therefore, God rightly directs His wrath at evil.

Theologian N. T. Wright explained:

The biblical doctrine of God's wrath is rooted in the doctrine of God as the good, wise, and loving creator, who hates—yes, hates, and hates implacably—anything that spoils, defaces, distorts, or damages his beautiful creation, and in particular anything that does that to his image-bearing creatures. If God does not hate racial prejudice, he is neither good nor loving. If God is not wrathful at child abuse, he is neither good nor loving. If God is not utterly determined to root out from his creation, in an act of proper wrath and judgment, the arrogance that allows people to exploit, bomb, bully, and enslave one another, he is neither loving, nor good, nor wise.[6]

The prophet Nahum explained the nature of God's wrath in this way: "The LORD avenges and is furious. The LORD will take vengeance on His adversaries, and He reserves wrath for His enemies; the LORD is slow to anger and great in power, and will not at all acquit the wicked" (Nah. 1:2–3).

TO PREACH THE GOSPEL

We know from Scripture that the seven-year Tribulation Period will expose unregenerate people, both Jews and Gentiles, to the wrath of God. The next question is this: How will those people respond?

Incredibly, God's Word indicates that the grinding *thlipsis* of the Tribulation will be wonderful news for many who are forced to endure it. Why? Because it will bring them to a place of submission before God. It will confront them with the reality of their sin and spur them to accept the salvation offered by Jesus Christ.

Amazingly, the Tribulation may produce the greatest harvest for God's kingdom in the history of our world. We'll explore this possibility more deeply in chapter 20. Just as the sun hardens clay and softens butter, God's wrath will harden some hearts and soften others. This shows us that the purpose of the Tribulation includes both conversion and punishment, depending on how the objects of God's wrath respond to it.

Speaking of our response to the Tribulation, I know this can seem like a bleak subject to study. Knowing that our world—and perhaps our loved ones—will endure seven long years of terror and chaos is a burden none of us wants to carry. Knowing those events may come quickly only raises the tension.

As the late Billy Graham has written, "We are like people under sentence of death, waiting for the date to be set. We sense that something is about to happen. We know that things cannot go on as they are. History has reached an impasse. We are now on a collision course. Something is about to give."[7]

Still, we can comfort ourselves in the knowledge that even something as terrible as the Tribulation is part of God's plan for history—for *His* story. Even during the worst circumstances imaginable, God is in control. He has planned out His will for the future, and His plans will never be thwarted.

CHAPTER 20

SALVATION IN THE TRIBULATION

He was seventeen, far too young to die. Yet Taha Erdem knew he was at the end of his short life. He'd been sleeping when the earthquake struck. He was violently shaken out of bed and buried by the debris of the four-story apartment building where he lived with his family. As the earth kept shaking, the youth watched the concrete slab of the roof edging closer and closer to his position, threatening to crush him to death.

Taha had the presence of mind to pull out his cell phone and record a video for his family and friends. He painfully moved the camera to his bruised face, hit the Record button, and said, "I think this is the last video I will ever shoot for you. I am dead if I am not wrong. There is close to [one thousand pounds] on top of my feet. My [feet] are gone. I could have hurt my head when I was getting it out of there. We are still shaking."

Then he said: "Death, my friends, comes at a time when one is least expecting it. There are many things that I regret. May God forgive me of all my sins."

What a message for the entire human race! Death often comes when we least expect it, which is also the way Christ will come for His people—like a thief in the night. Those who are left behind will have many regrets. They may feel they're as good as dead. They may think it's too late to be saved. But there's still time for God to forgive their sins.

Thankfully, it wasn't too late for Taha Erdem. About two hours after the earthquake, he was pulled from the rubble alive. Miraculously, so were all ten members of his family.[1]

In the same way, the grace of God will pull many people out of the rubble of the Tribulation. There will still be hope for those left behind after the Rapture. The gospel will still be available, even if the church is gone.

There will be at least four streams of gospel truth that will cut a channel through the Tribulation. In fact, it is possible that the spiritual awakening that will occur during the Tribulation will be the greatest evangelistic harvest the world has ever seen.

THE PREACHING OF THE 144,000

At the front lines of God's effort to bring Tribulation survivors to Himself will be 144,000 specially chosen Jewish evangelists. Here's how they are described in Revelation 7:2–4:

> Then I saw another angel ascending from the east, having the seal of the living God. And he cried with a loud voice to the four angels to whom it was granted to harm the earth and the sea, saying, "Do not harm the earth, the sea, or the trees till we have sealed the servants of our God on their foreheads." And I heard the number of those who were sealed. One hundred and forty-four thousand of all the tribes of the children of Israel were sealed.

God will ordain 144,000 Jews for a very special earth-to-heaven mission during the Tribulation. Only twelve Jews (Jesus' apostles) turned the first century upside down. In that coming day we will see what twelve thousand times twelve can do!

How many souls will be saved by the message of these evangelists? Here's what the Bible says:

> After these things I looked, and behold, a great multitude which no one could number, of all nations, tribes, peoples, and tongues, standing before the throne and before the Lamb, clothed with white robes, with palm branches in their hands. . . . Then one of the elders answered, saying to me, "Who are these arrayed in white robes, and where did they come from?". . . . So he said to me, "These are the ones who come out of the great tribulation, and washed their robes, and made them white in the blood of the Lamb." (Rev. 7:9, 13–14)

THE PROPHESYING OF THE TWO WITNESSES

In addition to the 144,000 Jewish evangelists, two more men will suddenly appear during the End Times and instantly command a worldwide audience. Revelation 11:3 says, "I will give power to my two witnesses, and they will prophesy one thousand two hundred and sixty days, clothed in sackcloth."

Most evangelical scholars believe these two witnesses are Moses and Elijah. Timothy Demy and John Whitcomb present strong reasons for this identification: "No two men in Israel's entire history would receive greater respect than Moses and Elijah. Moses was God's great deliverer and lawgiver for Israel (Deuteronomy 34:10–12). . . . So highly did the Jews of Jesus' day think of Elijah that when they saw Jesus' miracles, some people concluded that Elijah had returned."[2]

William R. Newell wrote, "They will testify unsparingly of human wickedness to men's very faces. . . . [They] will tell to the teeth of a horrid godlessness which is ready to worship the devil, just what they are before God."[3]

Halfway through the Tribulation, the two witnesses will be killed, and their bodies displayed in the streets of Jerusalem. But the Bible says, "Now after the three-and-a-half days the breath of life from God entered them, and they stood on their feet, and great fear fell on those who saw them" (Rev. 11:11).

As a stunned world watches, the two men—once again alive and unleashed—will hear a voice from heaven saying, "Come up here!" A cloud will envelop them, and they will be raptured to heaven as their enemies gape in astonishment (Rev. 11:12).

It's impossible to estimate how many Tribulation sinners will come to Christ as a result of the preaching of the two witnesses.

THE PROCLAMATION OF THE ANGEL

God will use a third resource to announce the good news of the gospel to the lost world during the Tribulation: His angel. The mercy and love of God is so vast that He will commission an angel to proclaim the message of His saving grace, making sure everyone has the opportunity to hear the good news. Even the Antichrist's grip on the world will not prevent the gospel from going forth. God will bypass demonic tyranny and announce it from the heavens.

We read about this in Revelation 14:6–7:

> Then I saw another angel flying in the midst of heaven, having the everlasting gospel to preach to those who dwell on the earth—to every nation, tribe, tongue, and people—saying with a loud voice, "Fear God and give glory to Him, for the hour of His judgment has come; and worship Him who made heaven and earth, the sea and springs of water."

The everlasting gospel and an earnest warning will peal forth from an angel flying over the earth! That's astounding to me, and it's a window into the heart of God. He will make sure everyone on earth hears the good news and has a chance to respond, even during the Tribulation.

THE PRESENCE OF BIBLES AND BIBLICAL MATERIALS

There is another means by which those who are left behind can hear the good news of God's grace and forgiveness: all the Bibles, devotional books, films, broadcasts, web pages, and literature that will be left behind. None of that will be raptured!

Henry Morris foresaw this reality, writing:

> Millions upon millions of copies of the Bible and Bible portions have been published in all major languages, and distributed throughout the world. . . . Removal of believers from the world at the rapture will not remove the Scriptures, and multitudes will no doubt be constrained to read the Bible. . . .
>
> Thus, multitudes will turn to their Creator and Savior in those days, and will be willing to give their testimony for the Word of God and even . . . their lives as they seek to persuade the world that the calamities it is suffering are judgments from the Lord.[4]

All this shows that God, in His mercy, will make sure people everywhere have an opportunity to hear the good news of the gospel of grace through preachers, witnesses, an angel, and Christian materials and Bibles.

It's important to understand that people will be saved during the Tribulation—that it's never too late to receive God's grace through Jesus Christ until the very moment before the Second Coming.

But we must also understand that following Jesus during the Tribulation will exact a high price, even death. In light of what we have already studied in this book, you might be wondering what will happen to a person who accepts Christ during the Tribulation and then dies before the seven-year Tribulation ends.

When a follower of Christ dies during the Tribulation Period, their body will remain here on the earth, but their soul will go immediately to heaven to be with God. To be absent from the body is to be present with the Lord (2 Cor. 5:8).

The book of Revelation gives us a glimpse of the souls of believers martyred during the Tribulation. It shows them waiting for God to exact vengeance on their persecutors who killed them. Read this passage in Revelation 6:9-12:

> When He opened the fifth seal, I saw under the altar the souls of those who had been slain for the word of God and for the testimony which they held. And they cried with a loud voice, saying, "How long, O Lord, holy and true, until You judge and avenge our blood on those who dwell on the earth?" Then a white robe was given to each of them; and it was said to them that they should rest a little while longer, until both the number of their fellow servants and their brethren, who would be killed as they were, was completed.

Seeing the incredible disasters on earth during the Tribulation, we can understand how these martyrs in heaven are praising the Lord with such fervor. Their troubles are over. They are home at last. This is in stark contrast to what happened to them on earth. They had been hungry, for they couldn't buy food without the mark of the Beast; they were thirsty, for the rivers were turned to blood; they were scorched by the burning sun. But now the agony of their lives is over and they are with the Lord.

When Jesus returns to earth at the end of the Tribulation, the bodies of believers who died during those seven years will be resurrected, and each will inhabit their new, heavenly body. Revelation 20:4 makes this clear: "Then I saw the souls of those who had been beheaded for their witness to Jesus and for the word of God, who had not worshiped the beast or his image, and had not received his mark on their foreheads or on their hands. And they lived and reigned with Christ for a thousand years."

One thing is crystal clear about salvation: if a person leaves this world without accepting Christ as Savior from sin, it's too late for that person to be saved. The soul of that person goes to hell forever. That's the plain and simple truth. There is no second chance for salvation after death. As the old saying goes, "As death finds you, eternity keeps you."

Hebrews 9:27 emphasizes the reality that "people are destined to die once, and after that to face judgment" (NIV).

Nothing can change your fate after death. There is no purgatory and no parole. The boundaries of destiny are forever fixed in the afterlife. Death removes any opportunity to change your mind about your eternal destiny. Death closes the door of salvation forever.

But is there ever a time *in this life* when it's too late to be saved? Is there a line a person can cross that closes the window of salvation? I believe the answer to this question is yes. The Bible contains a warning against all who reject Jesus Christ and receive the mark of the Antichrist during the Tribulation:

And then the lawless one will be revealed, whom the Lord will consume with the breath of His mouth and destroy with the brightness of His coming. The coming of the lawless one is according to the working of Satan, with all power, signs, and lying wonders, and with all unrighteous deception among those who perish, because they did not receive the love of the truth, that they might be saved. And for this reason God will send them strong delusion, that they should believe the lie, that they all may be condemned who did not believe the truth but had pleasure in unrighteousness. (2 Thess. 2:8–12)

Those who embrace the lies of the Antichrist and are duped and deceived by his wonders have no chance to be saved. Once the choice for the Antichrist is made, God will send a strong delusion to harden that choice and confirm the condemnation. There's no turning back from that fateful decision. It's irreversible and irrevocable. Such a choice is set forever in the concrete of eternity.

Revelation 14:9–11 says,

> If anyone worships the beast and his image, and receives his mark on his forehead or on his hand, he himself shall also drink of the wine of the wrath of God, which is poured out full strength into the cup of His indignation. He shall be tormented with fire and brimstone in the presence of the holy angels and in the presence of the Lamb. And the smoke of their torment ascends forever and ever; and they have no rest day or night, who worship the beast and his image, and whoever receives the mark of his name.

Dr. Arthur Compton was one of a committee of six scientists appointed by president Franklin D. Roosevelt to create the first atomic bomb. In a subsequent magazine article, Compton recalled the day in 1942 when he and other scientists conducted their first experiment in a squash court in Chicago. He described the different reactions— relief, concern, excitement. Everyone present realized a power had been unleashed that would change the course of history.

Compton knew that life on earth would never be the same. He concluded: "Man must now go the way of Jesus or perish."[5]

That's the choice for the world today, and it's your choice. Tragically, the world is perishing. But you can go the way of Jesus. Don't wait to receive Him. Time is passing. The Bible stresses the urgency to respond to the call of the gospel right now. Don't hope to be saved from the rubble of the Tribulation. Reach out to Christ right now, before the collapse comes.

The Lord tells us: "Behold, now is the accepted time; behold, now is the day of salvation" (2 Cor. 6:2).

Every page of the Bible says *today*.

Every tick of the clock says *today*.

Every beat of your heart says *today*.

Every obituary column seems to cry out *today*.

All of creation cries out: "Behold, *today* is the day of salvation."[6]

CHAPTER 21

AT ANY MOMENT

When you have lived in California as long as I have, you develop a healthy respect for earthquakes. Unlike other natural disasters that have built-in warning systems hours or even days in advance, there is no way to predict when or where an earthquake may strike.

But that hasn't stopped people from trying.

In 2022, a Dutch researcher named Frank Hoogerbeets made international news by accurately predicting a devastating earthquake in Turkey three days before it happened. Frank's method relies on the alignment of planets in our solar system—what he calls "planetary geometry."

Looking deeper, Frank's tweets and alerts are often as cryptic as fortune cookies, including, "We are slowly entering a time when the likelihood of M-8+seismic activity increases." And Frank's own website states, "There is no reliable method for predicting the exact time and location of earthquakes."[1]

Other earthquake-prediction methods are even stranger. Just a few months before Frank's prediction, a group of Mexican fishermen did their best to raise the alarm for a potential quake after catching a rare oarfish near Sinaloa. Oarfish are the largest bony fish in the sea, and they normally dwell much too deep to be caught.

Local legends state that oarfish only rise to the surface when a calamity is at hand, which is why they are often called "earthquake fish."[2]

After studying these and other methods, the United States Geological Survey put out a statement that says, "Neither the USGS nor any other scientists have ever predicted a major earthquake."[3]

Given that reality, those of us who live near geological fault lines must continue to expect that an earthquake is imminent. We must prepare as if "the big one" could occur at any moment. Just as an earthquake is imminent and could occur at any moment, so the coming of our Lord is also imminent and could occur at any moment.

In fact, one of the key teachings about the Rapture that is recorded in several places in Scripture is often called the doctrine of imminency.

When something is imminent, it could happen at any moment. There are no barriers that need to be removed or qualifications that need to be met before it occurs. Importantly, an event that is "imminent" is not necessarily "immediate." Saying an event is imminent does not mean it is guaranteed to occur in the immediate future, only that it *could* occur at any time.

In his definitive book on the Rapture, Renald Showers gives us an in-depth explanation of the word *imminent*:

> The English word "imminent" means "hanging over one's head, ready to befall or overtake one; close at hand in its incidence." Thus, an imminent event is one that is always hanging overhead, is constantly ready to befall or overtake a person, is always close at hand in the sense that it could happen at any moment.
>
> Other things may happen before the imminent event, but nothing else must take place before it happens. If something must take

place before an event can happen, that event is not imminent. The necessity of something else taking place first destroys the concept of imminency. When an event is truly imminent, we never know exactly when it will happen.[4]

Bible expositor A. T. Pierson wrote, "Imminence is the combination of two conditions . . . certainty and uncertainty. An imminent event is one which is certain to occur at some time, uncertain at what time. Imminent is not synonymous with impending. It is not exact to say what is imminent is near at hand; it may or may not be."[5]

I am highlighting this term because the Bible presents the Rapture as an imminent event—one that could take place at any moment. This chapter will show you where to find those claims in Scripture and why the doctrine of imminency is important for your everyday life.

THE PASSAGES THAT INTRODUCE IMMINENCY

We have explored Jesus' powerful promise to His followers in John 14 from several angles, but let's look once more at those verses through the lens of imminency:

"Let not your heart be troubled; you believe in God, believe also in Me. In My Father's house are many mansions; if it were not so, I would have told you. I go to prepare a place for you. And if I go and prepare a place for you, I will come again and receive you to Myself; that where I am, there you may be also." (vv. 1–3)

Look at the two action verbs at the core of that passage: "I go to prepare a place for you" and "I will come again and receive you to Myself." The first of those statements has already come to pass. After the resurrection, Jesus did not remain on earth but instead ascended to heaven. He left to prepare a place for us. The second of those promises is still to come. Jesus will return, and He gave no preconditions that must be fulfilled before that return. He could literally arrive at any moment.

That's imminency.

As one scholar has written: "Jesus mentions no signs that must precede the rapture. He spoke directly of a reunion of the apostles with their Lord, which would issue in an eternal 'at-home-ness' with both Jesus and the Father."[6]

Paul emphasized the imminence of Christ's return when he wrote his first epistle to the believers in Thessalonica:

> But you, brethren, are not in darkness, so that this Day should overtake you as a thief. You are all sons of light and sons of the day. We are not of the night nor of darkness. Therefore let us not sleep, as others do, but let us watch and be sober. For those who sleep, sleep at night, and those who get drunk are drunk at night. But let us who are of the day be sober, putting on the breastplate of faith and love, and as a helmet the hope of salvation. For God did not appoint us to wrath, but to obtain salvation through our Lord Jesus Christ. (1 Thess. 5:4–9)

Notice that Paul emphasized the salvation of his audience. He described the Thessalonians as "brethren" and "sons of light." They were believers. They were saved. For that reason, why was it important for them to "watch and be sober"? Their eternal futures had already been sealed—as is the case for Christians today—so what reason was there for them to maintain such readiness?

The answer is tied to the certainty of God's wrath. The day of God's judgment is coming. The believers in Thessalonica would not experience that wrath because of the Rapture. However, Paul charged them to invest themselves in the mission of expanding God's kingdom while they still had time. He wanted them to live out their calling as children of light precisely *because* the return of Christ was imminent.

Finally and appropriately, Jesus' last words in Scripture are recorded in Revelation 22:20, and they also emphasize the imminence of His return: "Surely I am coming quickly."

That is the reality we should remember as believers in Jesus. We don't need to wait for signs in order to carry out the work of Christ. He told us He is coming quickly. Sooner than later. At any moment.

While I was working on this chapter, a member of our church handed me a card that read, "I'm not looking for a sign, I'm looking for the Savior!"

Notice, also, the words that convey imminency in the following passages:

- "Lift up your heads, because your redemption draws near" (Luke 21:28).
- "We ourselves groan within ourselves, eagerly waiting for the adoption" (Rom. 8:23).
- "Eagerly waiting for the revelation of our Lord Jesus Christ" (1 Cor. 1:7).
- "We shall all be changed—in a moment, in the twinkling of an eye" (1 Cor. 15:51–52).
- "We also eagerly wait for the Savior, the Lord Jesus Christ" (Phil. 3:20).
- "For you yourselves know perfectly that the day of the Lord so comes as a thief in the night" (1 Thess. 5:2).
- "Looking for the blessed hope and glorious appearing of our great God and Savior Jesus Christ" (Titus 2:13).
- "You see the Day approaching" (Heb. 10:25).
- "The coming of the Lord is at hand" (James 5:8).
- "The Judge is standing at the door!" (James 5:9).
- "The end of all things is at hand" (1 Pet. 4:7).
- "Behold, I am coming quickly!" (Rev. 22:7).

THE PRONOUNS THAT INSIST
ON IMMINENCY

Every word in Scripture matters. Every letter. To quote Jesus, every "jot" and "tittle" (Matt. 5:18). There is a world of spiritual treasure to be found when we mine even the most minute elements of Scripture.

For example, look at the pronouns Paul used when writing to the Thessalonians: "*We* who are alive and remain until the coming of the Lord. . . . *We* who are alive and remain shall be caught up together with them in the clouds to meet the Lord in the air. And thus *we* shall always be with the Lord" (1 Thess. 4:15, 17).

Why did Paul keep saying "we"? Because he expected to be included in the Rapture. In the words of John MacArthur: "When the apostle Paul described the Lord's coming for the church, he used personal pronouns that show he clearly was convinced he himself might be among those who would be caught up alive to meet the Lord."[7]

Paul believed Christ would return during his lifetime. He *expected* Jesus to come back while he was still alive. More than that, he eagerly anticipated that return.

The fact that Jesus did not initiate the Rapture in the first century is not the point. What's important is understanding—as Paul did—that Christ *could* return at any moment. And that the imminence of that return should spur us to live as Paul did: focused each day on accomplishing God's work for God's kingdom.

THE PARABLES THAT
ILLUSTRATE IMMINENCY

To make His point about the imminency of His return, Jesus told several stories or parables.

His first story was about an *unexpected thief* (Matt. 24:43–44).

This is a story about a house that was broken into by a thief because the master of the house was not watching. The point that Jesus made was this: If the master of the house had known when the thief was coming, he would have watched and kept the theft from occurring. But since the master did not know the hour of the day when the theft would occur, his house was unexpectedly robbed.

Now watch how Jesus concluded His parable: "Therefore you also be ready, for the Son of Man is coming at an hour you do not expect" (v. 44).

The next story was about *two servants* (Matt. 24:45–51). This story is about two servants who worked for the same master. One of the servants was faithful and the other unfaithful. Their master went away from home and left the two servants in charge. The good servant faithfully served his master and provided food for his master's house. The evil servant convinced himself that the master was delaying his coming and, getting drunk, he beat up some of his fellow servants. Both of the servants were caught doing what they were doing when the master unexpectedly returned. The good servant was rewarded with a promotion and the evil servant was punished severely.

Like the master in the parable, our Master in heaven is coming at an unexpected time. It could be today or tomorrow . . . this century or the next. But we are always to be waiting, watching, and working until He comes.

The final story was about the *wise and foolish virgins* (Matt. 25:1–13). This parable of Jesus is "about ten virgins, five of whom are foolish and five wise. All ten virgins were anticipating the celebration of a wedding and the long and majestic parade to the house of the bridegroom. When the bridegroom came unexpectedly in the middle of the night, the foolish virgins had no oil for their lamps. By the time they purchased oil, it was too late, and they found themselves locked out of the wedding feast where the wise virgins had been admitted.

Neither group knew a fixed period within which the groom would return, but one group was ready, and the other was not."[8]

This is what Jesus said we should learn from this parable: "Watch therefore, for you know neither the day nor the hour in which the Son of Man is coming" (25:13).

In the Gospel of Luke, Jesus said something similar yet even more powerful: "Blessed are those servants whom the master, when he comes, will find watching. Assuredly, I say to you that he will gird himself and have them sit down to eat, and will come and serve them" (Luke 12:37).

THE PERSPECTIVE THAT INTERPRETS IMMINENCY

The imminency of Christ's return is more than just an incidental truth about the Rapture. Major books and manuscripts have been written to either defend this doctrine or attack it. Simply put, if the Bible teaches that Jesus can come back at any time, and that nothing needs to take place before He comes, then the idea that the church must go through the Tribulation before the Rapture occurs is found to be false.

The people of Taiwan understand the practical applications of imminence in a visceral way. For more than seventy years, Taiwan has been under threat of invasion from the Chinese Communist Party (CCP), and that threat has intensified after Russia's recent invasion of Ukraine.

"The question is not whether China will attack Taiwan but when," says Huoh Shoou-yeh, who is chairman of a defense ministry think tank. "Taiwan must be ready for a conflict at any time," he says, noting that the Taiwanese military is capable of mobilizing more than two hundred thousand soldiers within twenty-four hours.[9]

That's the kind of readiness we need to maintain as followers of Jesus. We, too, are on the cusp of an invasion—not hostile, but heavenly. Therefore, we must choose to remain ready for the glorious hour that may arrive at any moment.

CHAPTER 22

WHY THE DELAY?

I've traveled my fair share over the decades, and flight delays have challenged my patience. Yours too? When airlines give us a timetable, we build our plans around it and expect them to stay on schedule. But whenever I'm tempted to fly off the handle, I simply remember to be thankful I wasn't aboard United Airlines flight 857 from San Francisco to Shanghai in March 2012.

That plane departed San Francisco at 2:00 p.m. on a Sunday. Total flight time was scheduled at thirteen hours. Three hours in, however, the plane was diverted to Anchorage, Alaska. The problem had to do with the bathrooms. There weren't enough functional lavatories to ensure everyone's comfort on such a long flight.

When the plane landed in Anchorage, passengers were forced to remain on board for ninety minutes while air-traffic controllers arranged a gate. The travelers were given vouchers for a single meal and a hotel, then told to return the next day to resume their journey to Shanghai.

Another day, another delay. The new flight was scheduled to depart at 1:00 p.m. on a replacement plane, but the vehicle just sat there for more than two hours. Then, after boarding, passengers were informed the replacement plane was also malfunctioning. They pried themselves out of their seats, retrieved their luggage, and returned to the terminal once again.

On Tuesday, a third plane finally departed Anchorage and successfully delivered its passengers to Shanghai—three days late, but thankfully safe and sound.[1]

People don't like delays in general, but it's especially frustrating when we don't understand why we're being forced to wait. That's true of waiting during a trip, at a doctor's office, in the grocery line, in traffic, or for a package to arrive.

It's also true of waiting for God to deliver His promises—including His promise of the Rapture. After all, the very first verse of the book of Revelation says: "The Revelation of Jesus Christ, which God gave Him to show His servants—things which must shortly take place" (1:1).

Notice the word *shortly*. If I tell Donna, "I'm going to go down to the store for a gallon of milk, but I'll be back shortly," she wouldn't expect me to be gone for two days, let alone two thousand years!

The final chapter of Revelation uses the word "quickly" to describe the return of Christ that will initiate the End Times. In fact, you can find the word *quickly* used four times in Revelation 22. In verse 12, Jesus said, "Behold, I am coming quickly." And in verse 20 He repeated His promise, saying, "Surely I am coming quickly."

Soon! Quickly! For centuries, believers have echoed John's response to that promise: "Amen. Even so, come, Lord Jesus!" (v. 20).

Lord, come quickly! *Maranatha!*

We saw in the previous chapter that the Rapture is imminent, meaning it can happen at any moment. Yet our Lord Jesus has not yet returned. For two thousand years, Christians have watched and waited for the catalyst of the Rapture to coalesce into the next phase in God's prophetic plan. And we are still waiting.

It's fair to ask the question: *Why the delay?*

THE LORD'S PERSPECTIVE

Would you believe people were asking that same question even in the first century? When the apostle Peter wrote his second epistle to the churches in Asia Minor (modern-day Turkey), he likely did so from the depths of a prison in Rome. Condemned to die by Emperor Nero, Peter's goal for that letter was to confront false teachers who had permeated the church and to correct the doctrinal confusion they had caused.

Interestingly, one of the questions people in the early church seemed to be asking is the same one that puzzles us: *Why the delay?*

By that time it had been almost forty years since Jesus died, rose again, and ascended into heaven with the promise to "prepare a place" for His followers. The early church was aware of that promise, and many wondered why it was taking so long.

In fact, as Peter noted, false teachers were already using the delay to cast doubt on God's faithfulness and the dependability of Christ's promised return: "Scoffers will come in the last days, walking according to their own lusts, and saying, 'Where is the promise of His coming? For since the fathers fell asleep, all things continue as they were from the beginning of creation'" (2 Pet. 3:3–4).

Remember the definition of the biblical phrase "last days." It refers to the period between the end of Jesus' public ministry and the moment of the Rapture. The Christians of Peter's generation were part of the "last days," just as we are. In their time, as in ours, false teachers attempted to cast doubt upon the reality of Christ's return by pointing out that Christ had not yet returned as He had promised.

How did Peter respond?

First, by reminding his readers that our human perspective on time is different from God's perspective. He told them: "But, beloved, do not forget this one thing, that with the Lord one day is as a thousand years, and a thousand years as one day" (2 Pet. 3:8).

That verse contains an allusion to Psalm 90:4, which states: "A thousand years in Your sight are like yesterday when it is past, and like a watch in the night."

The psalmist's point (and Peter's as well) is simple and logical: because God is eternal, He experiences time differently than we do.

The Bible is God's Book, and the words represent His vocabulary. We have to understand how He is using the words, how He intends for us to understand them, and what He means by them from His perspective. We have to study Scripture in context.

New Testament scholar Doug Moo explained:

God views the passing of time from a different perspective than we do. We are impatient, getting disturbed and upset by even a short delay; God is patient, willing to let centuries and even millennia go by as He works out His purposes. Peter is not telling his readers that they are wrong to believe that Christ's return is "imminent." What he is telling them is that they are wrong to be impatient when it does not come as quickly as they might like or hope.[2]

The Bible teaches God exists in the past, present, and future at the same moment. For God, later is the same as earlier. The end is the same as the beginning. Now is the same as then.

This is a great mystery, and it's hard to wrap our heads around the concept of an eternal God. But if God were anything less than eternal, He would not, in actuality, be God. And, if one day with the Lord is like one thousand years, and one thousand years is like one day, then from God's perspective Jesus hasn't been gone for as long as it seems to us. Just two days!

"Loved ones," Peter said, in essence, "don't forget this one thing. This is important—this is significant. Remember that God doesn't work on our timetable. His plans are based on His perspective and His perception, not ours."

THE LORD'S PATIENCE

The second reason for the Lord's delay in returning to this earth is found in verse 9: "The Lord is not slack concerning His promise, as some count slackness, but is longsuffering toward us" (2 Pet. 3:9).

Some of the false teachers in the early church were claiming God is slow to carry out His promise—that He is unconcerned, that He doesn't care. But Peter said it's better to take God's delay in the other direction. This delay in the coming of Christ is not because of lack of concern but is actually a sign of how much He cares for and loves people. He's waiting because He's patient. He wants people to come to Him before it is too late.

In the book of Joel, we read, "Rend your heart, and not your garments; return to the LORD your God, for He is gracious and merciful, slow to anger, and of great kindness; and He relents from doing harm" (2:13).

Paul asked, "Do you despise the riches of His goodness, forbearance, and longsuffering, not knowing that the goodness of God leads you to repentance?" (Rom. 2:4).

John Piper wrote, "Since our God is immortal, does not age, does not forget, sees all history at a glance and is never bored, He clearly does not experience time like we do. . . . Don't fail to recognize this. It is no argument against Christ's second coming that almost 2,000 years have passed since His departure. From God's experience of time it is as though Christ just arrived at His right hand the day before yesterday."[3]

Another author said it like this: "Instead of casting doubt on his promise, God's seeming delay actually highlights his heart! His waiting isn't due to his impotence but to his mercy."[4]

The importance of this should not be lost on us. If Jesus had come in the year 500, or in the year 1500, or if He had come in, say, 1875, none of us would have yet been born. You would not have been able to enjoy your daily walk with Jesus Christ. You would not have been able to relish the promises in the Word of God. You would not have been able to look forward to eternal life. Had Jesus come in an earlier era none of us would have been around, none of us would have been caught up in the Rapture, and none of us would have been resurrected.

But because of God's patience, the epochs of time have been extended to include even us within His redemptive and glorious grace.

Thank You, Jesus, for Your patience!

THE LORD'S PREFERENCE

Finally, we come to God's desire regarding the timing of the Rapture. Jesus has delayed His coming because He is "not willing that any should perish but that all should come to repentance" (2 Pet. 3:9). That's God's preference.

In the book of Ezekiel, the Lord said, "Do I have any pleasure at all that the wicked should die . . . and not that he should turn from his ways and live?" (18:23).

God longs for people to come to repentance. He wants to give people every opportunity to change their minds and return to Him and to His ways. "True Christian repentance involves a heartfelt conviction of sin, a contrition over the offense to God, a turning away from the sinful way of life, and a turning towards a God-honoring way of life."[5]

Remember the story of the Prodigal Son. Even though the prodigal had wounded and abandoned his dad with disdain and disrespect, the father waited patiently for his wayward son to come back to him, loving him the whole time he was waiting, looking for him from the front porch, longing for him to come home.

That is God's preference for all people today—that we would end our rebellion and come back to Him.

Speaking of coming back, have you heard of the wonderful

partnership between Greyhound bus lines and the National Runaway Safeline—an organization that serves and supports youths who have run away from home? Because of this partnership, any child between the ages of twelve and twenty-one who has run away from their parents or guardians can receive a free ticket home.

Better still, the organizations provide more than transportation. They partner with the parents and the youth to create a plan for returning home safely—and for working through the issues that led the child to run away in the first place. The family is connected with people and resources in their community that provide long-term support.[6]

It's not possible for any person to physically run away from God. Our heavenly Father is present in every place and knows everything that can be known. But it is possible to turn away from God's goodness and love. To rebel against His authority. Even to reject Him and remove ourselves from the protection of His lovingkindness.

If that's the case for you, why not return today? There's no ticket necessary. No distance to travel or red tape to cut through. Just turn back.

God is always waiting to welcome you with open arms.

CHAPTER 23

DELIVERED BEFORE DESTRUCTION

The American embassy in Sudan is located in a well-fortified area just a stone's throw from the Blue Nile River on the western side of Khartoum. It's a relatively new complex of buildings, but it sits in a rough and violent city.

As I was writing this chapter, a team of special operations forces completed the difficult mission of evacuating the embassy. Chaos was descending on the city, and it was time to airlift the American diplomats to safety.

There were about one hundred people at the embassy, and it took less than an hour to get everyone out. The Navy's SEAL Team Six took part in the mission, which was cloaked in secrecy and executed in darkness. The evacuation was "fast and clean," using two MH-47 Chinook helicopters.

American officials said the deteriorating situation required the emergency evacuation because a storm of violence was heading toward the embassy gates.[1]

All of us who know Christ are His ambassadors, His representatives in a deteriorating world. Just before the storm of the Tribulation's violence hits the gates of the church, our great Commander is literally going to airlift us to safety, rescuing us before the storm.

We've talked about that rescue often in these pages—it's the Rapture. What you may be surprised to learn is that God has followed that pattern many times in history. Proverbs 11:8 says, "The righteous is delivered from trouble, and it comes to the wicked instead."

Psalm 144 says, "Part Your heavens, LORD, and come down. . . . Reach down your hand from on high; deliver me and rescue me" (vv. 5–7 NIV). While that's not a specific picture of the Rapture, I can visualize the Lord's hand reaching down to snatch us up in deliverance just in the nick of time.

The apostle Paul referred to this aspect of Christ's character when he urged us to "wait for His Son from heaven, whom He raised from the dead, even Jesus who delivers us from the wrath to come" (1 Thess. 1:10).

Here's how this worked out for two families in the Old Testament and what it all means for believers today. By studying the ways God acted to rescue His people in the past, we can learn much that will add to our understanding about God's future rescue of His people at the Rapture.

THE RESCUE OF NOAH

When speaking about His return in Luke 17, Jesus used two illustrations from the Old Testament—Noah and Lot. He said, "Just as it was in the days of Noah, so also will it be in the days of the Son of Man. . . . It was the same in the days of Lot. People were eating and drinking, buying and selling, planting and building. But the day Lot left Sodom, fire and sulfur rained down from heaven and destroyed them all. It will be just like this on the day the Son of Man is revealed" (vv. 26–30 NIV).

There's an interesting fact about the flood of Noah's day that's often overlooked. In the genealogies of Genesis 5, we see that Enoch was the father of Methuselah, who was the father of Lamech, who was the father of Noah (Gen. 5:21–28). Methuselah lived longer than anyone else in history—969 years. His father (who was Noah's great-grandfather), Enoch, was a preacher of righteousness. As we saw earlier in this book, he preached about the return of Christ and was raptured before the flood (Jude v. 14).

Bodie Hodge, an engineer and a student of Genesis, noticed something interesting about those two men: "If you match up the ages of the patriarchs, Methuselah died the same year as the Flood. . . . Methuselah was raised by a godly parent (Enoch) who walked with God and pleased God so that God took him away without death. In fact, Methuselah may have actually helped Noah in the construction phase of the Ark. But his death preceded the Flood."[2]

Pause a minute to let that soak in.

Enoch was raptured before the flood; Methuselah died just days before the flood. God delivered them both from the coming wrath, and together they represent those who will be raptured and resurrected when Jesus comes in the sky for His people.

And don't forget about Noah and his family. God also took them above the waters of the flood and rescued them from the storm of judgment that fell on the earth.

THE RESCUE OF LOT

Our Lord's other example was the family of Lot. In Genesis 19, two angels were sent by God to evacuate Lot and his family from the wicked city of Sodom before literal fires of judgment fell on that place. At dawn on that fateful day, the angels awoke Lot and his family and said,

"Hurry! Take your wife and your two daughters." The angels physically grabbed the hands of Lot's wife and daughters, dragging them from danger, "for the LORD was merciful to them" (vv. 15–16 NIV).

As soon as this little family was rescued from Sodom, the God of righteousness sent down bolts of fire that consumed the city in judgment.

Dr. W. A. Criswell, who was a constant student of biblical prophecy, said in a sermon on this subject, "Both of those men, Enoch and Lot, are very typical of God's people in this earth now. Enoch—glorious man who walked with God and was not, for God took him—Enoch was raptured, he was taken out before the judgment of the Flood came. . . . Lot was taken out also before the great judgment day of God came. . . . All of God's people . . . will be taken out before that awful day comes."[3]

Of course, these weren't isolated incidents. God's rescue of Noah and Lot is in keeping with the way He has worked throughout history. He spared the Hebrews in Egypt from the plagues of wrath that fell over Pharaoh's empire. The final plague—the death of the firstborn—came nowhere near the Jewish people who painted their doorposts with the blood of the Passover lamb. God made for them a way of escape.

Our same God brought the Israelite spies out of Jericho before judgment fell on that city. He brought Daniel out of the lions' den before the mouths of the lions were opened and devoured their prey. Jesus made sure His disciples were out of the garden of Gethsemane, terrified but safe, as He Himself was led away toward the cross.

We worship a Savior who saves!

THE RESCUE OF THE GODLY

Just as the family of Noah and the family of Lot were evacuated before the onslaught of judgment, so it will be with the family of the Lord.

Mirroring the words of Jesus, Peter also talked about this in detail when he wrote:

> If [God] did not spare the ancient world when he brought the flood on its ungodly people, but protected Noah, a preacher of righteousness, and seven others; if he condemned the cities of Sodom and Gomorrah by burning them to ashes, and made them an example of what is going to happen to the ungodly; and if he rescued Lot, a righteous man, who was distressed by the depraved conduct of the lawless . . . then the Lord knows how to rescue the godly from trials and to hold the unrighteous for punishment on the day of judgment. (2 Pet. 2:5–9 NIV)

The Lord knows how to rescue us from judgment. Of course He does! As Paul wrote to Timothy, his son in the faith, "For to this end we both labor and suffer reproach, because we trust in the living God, who is the Savior of all men, especially of those who believe" (1 Tim. 4:10).

That's why Paul, having described the Rapture, told the Thessalonians to "comfort one another with these words" (1 Thess. 4:18). We are under the power and protection of Jesus, our Savior.

I believe this is all a part of God's grace to us. He promised, "No temptation has overtaken you except such as is common to man; but God is faithful, who will not allow you to be tempted beyond what you are able, but with the temptation will also make a way of escape" (1 Cor. 10:13).

Our Lord has designed a way of escape, a rescue, an evacuation for His people at the end of the age of the gospel of grace. We call it the Rapture.

In this way, the Rapture is an extension of God's character. It reveals who He is and what He values. As the psalmist wrote, "He also brought me out into a broad place; He delivered me because He delighted in me" (Ps. 18:19).

The Lord delights in His church, in His family. He delights in you. Yes, we suffer trouble and tribulation in this world, but God always makes a way of escape for us because He delights in us. His deliverance isn't just reserved for the Rapture. He wants to deliver you right now from your anxiety about the future and from the worries that are crippling your life.

This theme circulates through Psalm 34 like a springtime fragrance: "I sought the LORD, and He heard me, and *delivered* me from all my fears. . . . The angel of the LORD encamps all around those who fear Him, and *delivers* them. . . . The righteous cry out, and the LORD hears, and *delivers* them out of all their troubles. . . . Many are the afflictions of the righteous, but the LORD *delivers* him out of them all" (vv. 4, 7, 17, 19).

The same One—the Lord Jesus Christ—who delivers us over and over from the perils of life will deliver His church at the end of the age, evacuating us and airlifting us to safety before the onslaught of Tribulation justice.

In her book *Beyond the Storm*, Debra B. Morton describes what happened to her family during Hurricane Katrina. She said her seventy-year-old dad and stepmom had been evacuated before the storm but went back home afterward, thinking all was now safe. When the nearby levee gave way, the water began rising in the house. "My father and stepmom (who was on dialysis), along with my sister, her husband, and their children, had to escape to the over one-hundred-degree attic for three days to avoid drowning. . . . There was nowhere to go."

How could they let anyone know they were trapped in the attic? The frightened little family could hear the chopping sound of helicopters above them, but they had no way of contacting their would-be rescuers.

According to Debra, one of the family members finally managed to open a small hole in the roof, just big enough to push a broken compact mirror through. "My father told me he felt it in his heart when on that third day the rescuers saw that little mirror reflection." He was right. They did, and the family was rescued on the third day.

"There was something about that third day," Debra said, "just like the resurrection story."[4]

Now, our Lord will not need for us to knock a hole in the roof and flash a mirror at Him. He knows where we are, every one of us at every moment. He rose on the third day to deliver us into His eternal kingdom, and He's coming to rescue us before the levee breaks and the flood of judgment washes over the earth.

We feel in our hearts that day is near!

CHAPTER 24

KEPT FROM
THE HOUR

As an actor and professional wrestler, John Cena knows how to entertain a crowd. He also knows how to keep a promise.

For more than twenty years, he has been an ambassador for the Make-A-Wish Foundation—an organization that serves children suffering from life-threatening diseases by connecting them with celebrities and once-in-a-lifetime experiences. These experiences can include meeting a hero, visiting a movie set, serving as an honorary fireman for a day, and so on.

According to the Make-A-Wish Foundation, John Cena has helped fulfill an incredible 650 wishes over a twenty-year period. No other celebrity has participated in more than 200 wishes. And Cena is still going—still volunteering. Whenever he hears of an opportunity to bless the life of an ill child, he takes it.

Speaking about his appreciation for the foundation, Cena said, "If you ever need me for this ever, I don't care what I'm doing, I will drop what I'm doing and be involved because I think that's the coolest thing. I just drop everything."[1]

The Rapture is a biblical promise stating that one day Jesus will drop everything, bring His people to Himself, and make our deepest dreams come true by welcoming us to His Father's house for all eternity.

It is my firm belief that this promise will be fulfilled before the onset of the terrible period we call the Tribulation, which makes me a pre-tribulationist. Yet I'd be remiss if I didn't acknowledge that not all Bible scholars agree with me about the timing of the Rapture or its place within God's eschatological calendar. The vast majority of biblical teachers believe in the Rapture itself, but there's honest disagreement about *when* this great event will occur.

Some students believe the Rapture will take place at the end of the Tribulation, almost simultaneous to the Second Coming of Christ. Those who hold this view are referred to as post-tribulationists. Others teach the Rapture will happen in the middle of the Tribulation, just before the Great Tribulation begins. They are mid-tribulationists. Also, a relatively new view suggests the Rapture will occur after the midpoint of the Tribulation but before God's seven bowls of wrath have been poured out on the earth. This is the pre-wrath view.

It's important to acknowledge the differences in these lines of thought, even though I do believe the preponderance of scriptural evidence makes it clear the Rapture of the church will take place *before* the Tribulation occurs, sparing us from the awful seven-year period described in Revelation 6–18.

In this chapter, we're going to closely examine one verse of Scripture that indicates a before-the-Tribulation Rapture. It's one of the most important verses in the entire New Testament on this subject and worthy of investigation.

Early in the book of Revelation, the Lord Jesus promised the church at Philadelphia:

"Because you have kept My command to persevere, I also will keep you from the hour of trial which shall come upon the whole world, to test those who dwell on the earth." (3:10)

Andrew M. Woods wrote, "Commentators of all stripes readily acknowledge that this verse represents the most significant verse in the debate over the timing of the rapture."[2]

Let's discover why.

THE SCOPE OF THIS PROMISE

First, let's add some context to Revelation 3:10. That verse expresses Christ's message to one of the seven churches to whom the book of Revelation is addressed—the church in the ancient city of Philadelphia. Its significance, however, isn't limited to that congregation. This wasn't just a promise having to do with regional persecution. Jesus wasn't telling the church in Philadelphia, "I'm going to keep you from persecution that's going to come into your vicinity."

Instead, He said, "I . . . will keep you from the hour of trial which shall come upon the whole world."

Jesus' promise is intended for all churches, everywhere, throughout all history. That's the scope of Revelation 3:10, and really all of Revelation. The messages to the seven churches are applicable to all the churches in the world. This is why we keep reading in Revelation 2 and 3: "He who has an ear, let him hear what the Spirit says to the churches" (2:7, 11, 17, 29; 3:6, 13, 22).

"Thus, the promise of being kept from the hour of testing is not limited to the church at Philadelphia," wrote Michael A. Rydelnik, "but was a promise for the universal church as well."[3]

There's an hour of trial ahead, not just for Asia Minor but for the globe. It will engulf the entire planet and all those "who dwell on the earth." John later declared that the trials of the Tribulation

Period will affect "all nations" (Rev. 12:5) and, again, "the whole world" (16:14).

According to Charles Ryrie, who was one of my professors at Dallas Theological Seminary:

> That this promise concerns the church's relation to the tribulation period is almost never debated. The reason is in the verse itself. This time of trial "is about to come on all the inhabited earth." It is worldwide, and on this inhabited earth; that is, on its people. It had not happened up to that time, for it was still in the future—"about to come." It is not a promise restricted to the church at Philadelphia in the first century any more than favorite promises like Philippians 4:13 or 4:19 or 1 Corinthians 10:13 were limited to the churches in the first century. Also, the risen Lord said in all seven letters in Revelation 2 and 3 that all the churches should heed what He said.[4]

THE SECURITY OF THIS PROMISE

Jesus' promise in Revelation 3:10 provides great security for His followers. Why? Because He isn't going to keep us *through* the Tribulation but *from* the Tribulation.

Some scholars teach that the church will go through the flames of persecution just as Shadrach, Meshach, and Abednego endured the flames of the fiery furnace. Those scholars believe Christ will be with us and keep us safe in the midst of it—that He will be present with us as we endure tribulation.

But that's not what the promise says. Jesus said: "I also will keep you from the hour of trial which shall come upon the whole world, to test those who dwell on the earth" (3:10).

Not *during* the trial or *in* the trial or *through* the trial but *from* the trial. This requires a removal before the trial ever occurs. Dr. Ryrie gave a vivid illustration of this distinction from a teacher's viewpoint:

As a teacher, I frequently give exams. Let's suppose that I announce an exam will occur on such and such a day at the regular class time. Then suppose I say, "I want to make a promise to students whose grade average for the semester so far is A. The promise is: I will keep you from the exam."

Now I could keep my promise to those A students this way: I would tell them to come to the exam, pass out the exam to everyone, and give the A students a sheet containing the answers. They would take the exam and yet in reality be kept from the exam. They would live through the time but not suffer the trial. This is post-tribulationism: protection while enduring.

But if I said to the class, "I am giving an exam next week. I want to make a promise to all the A students. I will keep you from the hour of the exam." They would understand clearly that to be kept from the hour of the test exempts them from being present during that hour. This is pre-tribulationism, and this is the meaning of the promise of Revelation 3:10. And the promise came from the risen Savior who Himself is the deliverer of the wrath to come (1 Thessalonians 1:10).[5]

If Revelation 3:10 only means the church will be kept safe during the Tribulation, then we have a problem as we read the rest of Revelation. During the Tribulation, especially during the first half of it, multitudes of people will flee to Christ and be saved. But they will not be safe! The ruthless government of the Antichrist will search them out and slaughter them in terrible ways (6:9–11; 11:7; 12:11; 13:7, 15; 14:13; 17:6; 18:24).

One commentator said, "If these are saints and tribulation saints, they are *not* being kept safe and Revelation 3:10 is meaningless."[6]

On the other hand, if believers will be raptured before the Tribulation, then what security we find in Revelation 3:10! Jesus' promise helps us sleep better and live with greater confidence. It enables us to anticipate our Lord's coming for us at any moment now.

THE SIMPLICITY OF THIS PROMISE

Surprisingly, this insight from Revelation 3:10 is centered on one simple little word. In the Greek language, it has just two letters: *ek*, which are translated "from" in Revelation 3:10.

This preposition is found over eight hundred times in the New Testament, and it's translated "out of" or "from" (or an equivalent phrase) in virtually every instance. Here is some context:

> *Ek* is rendered *out of* hundreds of times, as for example: "*Out of* Egypt have I called My Son" (Matthew 2:15); "first *cast out* the beam *out of* thine own eye" (Matthew 7:5); "for *out of* the heart proceed evil thoughts" (Matthew 15:19); "and [many bodies of the saints] came *out of* the graves after His resurrection" (Matthew 27:53); "I will spew thee *out of* My mouth" (Revelation 3:16).[7]
>
> The promise is clear and plain: "I . . . will keep you *from* the hour of testing." Not just from any persecution, but from the coming time that will affect the whole earth. (The only way to escape the time when events take place is not to be in a place where time ticks on. The only place that meets those qualifications is heaven).[8]

Sometimes we make studying Scripture way more complicated than it needs to be. God's promise is simple: He will keep us "from" (*ek*) the hour of trial that comes upon the whole world.

THE SIGNIFICANCE OF THIS PROMISE

With all that said, however, there is a significant truth we must accept: just because Christians will be spared from the torment described in Revelation 3:10, we are not exempt from trials and suffering beforehand. Actually, the Bible promises the exact opposite.

Jesus said, "If the world hates you, you know that it hated Me before it hated you" (John 15:18). He added, "In the world you will have tribulation; but be of good cheer, I have overcome the world" (16:33).

The apostle Paul wrote, "Yes, and all who desire to live godly in Christ Jesus will suffer persecution" (2 Tim. 3:12).

James told us, "My brethren, count it all joy when you fall into various trials" (1:2). And Peter said, "Beloved, do not think it strange concerning the fiery trial which is to try you, as though some strange thing happened to you" (1 Pet. 4:12).

Jesus' promise to rapture Christians before the Tribulation is a specific declaration that applies to a specific moment. We will be spared from the reign of the Antichrist. But in the meantime, we will still endure the persecution all of God's saints have endured throughout history.

In his book *Kept from the Hour*, Dr. Gerald B. Stanton helps us understand why Christians suffer now but won't suffer then: "Today, suffering is often the portion of the Christian, but not wrath. Wrath is reserved for unbelievers."[9]

The Tribulation represents the outpouring of God's wrath on the evil of this world. The Bible says, "God did not appoint us to wrath, but to obtain salvation through our Lord Jesus Christ" (1 Thess. 5:9).

Paul wrote, "Much more then, having now been justified by His blood, we shall be saved from wrath through Him" (Rom. 5:9).

As I studied this subject, I underlined these words from Dr. John F. Walvoord: "Paul is expressly saying that our appointment is to be caught up to be with Christ; the appointment of the world is for the Day of the Lord, the day of wrath. One cannot keep both of these appointments."[10]

Isn't that well put? The unsaved will keep the appointment with the day of wrath—the Tribulation. The saved will keep the appointment with Christ when we are drawn from the earth in the pre-tribulation Rapture.

Have you heard of "the Great Raid"? It took place near the end of World War II in 1945. After General Douglas MacArthur and US forces landed in the Philippines, orders went out from the Japanese military to kill any prisoners of war on the verge of being rescued. Many US soldiers were shot and burned alive within weeks or even days of potential freedom.

A camp called Cabanatuan was one of the largest facilities for prisoners of war—and one of the most notorious. Knowing that the Japanese were likely to kill the POWs if US forces got too close, MacArthur decided to send a secret rescue operation to liberate those prisoners before allowing his armies to advance.

The raid took place on January 30. More than a hundred Army Rangers and Filipino scouts trekked thirty-five miles behind enemy lines until they located the camp, overwhelmed the guards, and set the prisoners free. Most of those prisoners were too weak to walk, so more than a hundred wooden carts were used to wheel them quickly toward freedom.

In the end, 513 POWs were rescued on that day from certain death. The rescuing force suffered only two casualties, making the Great Raid one of the most successful rescue missions ever conducted.[11]

The Rapture will likewise be a rescue mission. The just judgment of God's wrath is on the way. It will crash against the sinfulness and unrighteousness of our world like waves smashing through sand.

Yet those who call on the name of the Lord shall be saved—not in the midst of those waves but from them. We shall be kept safe from the hour of God's wrath.

CHAPTER 25

DEAD SILENCE

Sherlock Holmes is history's favorite detective. As we all know, he solves his cases by noticing what others miss.

Remember the story of the dog that didn't bark? It started when a famous racehorse named Silver Blaze disappeared the night before the race. Then came the murder of the horse's trainer. Holmes investigated, and when a Scotland Yard inspector asked him what had caught his attention, he answered, "The curious incident of the dog in the nighttime."

"The dog did nothing in the nighttime," said the inspector.

"That was the curious incident," replied Sherlock.

Because the watchdog didn't bark, Holmes deduced the culprit was not a stranger to the dog but someone the dog recognized. He called this a "negative fact," and he later said he solved the case when he "grasped the significance of the silence of the dog."[1]

There are many times when silence is a powerful witness to the facts, and that's true when it comes to the Rapture of the church and the events of the Tribulation as we find them in the book of Revelation. So far in these pages, we've already established our conviction that the

Rapture occurs before the Tribulation. The "curious incident" of dead silence regarding the church in the core chapters of Revelation comes alongside that conclusion and helps corroborate it.

DEAD SILENCE ABOUT THE PRESENCE OF THE CHURCH

Many of us who study the book of Revelation have found it to be one of the best-organized books in the Bible. One particular verse in the first chapter gives us an outline of the entire book. The first half of the first chapter is the prologue, and the last part of Revelation 1 is John's initial vision of the glorified Jesus, who told him in verse 19: "Write the things which you have seen, and the things which are, and the things which will take place after this."

This is God's own framework to the book of Revelation.

The things you have seen. That's the first chapter and John's incredible opening vision of Jesus. John was on the island of Patmos in exile. He heard the blast of a trumpet and turned to see the glorious figure of the enthroned Christ, whom he described in magnificent detail. Christ spoke and explained the meaning of the symbols surrounding Him. The Lord told John to write down this opening vision he had seen.

The things which are. This refers to the next two chapters, Revelation 2–3, which contain seven short messages to the seven churches of Asia Minor. John oversaw these churches as an elder in exile. Each message describes the spiritual health of a given church, accompanied by commendations, reprimands, warnings, and rebukes. These messages are applicable throughout the entire age of the church, and they are important for us today.

The things which will take place after this. This refers to the core chapters of Revelation, which begin with Revelation 4 and continue through the end of the book. These chapters detail the events that will take place in the future. Almost everything in Revelation 4–18 has to do with the seven-year Tribulation, describing in great detail the pouring out of God's wrath upon the earth. Chapter 19 is devoted to the Second Coming of Christ at the end of the Tribulation.

Do you know what is conspicuously absent from these Tribulation chapters? *The church.* The word *church* appears nineteen times in Revelation 1–3, but not once in Revelation 4–18.

Why the silence? Because the church will no longer be on the earth. Believers will be removed before the Tribulation Period and taken to heaven by means of the Rapture. You cannot find the church anywhere from Revelation 4 to Revelation 18, the chapters that describe the seven years of Tribulation coming upon the earth.

I want you to see how the account of the Tribulation begins unfolding in Revelation 4. Verse 1 says: "After these things I looked, and behold, a door standing open in heaven. And the first voice which I heard was like a trumpet speaking with me, saying, 'Come up here, and I will show you things which must take place after this.'"

We shouldn't base our convictions about the Rapture of the church on a single verse, but since we have studied the primary Rapture passages already in this book, it's hard not to see some similarities. We have what Sherlock Holmes would call a meaningful clue. Actually, several meaningful clues.

To start, we see John confronted by heaven through the means of an open door. There is even the possibility that John was drawn up to heaven—that he experienced a precursor to the Rapture in the same way as Enoch and Elijah and Paul.

When did that happen? After "these things," which refers to the message John received for the churches in chapters 2 and 3.

Next, not only did John see an open door; he also heard a voice like a trumpet. Where have we heard that before? The great Rapture passages in 1 Thessalonians and 1 Corinthians both refer to the blast of a trumpet. In addition, John heard the command, "Come up here," which must surely be similar if not identical to the shout Jesus will give when He comes for us at the Rapture.

In short, the clues offered to us in the first verse of Revelation 4 point strongly to the conclusion that John's experiences were a preview of the Rapture. John Strombeck affirmed that idea without pressing the point out of proportion when he wrote, "No event recorded in Revelation can better represent the Rapture of the church" than John's being caught up to heaven in Revelation 4:1.[2]

While we're at it, here's another amazing coincidence: one phrase is repeated seven times in Revelation 2 and 3 at the conclusion of each of Christ's messages to His seven churches. That phrase is a convicting command: "He who has an ear, let him hear what the Spirit says to the churches" (2:7, 11, 17, 29; 3:6, 13, 22).

No similar phrase occurs again in Revelation until we come to chapter 13, the midpoint in the Tribulation when the Antichrist rises in all his demonic power to terrorize the world. At that point, we read in Revelation 13:9: "If anyone has an ear, let him hear."

What's missing? The writer no longer said, "What the Spirit says to the churches."

Why? Because the church is no longer around.[3]

Dr. Richard Mayhue wrote, "It is remarkable and totally unexpected that John would shift from detailed instructions for the church to absolute silence about the church . . . if, in fact, the church continued into the tribulation. If the church will experience the tribulation . . . then surely the most detailed study of tribulation events would include an account of the church's role. But it doesn't!"[4]

To summarize, the church is on earth in Revelation 1–3, then there is no record of anything being done by the church in chapters 4–18. Evangelism is carried out by 144,000 Jewish evangelists. The action centers around the nation of Israel. The Spirit says nothing to the church during these terrible years, for the church is in heaven. Only when we get to the account of the Second Coming of Christ in chapter 19 do we see Him coming with His people—the "armies in heaven" (Rev. 19:14).

Sherlock, are you putting together the clues?

DEAD SILENCE ABOUT THE PREPARATION OF THE CHURCH

Here's something else to think about: the New Testament is full of instructions for the church. In fact, from the first chapter of Romans until the fourth chapter of Revelation, the primary emphasis of the New Testament writers involves how we, as Christians on earth, should conduct ourselves. We're told about our morality, our theology, our faith, our behavior, our mission. We're even told how to react to the tribulations of life that we must endure. But those instructions suddenly stop when we come to Revelation 4.

There are no specific instructions given to the church in Revelation 4–18.

What's more, there's not a single passage in the New Testament that says something like, "During the Great Tribulation, here is what you should do. Here is how you should behave." If it were our lot to endure the wrath that will devastate the earth during those seven years, isn't it odd God never gave us one tidbit of information, encouragement, warning, or instruction on our preparation for it? The apostolic writers are strangely muted in giving any counsel to the church regarding our behavior during the Tribulation.

The reason for that omission is clear. The church will not be present at all when the Tribulation takes place.

John MacArthur agrees: "It would be inconsistent for the Scriptures to be silent on such a traumatic change for the church. If any time of the Rapture other than the pretribulational were true, one would expect the Epistles to teach the fact of the church in the tribulation, the purpose of the church in the tribulation, the conduct of the church in the tribulation. However there is no teaching like this whatsoever. Only a pretribulational Rapture satisfactorily explains such obvious silence."[5]

DEAD SILENCE ABOUT THE
PURPOSE OF THE CHURCH

Likewise, there is no account of the church's purpose during the Tribulation because the church has no purpose in the Tribulation. The Tribulation Period marks the final application of God's wrath upon Israel's transgressions, as we read in Ezekiel 20:37–38. God's wrath is reserved for apostate Israel—for those He nurtured and cherished and yet who departed from Him. The Tribulation Period is essentially a family matter between Israel and God.

It's also a time when God will bring judgment upon all the evil that's being perpetuated in and on the earth. According to Mark Hitchcock, "What is it about the Tribulation that necessitates our absence from this time? The Tribulation is the product of God's wrath upon wickedness. The book of Revelation clearly refers to God's wrath at least seven times (6:17–18; 14:8–10; 14:19; 15:7; 16:1, 19; 19:15)."[6]

The purpose of the Tribulation is to execute God's wrath on those who reject Him, and that helps us understand why He would want to get the church out of the way and to a place of safety—to a heavenly refuge where we'll be protected from that wrath. By simple logic, then, we can see why believers are to be spared the Tribulation. What would be the point of having to endure it? By turning to God for salvation, our rebellion has been forgiven and we have no need to be purged of it or punished for it.

In fact, the Bible clearly tells us that our salvation is a salvation *from* God's wrath. The apostle Paul wrote in his Rapture-rich book of 1 Thessalonians that we're to wait "for His Son from heaven, whom He raised from the dead, even Jesus who delivers us from the wrath to come. . . . For God did not appoint us to wrath, but to obtain salvation through our Lord Jesus Christ" (1:10; 5:9).

Romans 5:9 makes the same point: "Much more then, having now been justified by His blood, we shall be saved from wrath through Him."

Oh, our merciful Christ!

When God put Jesus on the cross, He exacted from Him the full penalty due for our sin. We have nothing left to pay. Accordingly, if we who have been cleansed by the blood of Jesus were to be put through the Tribulation—a time of punitive judgment from God—it would mean the price Christ paid on the cross was not enough; it would mean we still need the additional penalty of God's judicial wrath. The whole idea undermines the sufficiency of Christ's sacrifice for our sins.

Let me quote John Strombeck again: "One is forced to ask, how could the Lamb of God die and rise again to save the church from wrath and then allow her to pass through the wrath that He shall pour out upon those who reject Him? Such inconsistency might be possible in the thinking of men, but not in the acts of the Son of God."[7]

Dr. Tim LaHaye agreed:

> I simply cannot imagine the heavenly Bridegroom whispering to His chosen one: "Yes, My bride, My precious one, I love you so much that I gave My life for you. I want to nourish and cherish you. I want to take you home with Me and celebrate our marriage with joy and singing and feasting. I want to be with you forever. But before I bring you Home, I want you to experience seven years of the very fury of hell, and seven years of the terrible wrath of My Father. But try not to worry. I'll come back when it's all over."[8]

I mentioned earlier how silence can point to factual truth. Our legal system understands this. Most people are familiar with Miranda rights in the United States, and its famous phrase, "You have the right to remain silent." But there are times when a suspect's continued silence can be used as evidence in a court of law.

The legal concept is called "admission by silence," and it applies when a suspect has been approached or interviewed by law enforcement prior to being informed of their Miranda rights. In those cases, a suspect's refusal to deny wrongdoing can be construed as an admission of guilt.

For example, take the case of Richard Tom. He was convicted of gross vehicular manslaughter after slamming his car into the side of a woman's vehicle, killing one of her daughters and critically injuring another. During the hours Tom spent with officers prior to his arrest, he never asked about the wellbeing of the people he had struck. He never mentioned them. Prosecutors used his silence as evidence that he had behaved "without regard for the well-being of others."[9]

The silence of the church in Revelation 4–18 isn't evidence of wrongdoing, but of up-taking. It demonstrates the church will be snatched away from earth—and absent during the Tribulation Period.

We will be with Christ!

CHAPTER 26

RAPTURE AND RETURN

Did you know a mix-up in terms once cost the US government more than $150 million? In 1999, NASA launched a new Mars orbiter toward the Red Planet. After a journey of 286 days, the orbiter was poised to fire one final engine burst in order to establish a stable orbit around Mars. The engines did fire, but not correctly. The orbiter pushed too close to the planet and was slung by gravity back into space, where it became lost.

What happened? After an extensive review, NASA engineers determined that some of the orbiter's navigation commands were programmed by the manufacturer using standard American units—inches, feet, miles, and so on. That caused a problem because all of NASA's programs and instructions were based on the metric system.

Lorell Young, at the time president of the US Metric Association, summarized the issue succinctly: "In this day and age when the metric system is the measurement language of all sophisticated science, two measurement systems should not be used."[1]

Mix-ups in terminology can be harmful in any field, including our study of biblical prophecy and the End Times. Over the years I've noticed one particular misunderstanding that occurs regularly and often hinders the way people grasp God's prophetic plan: confusing the Rapture and the Second Coming. Many who read Scripture lump those two occurrences into the same moment—they think of Christians being caught up in the Rapture even as Christ descends from heaven to bring judgment on the earth. In reality, these are two separate terms that describe two distinct events.

As we'll see, there are many similarities between the Rapture and the Second Coming, and so the confusion is understandable. But in order to have a firm grasp of God's prophetic plan for the future, we need to notice the distinctions between these two events.

Rapture Passages	Second Coming Passages
John 14:1–3	Daniel 2:44–45; 7:9–14; 12:1–3
Romans 8:19	Zechariah 14:1–15
1 Corinthians 1:7–8; 15:51–53; 16:22	Matthew 13:41; 24:15–31; 26:64
Philippians 3:20–21	Mark 13:14–27; 14:62
Colossians 3:4	Luke 21:25–28
1 Thessalonians 1:10; 2:19; 4:13–18; 5:9, 23	Acts 1:9–11; 3:19–21
2 Thessalonians 2:1	1 Thessalonians 3:13
1 Timothy 6:14	2 Thessalonians 1:6–10; 2:8
2 Timothy 4:1	2 Peter 3:1–14
Titus 2:13	Jude 14–15
Hebrews 9:28	Revelation 1:7; 19:11–20:6; 22:7, 12, 20
James 5:7–9	
1 Peter 1:7, 13	
1 John 2:28–3:2	
Jude 21	
Revelation 2:25; 3:10	

Source: Thomas Ice, "Why the Rapture and the Second Coming Are Distinct Events," in *Pre-Trib Answers to Post-Trib Questions* (Aug.–Sept. 1994), 2.

Let's dig deeper by exploring four notable differences that will help us separate these two appearances of Christ.

DIFFERENT SETTINGS

First, the Rapture and the Second Coming will take place at different chronological times and in separate geographical places. They have different settings.

As we've seen throughout these pages, the Rapture is the first event in the prophetic content of the book of Revelation, and it is the next event on God's eschatological calendar. It is the opening salvo of the End Times. We don't know when the Rapture will occur—no person knows the day or the hour. Yet the signs of the times seem to indicate it will be coming soon.

On the other hand, we do know when the Second Coming will take place: seven years after the Rapture. Only then will Christ descend from His throne to inhabit our world once again in a physical way.

Here's another question that sometimes puzzles students of biblical prophecy: Since Christ will return to call up His saints in the Rapture and since the Rapture precedes the Second Coming, why is it called the Second Coming? Shouldn't it be the Third Coming?

The answer has to do with the physical locations of those two events. When Christ reenters our world at the Second Coming, He will begin that process in the atmosphere. As John wrote in Revelation:

> Look, he is coming with the clouds,
> and every eye will see him,
> even those who pierced him.
> And all the tribes of the earth will mourn over him.
> So it is to be. Amen. (1:7 csb)

Once He has alerted the world to His presence, Christ will continue His descent and alight on very specific geographical coordinates: the Mount of Olives. Remember the words of the angels after Jesus ascended into heaven: "They were looking intently up into the sky as he was going, when suddenly two men dressed in white stood beside them. 'Men of Galilee,' they said, 'why do you stand here looking into the sky? This same Jesus, who has been taken from you into heaven, will come back in the same way you have seen him go into heaven'" (Acts 1:10–11 NIV).

The prophet Zechariah was boldly specific in his promises about that future moment: "On that day his feet will stand on the Mount of Olives, east of Jerusalem, and the Mount of Olives will be split in two from east to west, forming a great valley, with half of the mountain moving north and half moving south" (14:4 NIV).

Christ's return at the Rapture will also begin in the atmosphere, but it will not progress to the ground. As we've already seen from 1 Thessalonians 4, the dead in Christ will rise first at that moment, and then "we who are still alive and are left will be caught up together with them in the clouds to meet the Lord in the air. And so we will be with the Lord forever" (v. 17 NIV).

DIFFERENT SIGNALS

As I've noted earlier in these pages, there will be no specific signs that signal the approach of the Rapture. Scripture is clear, and that moment will come "like a thief in the night" (1 Thess. 5:2 NIV).

Jesus told us: "Two men will be in the field: one will be taken and the other left. Two women will be grinding at the mill: one will be taken and the other left. Watch therefore, for you do not know what hour your Lord is coming" (Matt. 24:40–42).

The Second Coming is different. That event will be preceded by several signs that are well defined and impossible to miss.

Of course, the first concrete sign for the Second Coming will be the Rapture itself! Christ's return to gather His church—first those who have died, then those who are alive at that moment—will be the catalyst that initiates the Tribulation. For three and a half years, the Antichrist will consolidate power and draw the nations of the world together into a single system. A single government under the direct control of Satan.

Then, to borrow a common phrase, all hell will break loose. The final three and a half years of the Tribulation Period are often called the Great Tribulation. This will be a season of wars and rumors of wars, of pestilence and plague, of apostasy and persecution—all on a scale previously unimaginable in human history.

At the end of the Great Tribulation, the armies of the nations will assemble on the fields outside Megiddo in Israel. The purpose of those armies will be direct confrontation not only with Israel as a nation but with God Himself. The majority of humanity will align with Satan and the Antichrist in unmitigated rebellion against the living God.

And the living God will respond. The doors of heaven will be opened, and Christ will appear in full glory:

> I saw heaven standing open and there before me was a white horse, whose rider is called Faithful and True. With justice he judges and wages war. His eyes are like blazing fire, and on his head are many crowns. He has a name written on him that no one knows but he himself. He is dressed in a robe dipped in blood, and his name is the Word of God. The armies of heaven were following him, riding on white horses and dressed in fine linen, white and clean. Coming out of his mouth is a sharp sword with which to strike down the nations. "He will rule them with an iron scepter." He treads the winepress of the fury of the wrath of God Almighty. (Rev. 19:11–15 NIV)

DIFFERENT SCRIPTS

We have clear teaching from the Bible that Jesus does not change. He is "the same yesterday, today, and forever" (Heb. 13:8). Yet there does seem to be a sense in which Jesus operates in different roles when He interacts with our world at specific times. He emphasizes different elements of His character depending on the script or mission of the moment.

The Gospels primarily portray Jesus as the Lamb of God slain to cover the sins of the world. He is the Suffering Servant—the living personification of God's prophecies in Isaiah 53. Of course Jesus also operated as a Rabbi, teaching us in both word and deed what we need to know as His followers. But His main task was to rescue His people from their sin. He came as our Savior.

At the Second Coming, Jesus will operate from a much different role. He will return as the Conquering King. The Lion of Judah. Riding on His white horse and adorned with a robe dipped in blood, the One we know as Christ will reenter our world as the living personification of God's judgment and wrath against sin.

But there's a third role outlined for Jesus in the Scriptures: the Bridegroom of the church (Matt. 25:1–13). This is the script Jesus will primarily follow at the Rapture. In that brief moment, He will return, not as a sacrifice or as a conqueror but as the Lover of our souls.

DIFFERENT SPECTATORS

The Rapture and the Second Coming of Christ are two distinct events that will occur in different settings, be preceded by different signals, and follow different scripts. Here's another distinction: they will be observed by different spectators.

During the Rapture, only those who have accepted the salvation of Jesus Christ will be aware of His presence. He will appear only to His bride, the church. Of course, the rest of the world will see the *effects* of the Rapture—they will notice the huge number of people who literally disappeared in an instant—but they won't understand the cause.

In this way, Jesus will function as a "special ops" soldier at the Rapture. He will gather believers as part of a secret, quick-hitting rescue mission.

That will not be the case at the Second Coming. Rather than operating in stealth, Christ will return in splendor—and everyone will see. Remember Revelation 1:7, which promises:

> Look, he is coming with the clouds,
> and every eye will see him,
> even those who pierced him.
> And all the tribes of the earth will mourn over him.
> So it is to be. Amen. (CSB)

Similarly, the experience for Christians during the Rapture will be primarily passive. Believers both living and dead will be "caught up," but all the action will be taken by Christ.

We will be more involved at the Second Coming. When John foresaw Jesus bursting through the heavenly gates on His white horse, "the armies of heaven were following him, riding on white horses and dressed in fine linen, white and clean" (Rev. 19:14 NIV). That's us. You and me. We will actively join the armies of God in retaking this world for His kingdom.

The Rapture	The Return
The Lord will meet believers in the air.	The Lord will return to the Mount of Olives.
Only believers will see the Lord.	All humanity will see the Lord.
Raptured saints will be taken to heaven.	Raptured saints will return with the Lord to set up His kingdom on earth.
It could happen at any moment.	It will happen at the end of the Tribulation period.
There are no signs preceding it.	There are many signs preceding it.
It is not mentioned in the Old Testament.	It is predicted often in the Old Testament.
It will be a time of joy for believers.	It will be a time of mourning for unbelievers.
The Lord will come as a Bridegroom	The Lord will return as a King.
The Tribulation Period will follow it.	The Millennium will follow it.

One fascinating aspect of these truths is that there will be a generation of Jesus-followers who experience both the Rapture and the Second Coming within their lifetimes. These women and men will be alive at the moment of the Rapture, which means they will be caught up with Christ. Then, seven years later on earth, they will return with Christ as members of His heavenly host.

What a gift to experience such a double blessing!

And what a reminder that the Rapture and the Second Coming are both outworkings of the gospel. There has been a tendency throughout history to think of End Times events as bad news—as the end of something helpful that we wish would keep going.

This is not the case! The Rapture and the Second Coming are both important steps that must be taken to initiate the next phase of our lives: eternity. But it helps to come to terms with the terms, doesn't it?

He is coming again in no uncertain terms!

Vance Havner said, "When I studied arithmetic, I remembered that the answers were in the back of the book. No matter how I floundered among my problems, the correct solution was on the last page."[2]

Our world is floundering with many problems today, but the answers we need are on the Bible's last page: "'Surely I am coming quickly.' Amen. Even so, come, Lord Jesus!" (Rev. 22:20).

CHAPTER 27

SIGNS OF THE SECOND COMING

Drivers in the town of Greenville, South Carolina, received quite a shock as they approached the intersection of Wade Hampton Boulevard and Taylors Street on a sunny day in May. They found a large electronic road sign posted at that intersection, complete with traffic cones and construction barriers.

Everything looked official, but the sign's message was difficult to believe: "ZOMBIES AHEAD 2 MILES."

Turns out the sign had been hacked. Someone figured out the machine's password and secretly changed its message.[1]

Hacked road signs are an increasingly common nuisance along America's roadways, largely because more and more of those signs are equipped with modems; they can be accessed remotely. While sometimes humorous in the short term, this phenomenon is definitely dangerous in the long term. Why? Because signs play an important role in the modern driving experience. They tell us what's coming. They alert us to possible problems. And they help keep us safe.

The same is true for the "signs" identified throughout God's Word. Thankfully, those signs cannot be altered or adulterated!

THE BASICS OF BIBLICAL SIGNS

What is a biblical sign? The short answer is this: an event, symbol, place, or person whose existence or occurrence indicates something important in God's plan for the future. Importantly, these signs are identified in Scripture. They don't come from people's opinions or fortune-cookie interpretations. Rather, they are mortared into the very bedrock of God's Word.

There are any number of ways that signs can present themselves, but all express a particular meaning and point us to what is coming in the future. Jesus affirmed the existence of such signs, declaring there will be many of them: "And there will be signs in the sun, in the moon, and in the stars; and on the earth distress of nations, with perplexity, the sea and the waves roaring" (Luke 21:25).

Jesus referred to Himself as a sign: "Then the sign of the Son of Man will appear in heaven, and then all the tribes of earth will mourn, and they will see the Son of Man coming on the clouds of heaven with power and great glory" (Matt. 24:30).

Our Lord actually scolded the Pharisees and Sadducees because they were uninterested in the signs of the times:

> Then the Pharisees and Sadducees came, and testing Him asked that He would show them a sign from heaven. He answered and said to them, "When it is evening, you say, 'It will be fair weather, for the sky is red'; and in the morning, 'It will be foul weather today, for the sky is red and threatening.' Hypocrites! You know how to discern the face of the sky, but you cannot discern the signs of the times." (Matt. 16:1–3)

The gospels of Matthew, Mark, and Luke each contain a sermon, usually referred to as "the Olivet Discourse," in which Jesus presented a list of signs that describe the future of the world. Those signs illuminate the broad outline of the prophetic future. Indeed, this passage is so all-inclusive that many have called it the "mini-apocalypse." It is Jesus' overture to the book of Revelation.

Here is an excerpt from that discourse that is particularly important as we study the Rapture and other forthcoming events on God's eschatological calendar:

> Now as He sat on the Mount of Olives, the disciples came to Him privately, saying, "Tell us, when will these things be? And what will be the sign of Your coming, and of the end of the age?" And Jesus answered and said to them: "Take heed that no one deceives you. For many will come in My name, saying, 'I am the Christ,' and will deceive many. And you will hear of wars and rumors of wars. See that you are not troubled; for all these things must come to pass, but the end is not yet. For nation will rise against nation, and kingdom against kingdom. And there will be famines, pestilences, and earthquakes in various places. All these are the beginning of sorrows." (Matt. 24:3–8)

Here are six critical signs contained in Jesus' Olivet Discourse:

- Deception by false Christs (vv. 4–5)
- Disputes and warfare among nations (vv. 6–7)
- Disease and famine worldwide (vv. 7–8)
- Deliverance of believers to tribulation (v. 9)
- Defection of false believers (vv. 10–13)
- Declaration of the gospel to the whole world (v. 14)

These six signs cover the first three and one half years of the Tribulation and coincide with the book of Revelation. But while these signs will be fulfilled in the seven-year Tribulation Period, they will not start on a dime. They will build up over time.

I believe we are now seeing the prelude to these signs, which means understanding them to a greater degree will also increase our understanding of the Rapture.

THE BIRTH PAINS PRINCIPLE

Jesus employed a graphic picture in His Olivet Discourse—one that may have special significance to many women reading this book. He said, "All these are the beginning of sorrows." The Greek term translated as "sorrows" in Matthew 24:8 is the word *odin*, which literally means "birth pains"—the contractions that begin and increase during the birth of a baby.

Those contractions occur when the muscles of a woman's uterus tighten and release, which prepares her body to give birth. At first, the pains aren't intense at all. I'm told these initial stirrings are really more uncomfortable than painful. A woman may feel one such pain, then not feel another for twenty minutes or more. But as birth approaches, the pain gets a little more intense—and the pains get closer together. And when you reach a stage where the pain is very intense, and those pains are gripping you with regular frequency, you know you'd better get to the hospital, or you'll be giving birth in the back seat of the car.

Paul reminded the Thessalonians that the Rapture would come as a thief in the night—unexpectedly, quietly, and suddenly. Using the same figure Jesus used in the Olivet Discourse, but with a different sense, the apostle wrote: "But concerning the times and the seasons, brethren, you have no need that I should write to you. For you yourselves know perfectly that the day of the Lord so comes as a thief in the night. For when they say, 'Peace and safety!' then sudden destruction comes upon them, as labor pains upon a pregnant woman. And they shall not escape" (1 Thess. 5:1–3).

In 1 Thessalonians 5, Paul highlighted the sudden arrival of labor pains to describe the unexpected arrival of the Rapture. But Jesus used the metaphor in another way, highlighting the increasing intensity of labor pains to explain the unfolding of the Second Coming.

What Jesus wants us to know is this: the six signs that are going to happen in the future will not be all-of-a-sudden experiences. They will be like birth pains, with the frequency and intensity of each event gradually increasing. When we observe that pattern in the world, we've discovered the secret to understanding the signs of the times.

But here is where we must be very careful: the signs highlighted in Matthew 24 are not related to the Rapture, which is the return of Christ for His church. These are apocalyptic signs that point to the Second Coming of Christ. As we saw in chapter 26, this second advent will not be Christ coming *for* His saints in the Rapture; it will be Christ coming *with* His saints seven years after the Rapture to set up His kingdom on this earth.

There are no signs predicting the Rapture. Without any sign, without any warning, Jesus Christ will return to gather His saints and take them to heaven.

You might be wondering: If all these signs are not connected with the Rapture, and if I am going to be in heaven after the Rapture, why should I be concerned about the signs at all?

The broad answer to that question is that future events cast their shadows before them! The signs Jesus declared in Matthew 24—those that warn of His Second Coming—will begin to intensify prior to the Rapture. We will see a dramatic increase in deception, war, disease, persecution, apostasy, and the increased reach of the gospel. Those signs will give us a clue that the Rapture is near.

Perhaps this will help. Mark Hitchcock recalls this illustration from the prophetic teaching of the former president of Dallas Theological Seminary:

> Dr. John Walvoord used to share an apt illustration of how signs of the times relate to the Rapture and the Second Coming. He pointed out how there are all kinds of signs for Christmas. There are lights everywhere, decorations, Christmas trees, music, and even Santa in the mall. But Thanksgiving can sneak up on you. There are no real signs for Thanksgiving. Dr. Walvoord noted that the second coming of Christ is like Christmas. It will be preceded by many very specific signs that Scripture outlines. The Rapture, however, is like Thanksgiving. There are no specific signs for its coming. Yet, if it's fall and you already begin to see the signs of Christmas everywhere, and Thanksgiving has not arrived, then you know that Thanksgiving must be very near. The signs of "Christmas" seem to be appearing all around us today. The coming of Christ to rapture His church could be very near.[2]

This prophetic passage in Matthew 24 is described by many biblical scholars as the Bible's most important teaching on the future of our world. But if you read this discourse carefully, you will discover that it is not just for the world of tomorrow—it speaks to us where we are today.

As we study these verses in Matthew 24, three things should be apparent to us.

JESUS WANTS TO TEACH US ABOUT THE FUTURE

First, Jesus wants us to study the future. Jesus was in the habit of preparing His disciples for upcoming events even during His days upon this earth. As we've seen, He made a point of telling those around Him some of the things they could anticipate in the days ahead. So don't let anyone tell you that Jesus didn't bother about the future or that He was uninterested in prophecy. The facts say otherwise.

If the future was an important subject to Jesus, it should be important to us too! It should be something we are always studying and learning about. One theologian wrote, "Although we cannot know everything about the future, God knows everything about the future and he has in Scripture told us about the major events yet to come in the history of the universe. About these events occurring we can have absolute confidence because God is never wrong and never lies."[3]

Unless we have a firm grasp on what the Bible teaches about the future, His return, His glorious kingdom, and His eternal home, we cannot properly handle the strains of everyday life.

John Frame said, "So far as I can see, every Bible passage about the return of Christ is written for a practical purpose—not to help us to develop a theory of history, but to motivate our obedience."[4]

JESUS WANTS TO TRANSFORM US FOR THE FUTURE

Second, our Lord's prophetic ministry transforms us so we'll be able to meet the future. Jesus said, "These things I have spoken to you [about the future], that you should not be made to stumble" (John 16:1).

In other words, "If you grasp what I am telling you about the future, you won't fall all over yourself. You won't fall into the trap of running around in panic mode when you have no reason to be in panic mode."

In John 16:4 Jesus said this: "These things I have told you, that when the time comes, you may remember that I told you of them."

The days are coming when the hand of God will move across this globe in astounding ways. If we know the Word of God, we won't be taken by surprise. We won't find ourselves in a panic or gripped by sudden apprehensions.

Jesus said, in effect, "I've told you about these things so that when they happen, you won't be blown off course. You will have a sense of what God is up to."

If you are looking for a manual to the future that places no demands upon you today—a guidebook for days to come that has no bearing on days right now—you've come to the wrong place. I can't get excited about any book that inspires concern about future events but ignores what God wants us to do today. My study of prophecy convinces me that God intends knowledge of future events to help us "occupy today" with a sense of urgency until the Lord returns.

Paul Benware wrote, "A believer who gets out of bed in the morning thinking *My Lord Jesus could return today* will probably not let sin take root in his life. But Christians who rarely, if ever, reflect on the realities of the future life, the Lord's coming, and the judgment seat of Christ are far more vulnerable to temptation and sin. And perhaps that explains something of the sin and apathy seen in much of the church today."[5]

JESUS WANTS US TO TRUST HIM WITH THE FUTURE

Third, the signs of the End Times will help us trust our Savior—assuming we pay attention. If you have put your faith in Christ and have spent significant time in the Word of God, tough times can be like a magnet that draws you to the Lord. Nothing is going to happen, ever, that will catch Jesus Christ by surprise. He is able to help His children work through anything, and not a single thing is going to happen in the future that can change that fact.

Jesus' sufficiency is never more seen than in His communication to His disciples as He was preparing to leave them and return to heaven. He cared about these men, and His concern echoes in His words: "These things I have spoken to you, that in Me you may have peace. In the world you will have tribulation; but be of good cheer, I have overcome the world" (John 16:33).

These are familiar words to most of us, but I want you to look at them through a fresh pair of eyes. Notice Jesus' promise to the disciples was the promise of Himself. His peace was to be found in Him! "In Me you may have peace."

Jesus told His disciples that in the world they would have tribulation. What we often miss is what He *didn't* say.

Jesus did not say, "In the world you will have tribulation but I have overcome tribulation." No, Jesus said, "In the world you will have tribulation, but I have overcome the world." Jesus does not just overcome the event. He overcomes the environment in which the event occurs. Therefore, we can trust Him.

During the blitz in London in World War II, when German bombs were raining down on the city, the people there lived in constant fear. It's hard for us to imagine the kind of deep, pervasive anxiety—even terror—that results from continual bombardment.

During those dark days, one man's undaunted voice would regularly ring out from radios all over the nation, inspiring them to new hope and new belief. Their cause was just; their government was resolute; their armies would not fail them. The people listened and took heart.

What Winston Churchill did for the English during World War II, Jesus Christ does for us. He comes to us in the midst of the struggle, when the battle is almost unbearable and the circumstances look impossible. In the voice of absolute certainty, of power and strength beyond imagining, He speaks to us of peace and gives us the encouragement we need. He raises our morale and fills us with strength.

He says: "My peace I give to you; not as the world gives do I give to you. Let not your heart be troubled, neither let it be afraid" (John 14:27).

CHAPTER 28

THE SECOND COMING

Jenna Rose Alpern and her husband had just welcomed their first child into the world, which is an exciting time for any young couple. A time of transition and change. A time of growth. And in their case, time for a new apartment.

As residents of Jerusalem, Jenna and her husband were used to tight spaces. But with an infant on the scene, their current studio felt a little too tight. They needed something bigger.

After a quick online search, the young parents found a great apartment in a great location. The space had two bedrooms, high ceilings, and natural light filtering through windows from three sides of the building. It was everything they wanted, and they were eager to sign on the dotted line.

That's when Jenna's husband noticed the Messiah clause in their lease.

Yes, a Messiah clause. Near the bottom of the rental agreement, they read these words printed boldly in black and white: "Upon the coming of the Messiah, tenants agree to vacate the apartment within fifteen days."

You won't find that sentence on any legal documents in America, but such requirements are relatively common in Jerusalem. When Jewish homeowners rent their property in that city, they often include a clause that ensures they will be able to return and reign with the Messiah should He appear in their lifetime.

For Jenna Rose Alpern and her husband, who are themselves Jewish, the possibility of agreeing to such a term caused a few unexpectedly spiritual conversations. In her words: "[This] is what we are praying for, right? A basic tenet of Judaism being that we are eagerly awaiting and trying to bring Mashiach 'speedily, in our days.' Honestly, it's always been too huge a concept for me to wrap my head around, I'm embarrassed to admit."[1]

Mrs. Alpern is not alone in feeling the tension of conflicting priorities connected to the arrival of the Messiah. Nor are the Jewish people the only ones who find it difficult to wrap their minds around these concepts.

The major difference between Christian and Jewish thinking about the Messiah involves the number connected with His forthcoming appearance. Jews believe the next time the Messiah sets foot in Jerusalem will be the first time. Christians understand that *Mashiach*—the Hebrew term for Messiah—already knows the streets of that city. He walked them often. He died there, was buried there, and ascended into heaven from its highest hill after His resurrection.

We've studied the major signs that will precede the Second Coming. Now it's time to dig deeper into the incredible event that will occur seven years after the Rapture.

As Christians, we are quite familiar with our Lord's first coming to earth because we accept the record of the four gospels. The Bible clearly tells us He is coming to earth again. Though the exact expression "Second Coming of Christ" is not found in the Bible, Scripture makes the assertion in many places. For example, the writer of Hebrews said: "And as it is appointed for men to die once, but after this the judgment, so Christ was offered once to bear the sins of many. To those who eagerly wait for Him He will appear a second time, apart from sin, for salvation" (9:27–28).

One of the reasons some people are confused by the prophecies of Christ's Second Coming is the fact that the Old Testament prophets did not understand the first and second advents of Christ as separate events.

Their perception of these prophecies was like viewing a mountain range from a distance. They saw what appeared to be one mountain, failing to see that there was another equally high mountain behind it. The prophets saw both return of Christ either as one event or as very closely related in time.

One Bible scholar has written, "Words spoken in one breath, and written in one sentence, may contain prophetic events millennia apart in their fulfillment."[2]

It is evident that even Jesus' followers expected Him to fulfill the glorious promises relating to His Second Coming when He came the first time. Only after He ascended to heaven did they realize that they were living in the time between His two appearances, as if on a plain between two mountains.

Theologian John F. Walvoord explained:

From the present-day vantage point . . . since the first coming is history and the second coming is prophecy, it is comparatively easy to go back into the Old Testament and separate the doctrine of Jesus' two comings. In the first coming He came as a man, lived among people, performed miracles, ministered as a prophet as the Old Testament predicted, and died on the cross and rose again. All these events clearly relate to His first coming. On the other hand, the passages that speak of His coming to reign, judging the earth, rescuing the righteous from the wicked, and installing His kingdom on earth relate to His second coming. They are prophecy not history.[3]

The First Coming of Christ	The Second Coming of Christ
Jesus was born in obscurity.	Jesus will be seen by every eye.
Jesus was wrapped in swaddling clothes.	Jesus will be clothed royally in a robe dipped in blood.
Jesus was surrounded by cattle and common people.	Jesus will be accompanied by the massive armies of heaven.
The door of the inn was closed to Him.	The door of the heavens will be opened to Him.
Jesus' voice was the tiny cry of a baby.	Jesus' voice will thunder as the sound of many waters.
Jesus was the Lamb of God who came bringing salvation.	Jesus will be the Lion of the tribe of Judah who comes bringing judgment.

THE PRIORITY OF THE SECOND COMING

While it is true that Christians are most familiar with the first coming of Christ, it is the Second Coming of Christ that gets the most ink in the Bible. References to the Second Coming outnumber references to the first coming by a factor of eight to one. Scholars have identified 1,845 biblical references to the Second Coming, including 318 references in the New Testament. In the Old Testament, Christ's return is emphasized in no less than seventeen books, and New Testament authors speak of it in twenty-three of the twenty-seven books.

Incredibly, seven out of every ten chapters in the New Testament mention the Second Coming. And one out of every thirty verses in the New Testament teach us about the return of Christ to this earth.

In two of the first books written for the early church (1 and 2 Thess.), the return of Christ is taught in every single chapter. The Lord Himself referred to His return twenty-one times. The Second Coming is second only to salvation as the most dominant subject in the New Testament. The fact that Christ's Second Coming features so prominently in Scripture is an indication that this event is important to God—and that it should be important to us as well.

In the words of Dr. LaHaye: "If Jesus Christ does not return physically and literally to this earth to set up His kingdom, Christianity will turn out to be the greatest hoax in history. His return is so intimately tied to the most central doctrines of the Bible and the church that the validity of Christianity totally depends on it."[4]

THE PROPHECIES OF THE SECOND COMING

Here are seven key passages that predict the return of our Lord to this earth. These passages represent almost every section of the Bible, spanning the ages from Enoch in the book of Genesis to John the apostle in the book of Revelation.

ENOCH

According to Jude, Enoch was the first to predict the Second Coming of Christ: "Now Enoch, the seventh from Adam, prophesied about these men also, saying, 'Behold the Lord comes with ten thousands of His saints, to execute judgment on all, to convict all who are ungodly among them of all their ungodly deeds which they have committed in an ungodly way, and of all the harsh things which ungodly sinners have spoken against Him'" (vv. 14–15).

DANIEL

Daniel was known for his prophetic dreams, both about events in his lifetime and about things that would occur in the End Times. Here he described the return of the Son of Man (Christ): "I was watching in the night visions, and behold, One like the Son of Man, coming with the clouds of heaven! He came to the Ancient of Days, and they brought Him near before Him. Then to Him was given dominion and glory and a kingdom, that all peoples, nations, and languages should serve Him. His dominion is an everlasting dominion, which shall not pass away, and His Kingdom the one which shall not be destroyed" (Dan. 7:13–14).

ZECHARIAH

While many of the Old Testament prophets wrote about the Second Coming of Jesus Christ, it is Zechariah who has given us the clearest and most precise prediction of it: "Then the LORD will go forth and fight against those nations, as He fights in the day of battle. And in that day His feet will stand on the Mount of Olives, which faces Jerusalem on the east. And the Mount of Olives shall be split in two, from east to west, making a very large valley; half of the mountain shall move toward the north and half of it toward the south" (Zech. 14:3–4).

Notice how Zechariah dealt in specifics, even pinpointing the geographic location to which Christ will return: "In that day His feet will stand on the Mount of Olives" (14:4). The Mount of Olives is an explicitly identifiable place that retains its ancient name even today.

JESUS

While speaking from the Mount of Olives, Jesus affirmed His Second Coming to His disciples in dramatic and cataclysmic terms:

> "For as the lightning comes from the east and flashes to the west, so also will the coming of the Son of Man be.... Immediately after the tribulation of those days the sun will be darkened, and the moon will not give its light; the stars will fall from heaven, and the powers of the heavens will be shaken. Then the sign of the Son of Man will appear in heaven, and then all the tribes of the earth will mourn, and they will see the Son of Man coming on the clouds of heaven with power and great glory." (Matt. 24:27, 29–30)

THE TWO ANGELS

Immediately following Christ's ascension into heaven, two angels appeared to the stunned disciples and spoke words of comfort to them: "Men of Galilee, why do you stand gazing up into heaven? This same Jesus, who was taken up from you into heaven, will so come in like manner as you saw Him go into heaven" (Acts 1:11).

The next verse tells us, "They returned to Jerusalem from the mount called Olivet" (v. 12). Did you catch that? Jesus ascended to heaven from the Mount of Olives. According to the angels, Jesus will return to the very same spot—the Mount of Olives. The words of the angels conveyed both consolation for the disciples' present loss and confirmation of His future return.

The time of our Lord's return is uncertain, known only to God the Father: "Of that day and hour no one knows, not even the angels of heaven, but my Father only" (Matt. 24:36). But when the day comes, we can be sure that all eyes will be fixed on the sky above the Mount of Olives.

PAUL

In his second letter to the Thessalonians, Paul described what the Day of Judgment will be like: "The Lord Jesus is revealed from heaven with His mighty angels, in flaming fire taking vengeance on those who do not know God, and on those who do not obey the gospel of our Lord Jesus Christ. These shall be punished with everlasting destruction from the presence of the Lord and from the glory of His power, when He comes, in that Day, to be glorified in His saints and to be admired among all those who believe, because our testimony among you was believed" (2 Thess. 1:7–10).

JOHN

The prophecies of Christ's return are like bookends to John's book of Revelation. In the first chapter he wrote: "Behold, He is coming with clouds, and every eye will see Him, even they who pierced Him. And all the tribes of the earth will mourn because of Him" (v. 7).

And in the last pages of the last chapter—indeed, almost the last words of the New Testament—our Lord emphatically affirmed His Second Coming: "He who testifies to these things says, 'Surely I am coming quickly.' Amen. Even so, come, Lord Jesus!" (22:20).

Obviously, we have excellent reasons to anticipate the Second Coming of Christ. The Bible affirms it as a certainty, describing it in specific terms and with ample corroboration.

Many years ago in the city of Tokyo, a man named Eizaburo Ueno adopted an Akita puppy. That was his favorite breed of dog, and it had been his dream for many years to own one. He named it Hachiko—or "Hachi" for short. Instantly, man and man's best friend became inseparable. They shared a profound connection.

After a few weeks, Mr. Ueno began walking the dog to the local train station when he left for work each morning. Hachi spent most of the day at home but returned to the same train station every afternoon to greet his owner. Then they walked back to their house together.

This was their pattern for a period of years. Every day, Mr. Ueno and Hachi walked to the train station, and every day Hachi was waiting when Mr. Ueno arrived back from work.

One day, sadly, Mr. Ueno did not come back. He suffered a cerebral hemorrhage and died suddenly in his office.

Hachi was quickly adopted by the Ueno family's gardener and lived another ten years. But throughout his long life, he maintained his daily vigil. Every morning and every afternoon he returned to the same train station. There he spent hours each day waiting for his master's return.

Eventually the dog became a folk hero of sorts as his story spread throughout Japan. People named him Chuken Hachiko, "the faithful dog." Several movies have been made about the story. Today, there is even a bronze statue of Hachi outside that same train station. It's a popular spot for young people to take selfies.[5]

Like Hachi, followers of Jesus in today's world are awaiting our Master's return. And like Hachi, we don't know when that return will take place—but we do know where.

CHAPTER 29

SHOCK AND AWE

Do you remember "shock and awe"? That military strategy has been part of the United States Armed Forces' tactical approach since the 1990s. But the phrase itself became part of the national conversation during the 2003 invasion of Iraq.

The premise of "shock and awe" is that a sudden, overwhelming display of military force can paralyze the enemy's perception of the battlefield and destroy their will to fight. The idea is to throw a huge amount of offensive armaments toward your enemy with the goal of overwhelming them and short-circuiting their ability to respond.

That was America's strategy during the early days of Operation Iraqi Freedom. In a burst of power, the United States launched a coordinated combination of missile strikes and laser-targeted bombs. The immediate goal was not only to destroy Iraqi defensive weapons but also to convince Iraqi civilians that the United States and its allies were serious—that Saddam Hussein and his regime would soon be removed from power.

Less than five weeks later, coalition forces entered Baghdad, Iraq's capital, and secured the city.

We've explored the Rapture, the Tribulation, and the Second Coming as the next events in God's eschatological calendar. Now let's briefly explore the explosive moment that will occur alongside the Second Coming: the battle called Armageddon.

When Jesus leads His heavenly offensive against Satan and the Antichrist at that battle, He will follow a similar strategy as the US forces in Iraq—although He will have no part with conventional ammunition. His weapon will be glory. Christ's transcendent splendor and power will be fully aimed at the evil that has bedeviled humanity for so long.

In that final showdown, the rebellion of the Tribulation Period will come to a head. The Antichrist, the kings of the earth, and the souls that follow them will gather one last time to try to defeat Jesus Christ. Their armies will be made up of soldiers from the ten nations of the revived Roman Empire. The Antichrist, with the False Prophet at his side, will lead those massive armies in defying Christ's authority and right to rule—the ultimate revolt against God.

When Christ's return draws near, they will do everything they can to prepare for the battle of the ages. And they will fail spectacularly.

THE ADVENT OF CHRIST

The apostle John described this "shock and awe" moment that is to come: "Behold, He is coming with clouds, and every eye will see Him, even they who pierced Him. And all the tribes of the earth will mourn because of Him. Even so, Amen" (Rev. 1:7).

The first time Jesus came to earth, He appeared in obscurity. The second time, however, "every eye will see Him." The entire world will witness His return.

When Jesus arrives on earth the second time, His landing will dramatically herald the purpose of His coming. The moment His feet touch the Mount of Olives, that mountain will split apart, creating a broad passageway from Jerusalem to Jericho. As you can imagine, this will be an unprecedented geological cataclysm.

In describing it, Dr. Tim LaHaye wrote: "There will be a stellar Event. Celestial. Cosmic. Greater than earth. Greater than the heavens. And it will suck the air out of humanity's lungs and send men and women and kings and presidents and tyrants to their knees. It will have no need of spotlights, fog machines, amplified music, synthesizers, or special effects. It will be real."[1]

Thus Christ's return will be amplified by a spectacle that will make Hollywood disaster movies look like Saturday morning child's fare. The world will see and recognize its rightful Lord and King.

Whereas Jesus came the first time in humility and simplicity, this time His glory and majesty will be spectacularly displayed for all to see. In His coming, Christ will look like no other warrior in the history of the world. According to John: "His eyes were like a flame of fire, and on His head were many crowns. He had a name written that no one knew except Himself. He was clothed with a robe dipped in blood, and His name is called The Word of God" (Rev. 19:12–13).

Let's take a deeper look at that description. First, Jesus' eyes are flames of fire that burn up all that is false as He gazes upon the hearts and minds of mankind. This signifies the Lord's ability to see deeply into the hearts of men and deal with all injustice (1:14; 2:18; 19:12). His eyes will pierce through the motives of nations and individuals and judge them for what they really are.

Second, the head of the returning Christ is crowned with many crowns. When He came the first time, they mocked Him by putting a crown of thorns on His head. When He comes this time, His many crowns symbolize the reality that no rule, might, or authority will be able to stand against Him. He is the Supreme.

Third, Jesus' robe dipped in blood speaks of the redemption He secured for us on the cross as the Lamb that was slain. For all eternity we will celebrate the shed blood that brought about our redemption from the penalty of sin. Earlier in Revelation, John described Christ as "the Lamb slain from the foundation of the world" (13:8). In fact, Jesus will be represented to us as the Lamb of God throughout eternity.

In Revelation 19, the Lord is given the name "Faithful and True" (v. 11) and later "The Word of God" (v. 13). But as Christ leads His armies in victory, John saw a name written on His thigh: "KING OF KINGS AND LORD OF LORDS" (v. 16). We are familiar with this double name, but now it takes on its intended significance. Of all the kings on earth, Jesus is *the* King. Of all earthly lords (rulers, those in authority), He is *the* Lord. Every knee will bow before Him when He comes to earth (Isa. 45:23; Rom. 14:11; Phil. 2:10–11).

THE ARMIES OF CHRIST

Revelation 19:14 says, "And the armies in heaven, clothed in fine linen, white and clean, followed Him on white horses."

When Christ returns, He will bring His armies as part of His shock-and-awe campaign. Note the word in verse 14 is "armies," plural. It is not the "army" of heaven but the "armies." These armies are the believers from all the ages: the Old Testament saints, the New Testament saints, and the Tribulation saints—all the many legions of our Lord combined in one massive army.

Zechariah wrote: "The Lord my God will come, and all the saints with You" (14:5).

In his letters to the Thessalonians, Paul spoke of the saints who would accompany the Lord when He returned: "So that He may establish your hearts blameless in holiness before our God and Father at the coming of our Lord Jesus Christ with all His saints" (1 Thess. 3:13).

Jude echoed the same idea: "Listen! The Lord is coming with countless thousands of his holy ones" (v. 14 NLT).

All those who have died in the Lord, along with those who were raptured before the years of the Tribulation, will join with Jesus and participate in the battle to reclaim the world for the rule of Christ.

More important than who they are is how they are dressed. The white linen, clean and fine, represents the righteousness of those who are so clothed. Jesus wears the bloodstained garment so that we might wear the white linen of His righteousness.

But the saints are not the only armies of our Lord. Both Matthew and Paul told us that the angels will also descend with Christ: "When the Son of Man comes in His glory, and all the holy angels with Him, then He will sit on the throne of His glory" (Matt. 25:31).

And Paul described the moment "when the Lord Jesus is revealed from heaven with His mighty angels" (2 Thess. 1:7).

THE AVENGING OF CHRIST

In the first descriptive line of verse 11, we are given the central purpose for Christ's return to the earth: "In righteousness He judges and makes war" (Rev. 19:11).

Yes, Jesus will come to judge. He will come *as* the Judge of all things—including all people.

In the little epistle that immediately precedes the book of Revelation, Jude described the kind of world that Christ will find when He returns to the earth: "Now Enoch, the seventh from Adam, prophesied about these men also, saying, 'Behold, the Lord comes with ten thousands of His saints, to execute judgment on all, to convict all who are ungodly among them of all their ungodly deeds which they have committed in an ungodly way, and of all the harsh things which ungodly sinners have spoken against Him'" (vv. 14–15).

In two short verses, Jude used the word *ungodly* four times. This repetition is not accidental. Jude was emphasizing the fact that when Christ returns to the earth, His long-suffering patience will have run its course. He will come to impose judgment upon those who have defied Him.

Jesus will also render judgment against the leaders of the forces who opposed Him during the Tribulation. Namely, the Antichrist and his False Prophet: "Then the beast was captured, and with him the false prophet. . . . These two were cast alive into the lake of fire burning with brimstone" (Rev. 19:20).

When John used the word *captured* to describe what happens to the Beast and False Prophet, he was being very intentional. That word in Greek means "to grab" or "to snatch." When the time has come— when the cup of iniquity has been filled up—the Lord will snatch up the Beast and the False Prophet from the earth, and those two evil creatures will have the unwanted honor of actually going to hell before Satan, whose confinement occurs much later.

Perhaps surprisingly, Satan will not join the Beast and the False Prophet in hell until the end of the Millennium, one thousand years after the Second Coming: "The devil, who deceived them, was cast into the lake of fire and brimstone where the beast and the false prophet are. And they will be tormented day and night forever and ever" (20:10).

But why all this judgment and anger and wrath? Why must these things be part of God's plan for the future? If you are among those who struggle with the thought of God's wrath and judgment, these words from N. T. Wright may give you understanding:

The word *judgment* carries negative overtones for a good many people in our liberal and post-liberal world. We need to remind ourselves that throughout the Bible God's coming judgment is a good thing, something to be celebrated, longed for, yearned over. It causes people to shout for joy and the trees of the field to clap their hands. In a world of systematic injustice, bullying, violence, arrogance, and oppression, the thought that there might come a day when the wicked are firmly put in their place and the poor and weak are given their due is the best news there can be. Faced with a world in rebellion, a world full of exploitation and wickedness, a good God must be a God of judgment.[2]

As we consider God's "shock and awe" campaign during the Second Coming of Christ and the battle of Armageddon, the question is not "Why does Jesus have to be so judgmental?" Instead, the better question is "How could we call God good if He allowed evil to forever corrupt the world He created and pronounced to be good?"

In June 1944, the people of France had been suffering for four years under the tyranny of Adolf Hitler. His armies had invaded France in 1940 as part of his unholy ambition to turn all of Europe into a Nazi superstate. But then, on June 6, 1944, General Eisenhower commanded Allied troops to cross the channel from England and invade the fortified beaches of Normandy. Their purpose? To liberate the French nation from oppression.

Editor James M. Kushner described what happened on that fateful day, now known as D-Day:

> Before dawn, then throughout the rest of the day, sea, land, and air were rent by flashes, thunder, flying metal, parachutes, while fresh wounds in the earth and men erupted in sand and soil, blood and guts. Beaches turned red. Trees exploded, cattle perished, men breathed their last.
>
> D-day was just the first day. The battle for Normandy raged on well into August, and Paris was liberated August 25, 1944. The scarring of Normandy and the shedding of blood was the result of many men and their designs—either for conquest and occupation or for liberation.[3]

In many ways, what happened on D-Day offers a scaled-down preview of the world's final battle. Like World War II France, we suffer under the heel of a brutal tyrant who illegitimately occupies our world, imposing death, destruction, and misery. Like the oppressed citizens of France in the 1940s, we cry out for liberation from a cruel oppressor.

But we are assured in Revelation 19 that liberation will come. We have a Supreme Commander who has never lost a battle, and He is simply waiting for the strategic moment when He will descend and crush forever the forces that have invaded His world. Because He is "Faithful and True," we can rest assured that He will not fail. The Lion of Judah has conquered and will conquer on that final day.

CHAPTER 30

THE FINAL INVITATION

Belinda Luscombe recalled the time she lost a large sum of money by forgetting to claim stock options. "One day," she wrote, "I had $70,000 waiting to be claimed, and then about a month later when I realized I had forgotten to click on the 'exercise trade' button on my computer—poof!—the opportunity was gone."

Belinda's first, panicked thought was how she could tell her husband about her mistake. Then, the weight of her situation began to fully press down. In her words:

> It's hard to describe the feeling exactly. I imagine you could replicate the effects by lying on the ground and having a friend drop a bowling ball on your abdomen from atop a stepladder. There's a little shock, some confusion, pain, nausea, and a profound wish that this had happened to somebody else. For a while, it hurts to breathe.

"I had made something," she wrote, "it was there, but through sheer incompetence, it was gone. And it was All. My. Fault."[1]

I hope you never experience the gut-wrenching regret of losing tens of thousands of dollars from carelessness. But that pales in comparison to the soul-shattering terror of missing your opportunity to claim the eternal riches offered by Christ.

We've now spent twenty-nine chapters exploring the reality of the Rapture. A moment is coming when our world will change "in the twinkling of an eye." The Lord Jesus will appear in the clouds and gather His people to Himself—first those who've died in Him, and then those who are fortunate enough to witness His return in the sky.

As we've seen, that moment will mark the beginning of the end for this phase of human history. Once the Rapture occurs, our world will experience a seven-year countdown called the Tribulation that will end with *The End*—the battle of Armageddon. Any person who has not yet accepted God's free gift of salvation at that point will run out of time. The option will be closed.

If we procrastinate until the opportunity is gone, it will be All. Our. Fault.

The Bible ends with a final warning—a last invitation to Christ. You'll find it on the last page of the last book of the Bible: "Let him who thirsts come. Whoever desires, let him take the water of life freely" (Rev. 22:17).

Those may be the most important words you'll ever read. Let me show you why.

YOUR INVITATION IS READY

Who has the option to accept the riches of salvation through Christ? Anyone. Everyone! And yes, that certainly includes you! As we saw in chapter 12, heaven is restricted to those people who accept the gospel of Jesus Christ. But there are no restrictions when it comes to responding to that gospel.

In my decades as a servant of Jesus, I've had the privilege of sharing the gospel with thousands of people—many of them face-to-face. Often that message is received with joy—with eyes that brighten and lips that twitch upward into a smile of joy.

Sometimes, though, the person hearing the gospel lowers their head. Their eyes go to the floor, and they sigh with such weight and such sadness that it breaks my heart every time. Even when they don't say the words out loud, I know exactly what they're thinking: *It's not for me. If you only knew what I've done. If you only knew what was done to me. If you only knew what I'm capable of. I don't qualify.*

No! None of us qualify, and that's the point. That's the beauty of the gospel.

You don't have to be perfect to qualify for salvation. You don't have to be above average or ahead of the curve to pass through the gates of heaven—more good things than bad things on your ledger. You don't have to be good or pure or nice, nor do you have to be a certain age or a certain color or live in a certain place.

If you want to know God, if you want to experience His love and grace, and if you want to enjoy fellowship with Him for all eternity, all you have to be is thirsty.

Remember the words of Jesus' last invitation: "Let the one who is thirsty come; and let the one who wishes take the free gift of the water of life" (Rev. 22:17 NIV).

Two Bible translations say, "*Whoever* desires, let him come." Richard Baxter once wrote about the wonder of that word. "I thank God," he said, "for the word 'whosoever.' If God had said that there was mercy for Richard Baxter, I am so vile a sinner that I would have thought he meant some other Richard Baxter; but when he says 'whosoever' I know that it includes me, the worst of all Richard Baxters."[2]

I know "whoever" includes me. "David Jeremiah desires, so let him come." I've tasted of that living water, which is why I feel such eager anticipation for everything that is yet to come. Whether my journey takes me through the doorway of death or through the thrill of the Rapture, I know I will be with Christ.

Do you know? Have you tasted? If your answer is no, it's not too late—but time is short.

YOUR RESPONSE IS REQUIRED

As I said, there are no restrictions around the offer of salvation. But the gospel does require something of everyone in need of living water. Verse 17 says, "Let him take the water of life freely."

The only thing a thirsty person has to do is reach out and take the water. It's available to all, but we must make the choice to drink. *You* must make that choice.

Is it really that easy? We feel there must be something significant we have to say. There must be something more we have to do. We think there must be some level of maturity or goodness we have to attain—some kind of schooling or education we have to undergo.

No! Just come and drink. That's not a form of good works; it's just God's goodness and His grace. Reaching out and receiving a gift doesn't mean I did anything to earn the gift. The gift is offered freely—that's what makes it a gift. The response of the thirsty person is simply to take that which is offered freely by grace.

If there was anything you could do to help yourself get saved even a little bit, do you think God in heaven would have sent Jesus Christ to this earth to die on the cross for your sin? If there was any human way you could merit salvation or recommend yourself to God, do you think He would have paid the high price He did by giving His own Son as a sacrifice?

God sent Jesus Christ into this world because there's not a single thing any of us can do to save ourselves—nothing except to take the living water freely offered to us. We use various terms to refer to this process—*belief, trust, commitment*—but it means the same as "taking" the living water and drinking deeply.

The prophet Isaiah said,

> Is anyone thirsty?
> Come and drink—
> even if you have no money!
> Come, take your choice of wine or milk—
> it's all free!
> Why spend your money on food that does not give you strength?
> Why pay for food that does you no good?
> Listen to me, and you will eat what is good.
> You will enjoy the finest food. (55:1–2 NLT)

The apostle John borrowed from Isaiah's words to craft the final invitation of the Bible: "whoever desires, let him take the water of life freely."

Don't neglect to exercise your option, for this is truly the Bible's last word on the subject. The Rapture is real. Right now it is one day nearer than yesterday—one breath closer than your last exhalation. There is a moment in the future when all options will be removed and all fates sealed. We have to pray sincerely in a definite act of faith, "Dear Lord, I confess my sins, I'm so thirsty on the inside of my life, and I now receive Jesus Christ—the Living Water. Come into my life and help me live for You from this day forth!"

Presbyterian evangelist Benjamin Mills told of a friend of his, a pastor, who was preaching one night in his church. He invited people to come and kneel at the front of the room if they wanted to receive Christ as Savior. Several did so, and the pastor started to kneel and pray with them. But suddenly he was impressed to stand up and say he thought there was at least one more person who needed to come. Instantly, a young lady rose from the back seat and hurried forward, kneeling with the others and giving herself to Christ.

Two weeks later, this woman suffered a sudden fatal illness. On her deathbed, she said to the pastor, "I shall be glad through all eternity that you gave that last invitation that led me to Christ."[3]

Oh, you'll be thankful through all eternity that Jesus has given you one last invitation. I'm going to ask you as if I were sitting there beside you: Have you taken the living water that God offers in the person of Christ?

The Bible says, "Whoever calls on the name of the LORD shall be saved" (Rom. 10:13).

Let "whoever" be you!

CHAPTER 31

WHY STUDY PROPHECY?

For several years now, a Christian satire website called the Babylon Bee has made waves with content that is humorous, thought-provoking, and perhaps a little irreverent. Recent reports suggest they can add another adjective to that list: prophetic.

According to readers, several of the Bee's satirical articles are coming true. What the writers originally suggested as outrageous fiction has, over time, drifted into the realm of reality.

For example, one humorous headline read, "New, Less Problematic History Books Will Only Include What Happened in the Current Year." The article poked fun at the recent trend in educational circles to label historical figures and events as too dangerous or too controversial to share with vulnerable young minds. It was a silly concept.

But then "silly" became "serious" when CNN published an article titled, "Illinois Community Leaders Want to Abolish History Lessons in Schools."

During the COVID-19 pandemic, the Babylon Bee ran a fictitious article that proclaimed, "Triple-Masker Looks Down on People Who

Only Double Mask." Again, the point was to gently suggest that some people had perhaps gone a little overboard on cloth masks as a way to fight viral infections.

The Bee published that satirical piece in January 2021. The very next day, NBC News aired a segment on television that described "the benefits of triple masking."

In total, there have been ninety-two articles published on the Bee that eventually became prophetic—they came true in some form or fashion.[1]

Seth Dillon is the CEO of the Babylon Bee. When asked about the recent trend of his writers acting as prophets, he said: "The problem isn't that our satire is too close to reality; it's that reality is too close to satire, so our jokes keep coming true."[2]

Sadly, many people (including Christians) in our world think of biblical prophecy on a similar level as satire—interesting in some ways, but not particularly useful or applicable to "real life." I once heard someone say that Christians treat prophecy like the priest and the Levite treated the wounded man in the parable of the good Samaritan: they pass by on the other side. Some avoid prophecy because it seems difficult to understand. Others feel too overwhelmed by the present to think about the future.

I believe strongly that such an approach is mistaken. While many Christians are content to leave prophecy's pages shrouded in mystery and misunderstanding, the fact remains it is our only reliable source of information about tomorrow. God alone knows the end from the beginning, and He foretells the future with absolute accuracy. Incredibly, He has chosen to share many of those prophecies with us, if we will only heed what they say.

I'm reminded of an illustration I read in the book *Armageddon, Oil, and Terror*:

> Have you ever driven down a strange dark road in a blinding rainstorm? Every minute you wish you could see beyond the edge of the headlights to see what's ahead. If only you could know what was

coming next—could intuitively know what's out there or predict what you'll find at the next bend in the road. We long to see ahead, to know, perhaps to avert disaster.

Can someone see what's ahead by intuition or a special gift? Can a prophet know the future because the path of our lives is part of a larger drama scripted ahead of time? This is what the prophets of the Bible claim. Can we know where we are in that pattern of events foretold by prophets, written in Scripture or seen in apocalyptic visions of the future? In the uncertain storm of the days in which we live, all of us yearn to see beyond the headlights.[3]

Only biblical prophecy allows you to do that!

We've reached the final chapter in this exploration of the Rapture—the next event on God's prophetic calendar. I can't think of a better way to conclude these pages than by offering just a few additional reasons why it's worth our time as believers in Jesus to study biblical prophecy.

PROPHECY PERVADES SCRIPTURE

Perhaps the main reason why we should study biblical prophecy is that there wouldn't be much of the Bible left if we tried to ignore its predictive passages. Prophecy is pervasive throughout all of Scripture.

In the book *Christ's Prophetic Plans*, John MacArthur and Richard Mayhue have done excellent work in identifying just how much of the Bible is prophetic. Here are a few examples of what they found:

- Sixty-two of the Bible's sixty-six books contain predictive information, with Ruth, Song of Solomon, Philemon, and 3 John as the only exceptions. That's 94 percent.
- Breaking things down even further, there are a total of 31,124 verses in Scripture. Incredibly, 27 percent of those verses (8,352)

refer to prophetic issues. And 22 percent of all prophetic verses refer to Christ's Second Coming.

- Looking specifically at the End Times, there are approximately 333 specific biblical prophecies dealing with Christ's two advents. One-third describe His first coming, and two-thirds are connected to His Second Coming.[4]

If you value the Bible, then you need to value biblical prophecy.

PROPHECY PROVES GOD'S SOVEREIGNTY

Have you ever wished you could prove that God is who He says He is? That His Word is relevant and meaningful for our lives today?

You can! The prophetic passages of Scripture offer direct evidence that God knows everything and is in charge of everything. He is never surprised by anything, and whatever He says He will do, He does. He is sovereign, and He further proves that sovereignty every time His prophecies are fulfilled.

God Himself encouraged us to bank on the reliability of biblical prophecy in the book of Isaiah: "Remember the things I have done in the past. For I alone am God! I am God, and there is none like me. Only I can tell you the future before it even happens. Everything I plan will come to pass, for I do whatever I wish. . . . I have said what I would do, and I will do it" (46:9–11 NLT).

When we know the One who declares the beginning from the end, we can live every day with confidence.

PROPHECY PROMOTES THE BIBLE'S INTEGRITY

The confirmed accuracy of biblical prophecy boosts our confidence in God's sovereignty, and also in His Word. The more we study and understand the inerrancy of the Bible's prophetic passages, the more we trust every word of His Word.

Jesus used prophecy to validate His messiahship, for example. This is what He said to His disciples:

- "I tell you this beforehand, so that when it happens you will believe that I AM the Messiah" (John 13:19 NLT).
- "I have told you these things before they happen so that when they do happen, you will believe" (14:29 NLT).

Not only did Jesus perfectly prophesy about the future; He Himself was the fulfillment of prophecy. In the fullness of time, Jesus satisfied every detail of the prophets' predictions concerning the Messiah. He was a descendant of Abraham and the tribe of Judah (Gen. 12:3; 49:10). He came from David's family line (Isa. 9:7) and was born in Bethlehem (Mic. 5:2). His name was Immanuel; He was born of a virgin (Isa. 7:14). He based His ministry in Galilee, spoke in parables, and did wonders among the people (Isa. 9:1–2; 6:9–10; 61:1–2). He was betrayed, pierced for our sins, and crucified with criminals (Zech. 11:12–13; Isa. 53:5, 12). After His burial in a wealthy man's tomb, He rose again (Isa. 53:9–11).

Not a single one of the thirteen billion or so people who have lived on earth could even come close to fulfilling the 109 prophecies fulfilled by Christ. He stands alone in human history, and He stands on the foundation of God's prophetic Word. The study of messianic prophecy is a remarkable journey into ironclad evidence for the integrity of Scripture.[5]

The Old Testament Prophecy	The Description	The New Testament Fulfillment
Isaiah 7:14	Jesus would be born of a virgin.	Matthew 1:22–23
2 Samuel 7:12–16	Jesus would come from the line of David.	Matthew 1:1
Micah 5:2	Jesus would be born in Bethlehem.	Matthew 2:6; Luke 1:68–75; 2:4, 11
Isaiah 40:3; Malachi 3:1	A messenger would prepare the way for Jesus.	Matthew 11:10
Isaiah 61:1–2	Jesus would proclaim the Lord's favor.	Luke 4:21
Isaiah 49:1–7	Jesus would be the light to the Gentiles.	Luke 2:25–32
Zechariah 11:12–13	Jesus would be betrayed.	Matthew 27:6–10
Zechariah 9:9–10	Jesus would enter Jerusalem lowly and riding on a donkey.	Matthew 21:1–17; Mark 11:1–11; Luke 19:29–40; John 12:12–19
Isaiah 50:6–7	Jesus would come as a servant.	Matthew 5:17–18
Isaiah 53:3–12	Jesus would suffer and be despised.	Matthew 26:63
Psalm 118:22	Jesus would be rejected.	Matthew 21:42
Psalm 22:13–18	Jesus would be crucified.	Matthew 27:35, 39–44; John 20:25

PROPHECY PROTECTS US FROM FALSE TEACHING

One of the main reasons Jesus prophesied about the End Times was to protect us from false teaching. In Matthew 24:4–5, He warned, "Take heed that no one deceives you. For many will come in My name, saying, 'I am the Christ,' and will deceive many." This warning is so essential that Scripture repeats it in Mark 13 and Luke 21.

We live in a day when deception is common. Jesus said in John 16:1, "These things I have spoken to you, that you should not be made to stumble." Knowing what the Bible says about the future protects us from being deceived.

As much as God wants to place us under prophecy's umbrella of protection, the devil wants to keep us out. Satan knows that reading 2 Thessalonians 2 will reveal his scheme to spread apostasy in the Last Days. And if we read Revelation 20, we will know God has already assigned him to the lake of fire.

Seeing Satan as a defeated foe in the future helps us to be victorious over him today. Prophecy protects us from Satan's attacks.

PROPHECY PREPARES US FOR THE LAST DAYS

One of the great prophetic themes in the Bible is that God has a plan for history. That plan has phases, and the next phase is imminent. It can arrive at any moment.

Jesus told several parables to illustrate the importance of being prepared for His coming. One story was about a master of the house who had been robbed. If the master had known when the thief would come, he would have watched to prevent the robbery. The lesson is simple: be prepared. Always be ready for the Rapture, which will be as unpredictable as a thief in the night (1 Thess. 5:4).

Studying prophecy helps us prepare for the days ahead. Hardly a day goes by that we don't read about wars, rumors of wars, natural disasters, or lawlessness in the news. These grim realities can be disheartening. However, Jesus told His disciples to anticipate these events—that they would be signs that His return was on the horizon.

Tragedies never take God by surprise. Jesus said, "These things I have told you, that when the time comes, you may remember that I told you of them" (John 16:4).

Studying Bible prophecy gives us courage in chaotic times. Although life on earth will continue to get worse, the very pain of those trials reminds us the day of the Rapture draws near.

PROPHECY PROVIDES GUIDANCE FOR EVERY DAY

All prophecy is by definition focused on the future. Yet it would be a mistake to conclude that biblical prophecy has no value for the present. Quite the opposite is true!

In the opening chapters of Revelation, one sentence appears seven times: "He who has an ear, let him hear what the Spirit says to the churches" (2:7, 11, 17, 29; 3:6, 13, 22).

In other words, "Listen up! I have something to say, and it's important." Prophecy contains practical instruction for every Christian, every day.

In his book *World News and Bible Prophecy*, prophetic scholar Charles Dyer reminds us that "God gave prophecy to change our hearts, not to fill our heads with knowledge. God never predicted future events just to satisfy our curiosity about the future. He includes with His predictions practical applications to life. God's pronouncements about the future carry with them specific advice for the 'here and now.'"[6]

It would not be an exaggeration to say biblical prophecy drives evangelism and righteous living. Knowing what's coming encourages us to be ministry oriented, reaching out to the lost.

Not only that, living with an awareness of Christ's imminent return increases our desire to share the gospel. Prophecy elevates our perspective and energizes our walk with the Lord. God gave us prophecy to help us anticipate what is coming and to equip us for living in the world of the end.

PROPHECY PROMISES SPIRITUAL BLESSING

Did you know the book of Revelation is the only book in the Bible that promises a reward to its readers? This promise is found not just once but twice:

- "Blessed is he who reads and those who hear the words of this prophecy, and keep those things which are written in it; for the time is near" (1:3).
- "Blessed is he who keeps the words of the prophecy of this book" (22:7).

The Bible forms a guidebook that teaches us the sequence of events leading up to the return of Jesus Christ. Biblical prophecy can seem complex, but it doesn't have to be confusing if we understand what Scripture's predictions mean for our lives here and now.

John O'Neill worked for years as a counter-terrorism specialist for the FBI. He investigated many terrorist attacks, including a 1993 attack on the World Trade Center and various bombings throughout the Middle East.

In the late 1990s, O'Neill developed serious concerns about the growing threat of Al Qaeda as an organization and of Osama bin Laden as its leader. O'Neill even prevented an Al Qaeda attack against the Los Angeles International Airport in 2000.

O'Neill shared his deeper worries with US officials. He even told the Associated Press in 1997, "A lot of these groups now have the capability and the support infrastructure in the United States to attack us here if they choose to do so."

Sadly, his warnings were heard but not heeded. After retiring in August 2001, O'Neill accepted another position as chief of security at the World Trade Center. He was killed while attempting to help people evacuate the South Tower on September 11.[7]

The lesson from that story is that warnings are only helpful when they are acted upon. Knowledge of what's to come will benefit us only when we study it and allow it to influence our choices for today.

May that be the case for you and me. Let us never neglect the incredible gift we have received through the prophetic passages of God's Word.

Specifically, let us never neglect the key lesson of the Rapture:

Christ is coming soon! We are servants tasked with critical work in our Master's house; at any moment He may walk through the door. We are like young people awaiting the great Groom and His heavenly procession; when He comes, will He find us living wisely or foolishly?

The Rapture is both a warning and a promise—an admonition and a blessing. Each breath you take brings you one moment closer to the shout of Christ, the voice of the archangel, and the trumpet of God.

Whoever has ears, let them hear!

HAVE YOU BECOME RAPTURE READY?

After I wrote the last paragraph of this book and put down my pen, as it were, I had a nagging feeling something else was needed—just half a page.

Just for you. Personally. A final word about receiving Christ as your personal Savior and Lord and being truly rapture ready. What joy it would bring me to know you've not only heard the gospel but received it while reading this book.

I'd also like to hear from you if you need help making your commitment to Jesus.

Here's an easy way to let us know of your decision or questions. I invite you to explore DavidJeremiah.org/KnowingGod. We've designed a special section that will offer a number of helpful resources on knowing God and joining His mission in the world.

Around the world, friends sometimes part ways by saying, "If I don't see you again on earth, I'll see you in heaven!"

Let me part ways for now by saying, "I'll see you at the Rapture!"

And God bless you!

INDEX

SCRIPTURE INDEX

NOTES

INTRODUCTION

1. Erin A. Smith, "*The Late Great Planet Earth* Made the Apocalypse a Popular Concern," *HUMANITIES* 38, no. 1 (Winter 2017), https://www.neh.gov/humanities/2017/winter/feature/the-late-great-planet-earth-made-the-apocalypse-popular-concern.

2. Mark Hitchcock, *Could the Rapture Happen Today?* (Sisters, OR: Multnomah, 2005), 8.

CHAPTER 1

1. "Disappearance of Marvin Clark," Wikipedia, accessed May 25, 2023, https://en.wikipedia.org/wiki/Disappearance_of_Marvin_Clark.

2. Tyler Hooper, "B.C.'s Granger Taylor Left a Note Saying He Was Boarding an Alien Spaceship—Then He Disappeared," *CBC Docs POV*, accessed May 1, 2023, https://www.cbc.ca/cbcdocspov/features/bcs-granger-taylor-left-a-note-saying-he-was-boarding-an-alien-spaceship.

3. Tim LaHaye, *The Rapture* (Eugene, OR: Harvest House Publishers, 2003), 39.

CHAPTER 2

1. "Paul McCartney," *Empire*, accessed March 30, 2023, https://www.empireonline.com/people/paul-mccartney/.

2. Peter Ames Carlin, *Paul McCartney: A Life* (New York: Simon & Schuster, 2009), 306. See also Hannah Wigandt, "Paul McCartney Said the Lyrics of a 'Flaming Pie' Track Are Similar to the Beatles' 'It Won't Be Long,'" Showbiz CheatSheet, February 7, 2023, https://www.cheatsheet.com/entertainment/paul-mccartney-said-lyrics-flaming-pie-track-similar-the-beatles-wont-long.html/.

3. John F. Walvoord, *End Times: Understanding Today's World Events in Biblical Prophecy*, ed. Charles Swindoll (Nashville, TN: Word Publishing, 1998), 17.

4. Mark Hitchcock, *Could the Rapture Happen Today?* (Sisters, OR: Multnomah, 2005), 45.

5. Van Ho, *Too Young to Escape* (Toronto: Pajama Press, 2018), 127.

CHAPTER 3

1. Winston Churchill, "Blood, Toil, Tears and Sweat," International Churchill Society, accessed April 21, 2023, https://winstonchurchill.org/resources /speeches/1940-the-finest-hour/blood-toil-tears-sweat/.

2. Churchill, "Blood, Toil, Tears, and Sweat."

3. *Big Wisdom (Little Book): 1,001 Proverbs, Adages, and Precepts to Help You Live a Better Life* (Nashville, TN: W Publishing Group, 2005), 209.

4. Danielle Johnson, "Grab the Tissues: Watch Volusia Child's Surprise Homecoming with Brother in Military," *Daytona Beach News-Journal*, December 21, 2022, https://www.news-journalonline.com/story/news/good -news/2022/12/21/port-orange-student-gets-surprise-military-homecoming -from-brother/69740687007/.

CHAPTER 4

1. Cnaan Liphshiz, "Dutch Christian Boatmaker Aims to Sail His Exact Replica of Noah's Ark to Israel," *Times of Israel*, November 24, 2018, https://www. timesofisrael.com/dutch-christian-boatmaker-to-sail-his-life-size-replica-of -noahs-ark-to-israel/.

2. Katherine Weber, "Billy Graham: 'The Days of Noah' Are Returning to Earth," *Christian Post*, June 1, 2016, https://www.christianpost.com/news /billy-graham-the-days-of-noah-are-returning-to-earth.html.

3. Jeff Kinley, *As It Was in the Days of Noah* (Eugene, OR: Harvest House Publishers, 2014), 7–8.

4. Kinley, *As It Was in the Days of Noah*, 67.

5. Randi Minetor, *Death in Glacier National Park* (Lanham, MD: Rowman & Littlefield, 2016), loc. 719–36, Kindle.

6. Minetor, *Death in Glacier National Park*, Kindle location 833.

7. "Pornography Industry Statistics and Trends in 2023," Gitnux, March 24, 2023, https://blog.gitnux.com/pornography-industry-statistics/.

8. W. A. Criswell, *The Gospel According to Moses* (Nashville, TN: Broadman Press, 1950), 19.

9. Carla, "Man Dreams of Finding Jesus Behind a Door," Team Expansion, January 31, 2018, https://teamexpansion.org/man-dreams-finding-jesus -behind-door/.

CHAPTER 5

1. Mandalit Del Barco, "On 'Fanfare for the Common Man,' an Anthem for the American Century," NPR, July 19, 2018, https://www.npr.org/2018/07/19/629875534/on-fanfare-for-the-common-man-an-anthem-for-the-american-century.

2. "Aaron Copland, Fanfare for the Common Man," Kennedy Center, accessed March 20, 2023, https://www.kennedy-center.org/education/resources-for-educators/classroom-resources/media-and-interactives/media/music/aaron-copland--fanfare-for-the-common-man/.

3. "Aaron Copland, Fanfare for the Common Man."

4. Arnold G. Fruchtenbaum, *The Footsteps of the Messiah: A Study of the Sequence of Prophetic Events* (San Antonio, TX: Ariel Press, 2004), 144.

5. Fruchtenbaum, *The Footsteps of the Messiah.*

6. Fruchtenbaum, *The Footsteps of the Messiah.*

7. "Are the Sky Trumpets People Have Been Reporting Signs of the End Times?" Got Questions Ministries, accessed March 29, 2023, https://www.gotquestions.org/sky-trumpets.html.

8. Jessica Foley, "Kingston Residents Attempt to Explain Mysterious Early Morning Sounds," *Kingstonist*, January 17, 2023, https://www.kingstonist.com/news/kingston-residents-attempt-to-explain-mysterious-early-morning-sounds/.

9. "Keep Hearing Weird Trumpet-Like Sound from Sky. West End of Kingston," Reddit, January 17, 2023, https://www.reddit.com/r/KingstonOntario/comments/10e7aul/keep_hearing_weird_trumpet_like_sound_from_sky/.

10. John F. Walvoord, *End Times: Understanding Today's World Events in Biblical Prophecy*, ed. Charles Swindoll (Nashville, TN: Word Publishing, 1998), 28–29.

11. Roy B. Zuck, *The Speaker's Quote Book* (Grand Rapids, MI: Kregel Publications, 2009).

CHAPTER 6

1. "The Lord of the Rings, the Journey Doesn't End Here," TheLotrTV, February 24, 2015, YouTube video, https://www.youtube.com/watch?v=O_FmqI7QKck.

2. David Jeremiah, *What Are You Afraid Of?* (Carol Stream, IL: Tyndale House Publishers, 2013), 228.

3. Jeremiah, *What Are You Afraid Of?*, 234.

4. Robert J. Morgan, *The Lord Is My Shepherd* (New York: Howard Books, 2013), 116–17.

5. James M. Campbell, *Heaven Opened: A Book of Comfort and Hope* (New York: Revell, 1924), 178.

6. Michael P. Green, ed., *Illustrations for Biblical Preaching* (Grand Rapids, MI: Baker Book House, 1989), 91.

7. Peter J. Marshall, ed., *The Wartime Sermons of Dr. Peter Marshall* (Tulsa, OK: CrossStaff Publishing, 2005).

CHAPTER 7

1. Robert Krulwich, "Are Butterflies Two Different Animals in One? The Death and Resurrection Theory," NPR, August 1, 2012, https://www.npr.org /sections/krulwich/2012/08/01/157718428/are-butterflies-two-different -animals-in-one-the-death-and-resurrection-theory.

2. W. E. Vine and Terry Kulakowski, *Vine's Expository Dictionary of New Testament Words* (Grand Rapids, MI: Reformed Church Publications, 2015), 66.

3. Arnold G. Fruchtenbaum, *The Footsteps of the Messiah: A Study of the Sequence of Prophetic Events* (San Antonio, TX: Ariel Press, 2008), 144.

4. J. Vernon McGee, *First and Second Thessalonians* (Nashville, TN: Thomas Nelson Publishers, 1991), 78.

5. William Barclay, *At the Last Trumpet* (Louisville, KY: Presbyterian Publishing Company, 1998), 62.

6. A. T. Pierson, *The Gospel*, vol. 3 (Grand Rapids, MI: Baker Book House, 1978), 136.

7. Adapted from Philip Yancey, "What's a Heaven For?," *Christianity Today*, October 26, 1998, www.christianitytoday.com/ct/1998/october26/8tc104.html.

8. Hank Hanegraaff's *Resurrection: The Capstone in the Arch of Christianity* (Nashville, TN: Thomas Nelson, 2000), xi–xii.

CHAPTER 8

1. Agatha Christie, *An Autobiography* (New York: HarperCollins, 2010), Kindle.

2. Arnold G. Fruchtenbaum, *The Footsteps of the Messiah: A Study of the Sequence of Prophetic Events*, rev. ed. (San Antonio, TX: Ariel Ministries, 2010), 651.

3. Gretty Garcia, "There's a Secret Royal Letter from Queen Elizabeth II That Can't Be Opened Until 2085," *Good Housekeeping*, September 20, 2022, https://www.goodhousekeeping.com/life/entertainment/a41295930/queen -elizabeth-secret-letter-2085/.

CHAPTER 9

1. Vanessa Barford and Lucy Townsend, "Eugen Sandow: The Man with the Perfect Body," BBC News, October 19, 2012, https://www.bbc.com/news /magazine-19977415.

2. Matthew Henry, *Matthew Henry's Commentary on the Whole Bible (Complete)*, Bible Study Tools, accessed April 4, 2023, https://www.biblestudytools.com /commentaries/matthew-henry-complete/1-corinthians/15.html.

3. "The State Funeral of Her Majesty Queen Elizabeth II," Westminster Abbey, accessed May 26, 2023, https://www.westminster-abbey.org/media/15467 /order-of-service-the-state-funeral-of-her-majesty-queen-elizabeth-ii.pdf.

CHAPTER 10

1. Sylvia Wrigley, *Without a Trace* (EQP Books, 2019); M. S. Morgan, *Foxtrot 94: Tragic Accident or UFO Conspiracy?* (self-pub., 2022); "William Schaffner," Wikipedia, accessed April 4, 2023, https://en.wikipedia.org/wiki /William_Schaffner.

2. Mark Hitchcock, *The End: A Complete Overview of Bible Prophecy and the End of Days* (Carol Stream, IL: Tyndale House Publishers, 2012), 29–30.

3. Tim LaHaye, *No Fear of the Storm: Why Christians Will Escape All the Tribulation* (Sisters, OR: Multnomah Press, 1992), 35.

4. Hal Lindsey, *The Late Great Planet Earth* (Grand Rapids, MI: Zondervan, 1970).

5. "Longest Domino Wall," Guinness World Records, accessed May 26, 2023, https://www.guinnessworldrecords.com/world-records/longest-domino -wall#:~:text=The%20longest%20domino%20wall%20is,USA%2C%20on%20 2%20April%202022.

6. Harold Wilmington, *The King Is Coming* (Carol Stream, IL: Tyndale House Publishers, 1981), 8.

CHAPTER 11

1. Levi is another possibility if we review Malachi 2:6–7.

2. C. S. Lewis, *The World's Last Night* (New York: HarperOne, 2017), loc. 1239, 1258, Kindle.

3. Jo Woolf, "Shackleton and the Men on Elephant Island: A brotherhood of the Sea," Royal Scottish Geographical Society, accessed May 25, 2023, https:// www.rsgs.org/blog/shackleton-and-the-men-on-elephant-island-a -brotherhood-of-the-sea.

4. "Ernest Shackleton," National Library of Scotland, accessed May 25, 2023, https://www.nls.uk/learning-zone/geography-and-exploration/shackleton -and-wordie/ernest-shackleton/.

CHAPTER 12

1. Cody Taylor, "Pistons' Dwane Casey Explains Passport Situation with Jalen Duren," *Rookie Wire*, January 19, 2023, https://therookiewire.usatoday.com /2023/01/19/pistons-dwane-casey-jalen-duren-paris-passport/.

2. Michael Foust, "Did Billy Graham Say People 'Born Christian'?" *Baptist Press*, February 2, 2011, https://www.baptistpress.com/resource-library/news/did -billy-graham-say-people-born-christian.

3. "Knott's Berry Farm Ride Stuck 148 Feet in Air; 21 Riders Rescued," ABC7

Eyewitness News, December 31, 2016, https://abc7.com/knotts-berry-farm
-ride-stuck-sky-cabin-rescue/1679992.

CHAPTER 13

1. Ada Calhoun, "'It Could Be Huge: It Could Be a Nightmare': Attempting the Largest Family Reunion in the World," *Guardian*, March 17, 2018, https://www.theguardian.com/lifeandstyle/2018/mar/17/huge-nightmare-biggest-family-reunion-world-record-attempt.
2. "Lilly Family Reunion," accessed April 3, 2023, https://lillyreunion.org/.

CHAPTER 14

1. Charles Haddon Spurgeon, "Watching for Christ's Coming," Spurgeon Gems, accessed June 26, 2023, http://www.spurgeongems.org/vols37-39/chs2302.pdf.
2. Wayne Grudem, *Systematic Theology* (Grand Rapids, MI: Zondervan, 1994), 1093.
3. John F. Walvoord, *End Times: Understanding Today's World Events in Biblical Prophecy*, ed. Charles R. Swindoll (Nashville, TN: Word Publishing, 1998), 38.
4. Renald Showers, *Maranatha: Our Lord, Come!: A Definitive Study of the Rapture of the Church* (Belmawr, NJ: Friends of Israel Ministry, 1995), 148.
5. Ruthanna Metzgar, "It's Not in the Book!," Eternal Perspective Ministries, March 29, 2010, https://www.epm.org/resources/2010/Mar/29/Its-Not-in-the-Book/.

CHAPTER 15

1. Genny Glassman, "TikTok Mom Sobs After Seeing What Her Son Packed for His Trip to 'Heaven' to Visit His Dad," Café Mom, February 3, 2022, https://cafemom.com/parenting/tiktok-son-packed-for-his-trip-to-heaven.
2. John MacArthur, *Safe in the Arms of God* (Nashville, TN: Thomas Nelson, 2003), 81.
3. Quoted by Woodrow Kroll, "Is My Child in Heaven?" (Lincoln, NE: Back to the Bible, 1996).

CHAPTER 16

1. Tim McGraw, vocalist, "Live Like You Were Dying," words and music by James Timothy Nichols and Craig Michael Wiseman, track five on Tim McGraw, *Live Like You Were Dying*, Curb Records, 2004.
2. "Dying Professor's Lecture of a Lifetime," ABC News, accessed April 20, 2023, https://abcnews.go.com/GMA/story?id=3633945&page=1.
3. Vance Havner, *In Times like These* (Old Tappan, NJ: Fleming H. Revell Company, 1969), 29.

4. Charles Haddon Spurgeon, "Wake Up! Wake Up!," in *The Metropolitan Tabernacle Pulpit: Sermons Preached and Revised* (London: Passimore & Alabaster, 1879), 657.

5. Ray Stedman, *Expository Studies in Romans 9–16: From Guilt to Glory*, vol. 2 (Waco, TX: Word, 1978), 136.

6. Quoted in Leon Morris, *The Epistle to the Romans* (Grand Rapids, MI: William Eerdmans Publishing Company, 1988), 474.

7. *Saving Private Ryan*, directed by Steven Spielberg, written by Robert Rodat, featuring Tom Hanks and Matt Damon (Universal City, CA: Dreamworks, 1998).

CHAPTER 17

1. Charles G. Davis, "Heaven, Texas," Texas State Historical Association, January 1, 1995, https://www.tshaonline.org/handbook/entries/heaven-tx.

2. Lauren Sloss, "National Park Booking App Leaves Users Feeling Lost in the Woods," *New York Times*, July 29, 2022, https://www.nytimes.com/2022/07/29/travel/nps-recreation-gov.html.

CHAPTER 18

1. Deyan Georgiev, "How Much Time Does the Average American Spend on Their Phone in 2023?," *Techjury* (blog), updated June 23, 2023, https://techjury.net/blog/how-much-time-does-the-average-american-spend-on-their-phone/#gref.

2. Lonnie Lee Hood, "Hong Kong Puts Street Lights on the Ground Because People Won't Stop Looking at Their Phones," The_Byte, August 24, 2022, https://futurism.com/the-byte/hong-kong-street-lights-phones.

3. Christina Hodgson, "Pedestrians Can Face Huge Fines for Distracted Walking in Spain," *Olive Press*, May 13, 2023, https://www.theolivepress.es/spain-news/2023/05/13/pedestrians-can-face-huge-fines-for-distracted-walking-in-spain/.

4. Joan Lowy, "Distracted Walking: Smartphone Wielding Pedestrians Stumble into Danger," *Christian Science Monitor*, July 30, 2012, https://www.csmonitor.com/USA/Latest-News-Wires/2012/0730/Distracted-walking-Smartphone-wielding-pedestrians-stumble-into-danger.

5. Randy Alcorn, *Heaven* (Carol Stream, IL: Tyndale House Publishers, 2004, 455).

6. C. S. Lewis, *The Complete C. S. Lewis Signature Classics* (New York: HarperOne, 2002), 114.

7. C. S. Lewis, *Mere Christianity* (San Francisco, CA: HarperSanFrancisco, 2001), 134–35.

CHAPTER 19

1. Neil MacFarquhar and Andrew E. Kramer, "Russians Pound Ukrainian Cities, As Biden Rallies Anti-Kremlin Alliance," *New York Times*, March 21, 2022, https://www.nytimes.com/2022/03/21/world/europe/kyiv-mariupol -bombed.html.
2. MacFarquhar and Kramer, "Russians Pound Ukrainian Cities."
3. MacFarquhar and Kramer, "Russians Pound Ukrainian Cities."
4. A. T. Robertson, *Word Pictures in the New Testament*, s.v. "Matthew 13:21," Christian Classics Ethereal Library, accessed June 6, 2016, https://ccel.org /ccel/robertson_at/word/word.
5. J. Dwight Pentecost, quoted in Mark Hitchcock, *The End: A Complete Overview of Bible Prophecy and the End of Days* (Carol Stream, IL: Tyndale House, 2012), 235.
6. N. T. Wright, quoted in "The Necessity of God's Wrath," *Preaching Today*, accessed June 13, 2016, http://www.preachingtoday.com/illustrations/2009 /september/6092809.html.
7. Billy Graham, "10 Quotes from Billy Graham on the End Times," Billy Graham Library, April 8, 2021, https://billygrahamlibrary.org/blog-10 -quotes-from-billy-graham-on-end-times/.

CHAPTER 20

1. Rachel Lang, "Teen Shares Tearful Goodbye Video Before Pulled Out Alive from Turkey Earthquake Rubble," UNILAD, February 19, 2023, https://www.unilad.com/news/teen-shares-last-words-on-social-media -before-rescue-turkey-earthquake-411808-20230219.
2. Timothy J. Demy and John C. Whitcomb, "Witnesses Two," in *The Popular Encyclopedia of Bible Prophecy*, eds. Tim LaHaye and Ed Hindson (Eugene, OR: Harvest House, 2004), 402–3.
3. William R. Newell, *Revelation: Chapter by Chapter* (Chicago: Moody Press, 1935), 152.
4. Henry M. Morris, *The Revelation Record* (Carol Stream, IL: Tyndale House Publishers, 1983), 119.
5. Tim Chester, *The Ordinary Hero* (Nottingham, England: Intervarsity Press, 2009), 207.
6. Paul W. Powell, *The Night Cometh* (Tyler, TX: Paul W. Powell, 2002), 9.

CHAPTER 21

1. Frank Hoogerbeets, FrankHoogerbeets.com, accessed June 12, 2023.
2. Patrick Walsh, "Fishermen Fear Imminent Earthquake After Catching Rare Oarfish," MSN, November 2, 2022, https://www.msn.com/en-us/news/world

/fishermen-fear-imminent-earthquake-after-catching-rare-oarfish/ar-AA13F6s4?li=BBnb7Kz.

3. "Frequently Asked Questions," United States Geological Survey, accessed June 12, 2023, https://www.usgs.gov/faqs/can-you-predict-earthquakes.

4. Renald Showers, *Maranatha: Our Lord, Come!: A Definitive Study of the Rapture of the Church* (Bellmawr, NJ: Friends of Israel Ministry, 1995), 127.

5. A. T. Pierson, "Our Lord's Second Coming, a Motive to World Wide Evangelism," in *Prophetic Studies of the International Prophetic Conference, Chicago, November 1886*, ed. George Carter Needham (Chicago: Fleming H. Revell, 1886), 27.

6. Wayne A. Brindle, "Biblical Evidence for the Imminence of the Rapture," *Bibliotheca Sacra* 158 (April–June 2001): 138–51.

7. John MacArthur, *The Second Coming* (Wheaton, IL: Crossway, 1999), 52.

8. Robert L. Thomas, "The Rapture and the Biblical Teaching of Imminency," *Evidence for the Rapture: A Biblical Case for Pretribulationism*, ed. John. F. Hart (Chicago: Moody Publishers, 2015), 27.

9. "Taiwan Must Be Ready for a Chinese Invasion 'At Any Time,' Experts Say," *Radio Free Asia*, November 3, 2022, https://www.rfa.org /english/news/southchinasea/taiwan-invasion-readiness-11032022034156 .html.

CHAPTER 22

1. Mike M. Ahlers and Lizzie O'Leary, "Broken Toilets Strand United Passengers in Alaska," CNN, March 21, 2012, https://www.cnn.com/2012/03 /21/travel/alaska-passengers-stranded/index.html.

2. Douglas J. Moo, *The NIV Application Commentary 2 Peter, Jude* (Grand Rapids, MI: Zondervan, 1996), 260.

3. John Piper, quoted by Chris Mueller, "Why Is Christ Taking So Long to Return?," Media Library, accessed May 10, 2023, https://media.faith-bible.net /scripture/2-peter/why-is-christ-taking-so-long-to-return.

4. James Shaddix, *Exalting Jesus in 2 Peter, Jude* (Nashville, TN: B&H Publishing Group, 2018), 121.

5. Sam Storms, "The Christian and Repentance," The Gospel Coalition, accessed May 29, 2023, https://www.thegospelcoalition.org/essay/the -christian-and-repentance/.

6. Elizabeth Wolfe and Saeed Ahmed, "Greyhound Is Giving Free Tickets to Runaways Who Want to Return Home," CNN, December 31, 2019, https:// www.cnn.com/2019/12/31/us/greyhound-runaway-kids-home-free-ticket -trnd/index.html.

CHAPTER 23

1. Based on multiple news reports the week of April 27, 2023.
2. Bodie Hodge, "Methuselah: When Did He Die?," Answers in Genesis, July 30, 2010, https://answersingenesis.org/bible-timeline/genealogy/when-did-methuselah-die/.
3. W. A. Criswell, "God's Churches and the Great Tribulation," W. A. Criswell Sermon Library, accessed June 25, 2023, https://wacriswell.com/sermons/1961/god-s-churches-and-the-great-tribulation/.
4. Debra B. Morton, *Beyond the Storm: How to Thrive in Life's Toughest Seasons* (Nashville, TN: Nelson Books, 2019), 24–25.

CHAPTER 24

1. "John Cena Sets Record for Most Wishes Granted Through Make-A-Wish Foundation," *MovieGuide*, September 30, 2022, https://www.movieguide.org/news-articles/john-cena-sets-record-for-most-wishes-granted-through-make-a-wish-foundation.html.
2. Andrew M. Woods, "John and the Rapture: Revelation 2–3," in *Evidence for the Rapture: A Biblical Case for Pretribulationism*, ed. John F. Hart (Chicago: Moody Publishers, 2015), 196.
3. Michael A. Rydelnik, "Israel: Why the Church Must Be Raptured Before the Tribulation," in Hart, *Evidence for the Rapture*, 264.
4. Charles Ryrie, *Come Quickly, Lord Jesus: What You Need to Know About the Rapture* (Eugene, OR: Harvest House Publishing, 1996), 130–31.
5. Ryrie, *Come Quickly, Lord Jesus*, 137–38.
6. Arnold G. Fruchtenbaum, *The Footsteps of the Messiah: A Study of the Sequence of Prophetic Events* (Tustin, CA: Ariel Ministries, 2003), 153.
7. *Our Hope Magazine*, August 1950, 86.
8. Ryrie, *Come Quickly, Lord Jesus*, 137.
9. Gerald B. Stanton, *Kept from the Hour* (Miami Springs, FL: Schoettle Publishing, 1991), 44–45.
10. John F. Walvoord, *The Thessalonian Epistles* (Grand Rapids, MI: Zondervan, 1974), 54.
11. Val Lauder, "Remember 'The Great Raid' of 1945," CNN, January 29, 2015, https://edition.cnn.com/2015/01/29/opinion/lauder-great-raid-cabanatuan-pow-camp-1945/index.html.

CHAPTER 25

1. Arthur Conan Doyle, *The Memoirs of Sherlock Holmes*, vol. 1 (Leipzig: Bernhard Tauchnitz, 1894), 50, 58.
2. J. F. Strombeck, *First the Rapture: The Church's Blessed Hope* (Grand Rapids, MI: Kregel, 1992), 185–86.

3. Tim LaHaye, *No Fear of the Storm* (Sisters, OR: Multnomah Press, 1992), 45–46.

4. Richard Mayhue, "Why a Pretribulation Rapture?," in *Christ's Prophetic Plans: A Futuristic Premillennial Primer*, ed. John MacArthur and Richard Mayhue (Chicago: Moody Publishers, 2012), 89.

5. Mayhue, "Why a Pretribulation Rapture?," 91.

6. Mark Hitchcock, *The End: A Complete Overview of Bible Prophecy and the End of Days* (Carol Stream, IL: Tyndale House Publishers, 2012), 154–55.

7. J. F. Strombeck, *First the Rapture: The Church's Blessed Hope* (Grand Rapids, MI: Kregel, 1992), 133.

8. LaHaye, *No Fear of the Storm*, 57.

9. Steven Greenhut, "Your Silence May Be Admission of Guilt," *San Diego Union Tribune*, August 18, 2014, https://www.sandiegouniontribune.com /news/politics/sdut-suspect-silence-admission-guilt-california-court -2014aug18-story.html.

CHAPTER 26

1. Robin Lloyd, "Metric Mishap Caused Loss of NASA Orbiter," CNN, September 30, 1999, http://www.cnn.com/TECH/space/9909/30/mars .metric.02/.

2. Vance Havner, "Second Coming of Christ—Quotes, Devotionals & Illustrations," *Precept Austin*, accessed June 7, 2023, https://www .preceptaustin.org/second_coming_of_christ.

CHAPTER 27

1. Carla Field, "Greenville Traffic Sign Warns of Zombies," NBC News WYFF, May 7, 2018, https://www.wyff4.com/article/greenville-traffic-sign-warns-of -zombies/20257749#.

2. Mark Hitchcock, *The End: A Complete Overview of Bible Prophecy and the End of Days* (Carol Stream, IL: Tyndale House Publishers, 2012), 109.

3. Wayne Grudem, *Bible Doctrine: Essential Teachings of the Christian Faith* (Grand Rapids, MI: Zondervan, 2014), 427.

4. John M. Frame, *Systematic Theology: An Introduction to Christian Belief* (Phillipsburg, NJ: P&R Publishing, 2013), 1094.

5. Paul N. Benware, "Introduction: The Critical Importance of Bible Prophecy," in *Understanding the End Times* (Chicago: Moody Publishers, 2006).

CHAPTER 28

1. Jenna Rose Alpern, "A Rental Contract for the End of Days," *Times of Israel*, February 10, 2014, https://blogs.timesofisrael.com/only-in-israel/.

2. Lehman Strauss, "Bible Prophecy," Bible.org, accessed November 27, 2007, http:/www.bible.org. phph.page_id=412.

3. John F. Walvoord, *End Times* (Nashville, TN: Word Publishing, 2002), 89.

4. Tim LaHaye, *No Fear of the Storm: Why Christians Will Escape All the Tribulation* (Sisters, OR: Multnomah Press, 1992), 79.

5. Maria Wulff Hauglann, "The Amazing and True Story of Hachiko the Dog," Nerd Nomads, May 4, 2021, https://nerdnomads.com/hachiko_the_dog.

CHAPTER 29

1. Tim LaHaye, *The Rapture* (Eugene, OR: Harvest House Publishing, 1998), 143.

2. N. T. Wright, *Surprised by Hope* (New York: HarperCollins, 2008), 137.

3. James M. Kushner, "Onward Christian Soldiers," Fellowship of St. James, accessed April 18, 2023, http://campaign.120.constantcontact.com/render?ca=fa215191-1d64-43db-8712-3e2c19d76878cc=a9340410-417c.

CHAPTER 30

1. Belinda Luscombe, *Marriageology: The Art and Science of Staying Together* (New York: Random House, 2019), 90.

2. Richard Baxter, quoted in Bryan Chapell, *The Wonder of It All: Rediscovering the Treasure of Your Faith* (Wheaton, IL: Crossway Books, 1999), 189.

3. Benjamin Fay Mills, "The After-Meeting: Drawing the Net," *Independent* 47, no. 2425 (May 23, 1895): 2.

CHAPTER 31

1. "Book of Prophecy," Babylon Bee, accessed May 29, 2023, https://babylonbee.com/book-of-prophecy.

2. Kassy Dillon, "When Satire Becomes Reality: Nearly 100 Babylon Bee Joke Stories Have Come True," Fox News, March 26, 2023, https://www.foxnews.com/entertainment/satire-reality-nearly-100-babylon-bee-joke-stories-come-true.

3. John F. Walvoord and Mark Hitchcock, *Armageddon, Oil, and Terror* (Carol Stream, IL: Tyndale House Publishers, 2007), 1–2.

4. Richard Mayhue, "Introduction: Why Study Prophecy?," in *Christ's Prophetic Plans: A Futuristic Premillennial Primer* (Chicago: Moody Publishers, 2012), 14.

5. Tim LaHaye, *A Quick Look at the Rapture and the Second Coming* (Eugene, OR: Harvest House Publishers, 2013), 11.

6. Charles Dyer, *World News and Bible Prophecy* (Carol Stream, IL: Tyndale House Publishers, 1995), 270.

7. "John O'Neill's FBI Jacket and Passport Embody His Enduring Fight Against Terrorism," 9/11 Memorial and Museum, accessed May 5, 2023, https://www.911memorial.org/connect/blog/john-oneills-fbi-jacket-and-passport-embody-his-enduring-fight-against-terrorism.

ACKNOWLEDGMENTS

This story originated with Almighty God and features His Son, the Lord Jesus Christ. David Jeremiah wrote the screenplay with assistance from Rob Morgan and Sam O'Neal. Beau Sager is the producer and director, and Katie Long is the illustrator.

The Great Disappearance is released by HarperCollins Christian Publishing under the W Publishing imprint. Mark Schoenwald, President and CEO; Damon Reiss, Publisher.

And it is circulated by Turning Point Media. David Michael Jeremiah, President; Paul Joiner, Creative Director; and BethAnne Hewett, Executive Secretary.

David Jeremiah is represented by Sealy Yates of Yates and Yates!

ABOUT THE AUTHOR

DR. DAVID JEREMIAH is the founder of Turning Point, an international ministry committed to providing Christians with sound Bible teaching through radio and television, the internet, live events, and resource materials and books. He is the author of more than fifty books, including *Where Do We Go from Here?*, *Forward*, *The World of the End*, and *The Book of Signs*.

Dr. Jeremiah serves as the senior pastor of Shadow Mountain Community Church in El Cajon, California. He and his wife, Donna, have four grown children and twelve grandchildren.

stay connected to the teaching of

DR. DAVID JEREMIAH

·······

Publishing | Radio | Television | Online

FURTHER YOUR STUDY OF THIS BOOK

· · · · · · · ·

The Great Disappearance **Resource Materials**

To enhance your study on this important topic, we recommend the
correlating audio message album, study guide, and DVD messages from
The Great Disappearance series.

Audio Message Album

The material found in this book originated
from messages presented by Dr. Jeremiah.
These messages are conveniently packaged
in an accessible audio album.

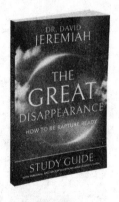

Study Guide

This 144-page study guide correlates with
the messages from *The Great Disappearance*
series by Dr. Jeremiah. Each lesson
provides an outline, an overview, and
group and personal application questions.

DVD Message Presentations

Watch Dr. Jeremiah deliver *The Great
Disappearance* original messages in this
special DVD collection.

To order these products, call us at 1-800-947-1993
or visit us online at www.DavidJeremiah.org.

MORE PROPHECY RESOURCES FROM DR. JEREMIAH

· · · · · · · ·

The Book of Signs

The Bible tells us to watch out for the signs in our world that will foreshadow the End Times. But what are these signs and what do they mean? In *The Book of Signs,* Dr. Jeremiah takes an in-depth look at the prophecies in Scripture and how they correlate with the events of our time. As you read *The Book of Signs,* you will see not only how God's Word offers insights into the future, but also how Scripture builds faith through the events of the past and encouragement in the uncertainty of the present.

Where Do We Go From Here?

The prophetic passages of Scripture are God's transfusion of hope to our hearts. They show us that God is sovereign, no matter what may be building up or crashing down around us. And you don't have to be a biblical scholar to see how Scripture predicted many of the events surrounding us. The prophecies about tomorrow reveal much about the problems of today, and in *Where Do We Go From Here?,* Dr. Jeremiah takes us on a tour of today's major issues, showing us where we are, what they mean, and what we should do next.

STAY CONNECTED TO DAVID JEREMIAH

· · · · · · · ·

**Take advantage of three great ways to let Dr. David Jeremiah
give you spiritual direction every day!**

Turning Points Magazine and Devotional

Receive Dr. Jeremiah's magazine,
Turning Points, each month:
- Thematic study focus
- 52 pages of life-changing reading
- Relevant articles
- Daily devotional readings and more!

Request *Turning Points* magazine today!
(800) 947-1993 | DavidJeremiah.org/Magazine

Daily Turning Point E-Devotional

Receive a daily e-devotion from Dr. Jeremiah
that will strengthen your walk with God and
encourage you to live the authentic Christian life.

Sign up for your free e-devotional today!
www.DavidJeremiah.org/Devo

Turning Point Mobile App

Access Dr. Jeremiah's video teachings,
audio sermons, and more . . . whenever and
wherever you are!

Download your free app today!
www.DavidJeremiah.org/App

—